THE LIFE OF THE APOSTLE PAUL
The Apostle to the Nations

PAUL SAID, "BE IMITATORS OF ME, JUST AS I ALSO AM OF CHRIST."—1 CORINTHIANS 11:1

JAMES STALKER AND EDWARD D. ANDREWS
UPDATED AND EXPANDED EDITION

CHRISTIAN PUBLISHING HOUSE CLASSICS

THE LIFE OF THE APOSTLE PAUL

The Apostle to the Nations

Updated and Expanded

James Stalker and Edward D. Andrews

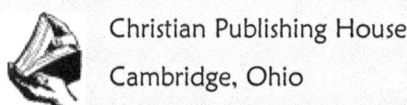

Christian Publishing House
Cambridge, Ohio

Copyright © 2016 Christian Publishing House

All rights reserved. Except for brief quotations in articles, other publications, book reviews, and blogs, no part of this book may be reproduced in any manner without prior written permission from the publishers. For information, write, support@christianpublishers.org

THE LIFE OF THE APOSTLE PAUL: *The Apostle to the Nations* [Updated and Expanded]

Authored by James Stalker and Edward D. Andrews

ISBN-13: **978-1-945757-16-7**

ISBN-10: **1-945757-16-7**

INTRODUCING The Apostle Paul 1
CHAPTER I His Place In History 25
CHAPTER II His Unconscious Preparation for His Work 30
CHAPTER III His Conversion 41
CHAPTER IV His Gospel 47
CHAPTER V The Work Awaiting the Worker 55
CHAPTER VI His Missionary Travels 60
  The First Journey 60
  The Second Journey 65
  The Third Journey 72
CHAPTER VII His Writings and His Character 75
CHAPTER VIII Picture of a Pauling Church 83
CHAPTER IX His Great Constroversy 90
CHAPTER X First and Second Imprisonments at Rome 98
  Hints to Teachers and questions to Bible Students 109
CHAPTER XI Who Authored the Book of Hebrews: A Defense for Pauline Authorship 111
  Edward D. Andrews 111
APPENDIX A The Conversion of Saul 121
  Edward D. Andrews 121
APPENDIX B Gamaliel Taught Saul of Tarsus 132
APPENDIX C Citizenship, the rights and privileges of 135
APPENDIX D Areopagus, A Unique Athenian Rock 139
APPENDIX E The Unknown God 142
APPENDIX F Athens, the "City of Many Gods" 144
APPENDIX G Gallio, the Proconsul of Achaia 147
APPENDIX H Vow, Paul's Observance of Law as to Vows ... 148
APPENDIX I Thorn In the Flesh 152
APPENDIX J Governor Felix Fails to Pass Judgment 154

APPENDIX K Shipwreck, Paul and His Traveling Companions **155**

APPENDIX L Timothy, A Genuine Child in the Faith **162**

APPENDIX M Titus, A Fellow Worker..................................**164**

APPENDIX N Why Has God Permitted Suffering and Evil? ..**166**

Edward D. Andrews... 166

APPENDIX O Why is Life So Unfair? **176**

Edward D. Andrews... 176

APPENDIX P Does God Step in and Solve Our Every Problem Because We are Faithful? **203**

Edward D. Andrews... 203

APPENDIX Q How Are We to Understand the Indwelling of the Holy Spirit?...**210**

Edward D. Andrews... 210

INTRODUCING The Apostle Paul

Paul, The Apostle.

Known as Saul of Tarsus before his conversion to Christianity and the most influential leader in the early days of the Christian church. Through his missionary journeys to Asia Minor and Europe, Paul was the primary instrument in the expansion of the gospel to the Gentiles. Moreover, his letters to various churches and individuals contain the most thorough and deliberate theological formulations of the NT.

Most of the biographical material available comes from the Book of Acts. Though modern critics question the reliability of this narrative, there is every good reason to use it as the basis for outlining Paul's life. Moreover, the teachings of Paul, as set forth in his letters, are best summarized within the historical framework provided by the Acts narrative.

Background and Conversion.

Date of Birth. Little is known of Paul's life prior to the events discussed in Acts. He is first mentioned in chapter 7 in connection with the execution of Stephen. According to verse 58, "the witnesses laid their clothes at the feet of a young man named Saul." The term "young man" probably indicates someone in his 20s, though this is uncertain.

The events mentioned in Acts 7 may have occurred as early as A.D. 31 if Jesus' death took place during the Passover of A.D. 30. On the other hand, if Jesus' death is dated in the year 33[1] then those events could have taken place no earlier than 34, but no later than 37. (Second Cor 11:32, 33 states that when Paul escaped from Damascus that city was being ruled by the Nabataean king Aretas, who died in the year 40. Since, according to Gal 1:17, 18, Paul left Damascus three years after his conversion, the year 37 must be regarded as the latest possible date for Stephen's death.)

Using the year 34 as an approximate date for the time when Saul is described as a "young man," and assuming that Saul was no older than 30 years at that time, then it can be concluded his birth took place no earlier than A.D. 4. And since it is very unlikely that he was younger than 20, A.D. 14 can be set as the latest possible date for his birth. This conclusion is supported by the knowledge that Paul studied under the famous Gamaliel I (Acts 22:3), who according to some scholars became a member

---

[1] Edward D. Andrews dates Jesus' death to Nisan 14, A.D. 33 (c. 3:00 p.m., Friday) Golgotha, Jerusalem

of the Sanhedrin about A.D. 20. If Paul was 15 years old when he entered the school, the range of A.D. 4–14 for his birth fits all the information available. So it can be said with a degree of accuracy that Saul was born in the city of Tarsus about A.D. 9, but any estimates about his age should allow a leeway of 5 years either way.

Upbringing. The city of Tarsus was a major population center in the province of Cilicia in the southeastern region of Asia Minor. Lying on a significant commercial route, Tarsus felt the influence of current cultural movements, particularly Stoic philosophy. It is difficult to determine to what extent Greek thought affected Paul as a child. There is a possibility that his family had become "Hellenized"—after all, Paul was born a Roman citizen (it is not know how his father or ancestors acquired citizenship, though military or other notable service is a strong possibility); accordingly, he was given not only a Hebrew name (*Shaul*) but also a Roman cognomen (*Paulus*, though some have argued that he adopted this Roman name at a later point). At any rate, the fact that in his letters he shows great ease in relating to Gentiles suggests that he obtained a Greek education while in Tarsus.

A scene from Asia Minor, the location of Paul's birth (Tarsus) and much of his ministry.

On the other hand, he describes himself as one "circumcised on the eighth day, of the people of Israel, of the tribe of Benjamin, a Hebrew born of Hebrews" (Phil 3:5), and such a characterization, particularly the last phrase, perhaps served to distinguish him from those Jews in the Dispersion who freely adopted Greek ways. Moreover, according to Acts 22:3, he was actually brought up in Jerusalem (possibly in his sister's house, cf. Acts 23:16), and some scholars infer from that statement that

2

Paul was brought up in a totally Jewish environment from earliest childhood.

It is worthwhile pointing out that Gamaliel is represented in later rabbinic literature as a teacher who had considerable appreciation for Greek culture. Besides, soon after his conversion, Paul spent at least 10 years ministering in Tarsus and its environs (cf. Acts 9:30; Gal 1:21; 2:1; see below). These questions are interesting for more than historical reasons. One of the most basic issues debated among modern interpreters of Paul is whether he should be viewed primarily as a Greek or as a Hebrew. The latter position has, with good reason, become more and more prominent, but the strong Hellenistic elements that formed part of the apostle's total character should not be overlooked.

From Pharisaism to Christianity. In addition to the statement in Philippians 3:5, Paul makes some biographical comments in Galatians 1:13, 14: "For you have heard of my previous way of life in Judaism, how intensely I persecuted the church of God and tried to destroy it. I was advancing in Judaism beyond many Jews of my own age and was extremely zealous for the traditions of my fathers." It is clear that Paul had made a total religious commitment to his Pharisaic heritage. But what precisely did that mean? The difficulty in answering that question arises from two problems. One is the issue of how 1st-century Pharisaism should be characterized; the other is the debate that has raged over the relation between Paul's religious background and his conversion to Christianity.

The first issue may be dealt with briefly. Paul's own statement in Galatians 1:14 provides an important key, namely, his reference to "the traditions of my fathers." That phrase is equivalent to "the traditions of the elders," used by the Pharisees to criticize Jesus' conduct (Mk 7:5). It refers to the rabbinic "oral law," a body of legal biblical interpretation that played an authoritative role among the Pharisees. Unfortunately, much of that interpretation was characterized by a tendency to relax the stringency of God's commands, and the Pharisees were often in danger of thinking that they had satisfied the divine requirements (cf. esp. Mt 5:20, 48; Lk 19:9–14). This religious background is clearly reflected in Philippians 3:9, where Paul, obviously referring to his pre-Christian experience, speaks of "a righteousness of my own that comes from the law."

This fact leads naturally to the second difficulty: how do we relate Paul's background to his conversion? Some scholars have argued forcefully that Protestants have interpreted Paul's conversion in the light of Martin Luther's experience. This reading, they add, is quite misleading, for there is no evidence that Paul was moved to embrace Christianity out of a sense of guilt. In fact, they say the term "conversion" should not even be used since Paul himself speaks rather of a "call" (e.g., Gal 1:15).

There are some valid insights in the charge that Protestantism has placed too much emphasis on "the introspective conscience of the West" (so Krister Stendahl), but it would be a serious mistake to suggest that Luther and the Reformers misunderstood Paul's experience at a fundamental level. Part of the debate focuses on the meaning of Romans 7:7–25, especially such a statement as the following: "Once I was alive apart from law; but when the commandment came, sin sprang to life and I died" (v 9). Whether this and subsequent verses should be understood as biographical or not is a question that has divided exegetes for a long time.

However, the significance of Philippians 3 is clear. In verse 6 of that chapter Paul characterizes his pre-Christian life as "blameless" with reference to legal obedience. Since he can hardly mean that he was (or had earlier thought he was) free from sin, the statement reflects the same attitude expressed by the Pharisee in the parable of Luke 18:9–14, namely, religious self-satisfaction and a lack of sense for the need to cry out for divine mercy. Whether Paul went through a period of guilt (comparable to Luther's) before he surrendered to the claims of the gospel is not known. What matters is that he came to view the knowledge of Jesus Christ as incomparably superior to what he had earlier known. In the light of the gospel, his previous advantages and accomplishments, great as they were, could only be regarded as rubbish (Phil 3:7, 8).

With regard to Paul's pre-Christian attitude to the gospel, one thing is certain—he was opposed to it with his whole heart. In his apostolic letters he speaks of his previous hatred for the church (e.g., Gal 1:13; Phil 3:6). Paul does not say explicitly why he felt this way, but there are some hints. In 1 Corinthians 1:23, for example, he speaks of the crucifixion of Christ as a stumbling block to the Jews; and in Galatians 3:13 he quotes Deuteronomy 21:23 ("Cursed is everyone who is hung on a tree") as evidence that Christ, by dying on the cross, became a curse for us. It seems reasonable to infer that Paul, along with many other Jews, viewed the preaching of the gospel as blasphemy. How could these Christians regard as Messiah (God's anointed) a lowly man who suffered a criminal's death and received the divine curse itself? Not surprisingly, this theme would become a basic one in Paul's own proclamation of the gospel.

At any rate, Paul did become a Christian, and thanks to the Book of Acts we are well informed regarding this event. According to chapter 8, not only did he give approval to Stephen's stoning, but soon after that he "began to destroy the church. Going from house to house, he dragged off men and women and put them in prison" (vv 1, 3). Not satisfied, he decided to pursue the disciples as far away as Damascus. The sequel is familiar to all Bible students. As he and his traveling party approached Damascus, a light flashed and a voice said to him, "Saul, Saul, why do you persecute me?" The One speaking identified himself as "Jesus, whom you are persecuting" (Acts 9:1–5; cf. also 22:4–8 and more fully 26:9–18). Unable to see anything, he followed the Lord's instructions and waited in Damascus. Ananias, a disciple, was sent to speak to Paul, restore his sight, and baptize him (Acts 9:6–19).

The street called "straight" (Acts 9:11) in Damascus.

Early Ministry.

Damascus. To the surprise of everyone who had heard of Paul's enmity toward the church, the new apostle began to preach the gospel vigorously and convincingly. According to Galatians 1:17, 18, Paul spent some three years in Damascus and its environs. His ministry, however, eventually drew opposition and he had to escape from Damascus. Upon his return to Jerusalem, the Christians at first could not bring themselves to trust the one who had earlier persecuted them so fiercely, but Barnabas, a highly respected leader in the church, made it possible for Paul to receive a hearing (Acts 9:23–27).

Jerusalem. At once he resumed his preaching, and the Acts narrative gives us a significant clue regarding the distinctiveness of Paul's ministry. According to 9:29 Paul "talked and debated with the Grecian Jews, but they tried to kill him." The significance of this statement is that it draws a suggestive parallel between Paul's preaching and Stephen's ministry. The story that describes Stephen's selection as a deacon is set in the context of conflicts within the church between Greek-speaking, partially Hellenized Jews and those who spoke Hebrew or Aramaic (Acts 6:1; the latter were natives of Palestine and probably stricter in their observance of the Jewish ceremonies). Since Stephen himself belonged to the Greek-speaking community, this is where he took his ministry; indeed, he spoke powerfully as he presented the gospel to the Jews of Cyrene, Alexandria, and other foreign places (vv 8, 9).

To judge by the Jews' subsequent accusations (that he spoke against the temple and the OT customs, vv 11–14), it seems that an important theme in Stephen's preaching was the newness of the gospel message and therefore the secondary importance of the Jewish traditions. This is probably the best explanation for the violent reaction of the Jews against him. Up to this point, the Jewish leaders, though annoyed by the preaching of the apostles, put up with it (see esp. Acts 5:27–40). Now, however, that preaching may have taken a new twist that threatened in a fundamental way the Jewish establishment. So significant was this turn of events that it led to Stephen's death and the persecution of the Christians.

It can be said that, in a very important sense, Paul took up Stephen's mantle. Bible students have long recognized that Luke, as he wrote the Book of Acts, appears to picture Stephen as a precursor of the great apostle to the Gentiles. More recently, scholars have become increasingly aware of the significance of this connection in the light of the serious Jewish-Gentile conflicts experienced by the early church. During its first years the Christian church was totally Jewish and it was taken for granted that it would remain so. In spite of persecution from their countrymen, it does not seem to have occurred to the early Christians that the gospel might affect their evaluation of Jewish observances. They continued to circumcise their boys, to attend the sacrifices at the temple, to keep the sabbath, to make Nazirite vows, to avoid association with Gentiles, and so on.

Probably because of his Hellenistic background, Stephen was apparently one of the first Christian leaders to raise questions about these matters. Perhaps reflecting Jesus' own remarks about the transitory character of the temple (cf. Jn 2:19; 4:21-24), Stephen challenged his hearers' assumptions in clear terms (Acts 7:44-53). Paul too had a Hellenistic background, and one wonders whether his earlier enmity toward Stephen may have been occasioned in part by fear that Stephen was possibly correct. Whether guilt over Stephen's death played a part in Paul's conversion—and in his later decision to take up the ministry to Hellenistic Jews—is much too speculative.

What matters is that Paul did in fact pick up where Stephen had left off. This ministry once again aroused the ire of the Jews, and so the believers in Jerusalem, concerned for Paul's life and no doubt fearing that a new wave of persecution might be unleashed, sent the apostle off to Tarsus (Acts 9:30). According to Galatians 1:18-24, Paul's stay in Jerusalem had lasted only two weeks, and most of the Christians there and in the outlying areas had no personal acquaintance with him. Subsequent events suggest strongly that from the beginning of his ministry Paul's distinctive interests and emphases created special tensions. While it would be an exaggeration to say that the Jerusalem church was opposed to him (note esp. Gal 1:24), it is certain that some individuals and groups entertained doubts about his ministry. The Christians in Judea had no desire to break off their ties with Judaism, and preachers like Paul who emphasized the antithesis between it and the gospel could easily be perceived as troublemakers or worse.

Tarsus and Antioch. The time Paul spent in Tarsus and other parts of Cilicia must be regarded as "dark years" in his ministry, since virtually nothing is known about his activities during this period. Luke gives us no information in Acts, and the casual reader might infer that this was a relatively brief period. In Galatians 2:1, however, Paul says that 14 years elapsed from the time of his conversion (or possibly from the time he was sent off to Tarsus) to the time of an important meeting with the Jerusalem apostles. The identification of this visit to Jerusalem is a major point of controversy among scholars, but even if the earliest possible date for it is taken, the year A.D. 46, it appears that Paul spent at the very least 9 years in Tarsus before he became a prominent figure in the early church. It has been suggested that some of the experiences listed by Paul in 2 Corinthians 11:23-27 (perhaps also the revelations mentioned in 12:1-10) may have taken place during these "dark years," but even if this thesis is correct, there are little more than generalities to back it up. It is a most intriguing fact that the great apostle to the Gentiles spent the first decade of his ministry in relative obscurity, virtually unknown by the vibrant early church in Jerusalem.

At least one leader in the Jerusalem church, however, had not forgotten Paul. Barnabas—himself a Hellenistic Jew from Cyprus—was sent by the church to Antioch of Syria, a large metropolitan center in the Middle East and the third largest city in the Roman Empire. The Christians in Jerusalem had heard that the gospel was being preached with great success in Antioch. Some of them probably were concerned about reports that this evangelistic effort had been extended to the "Greeks," and this represented quite an innovation.

Some time earlier Peter had by revelation brought the gospel to Cornelius, a "God-fearer," that is, a Gentile who was sympathetic to Judaism and probably attended the synagogue services but who was not willing to adopt Judaism completely. The Christians who accompanied Peter were astonished to find out that a non-Jew was granted the gift of the Holy Spirit (Acts 10:44–46), and when the church in Jerusalem heard about his visiting a Gentile, Peter was under considerable pressure to explain his actions (11:1, 3). His explanation satisfied the church (see v 18), but obviously not everyone was happy.

In any case, the news that Antiochene Gentiles (presumably "God-fearers" too, though there is some disagreement about this) were being received into the church suggested that some supervision might be required. The Jerusalem leaders wisely chose Barnabas, no doubt because he, like some of the "evangelists" in Antioch, was from Cyprus; certainly someone was needed who enjoyed the confidence of both parties. Barnabas was greatly encouraged by what he saw in Antioch (Acts 11:22–24). The work was so large and promising that he traveled to nearby Tarsus and persuaded Paul to help him with this work. "So for a whole year Barnabas and Saul met with the church and taught great numbers of people" (Acts 11:26).

Because of the great famine of a.d. 46, predicted by the prophet Agabus, the Christians in Antioch sent a gift to Jerusalem by the hand of Barnabas and Paul (Acts 11:27–30). According to some scholars, this "famine visit" is to be identified with that related by Paul in Galatians 2:1–10. In any case, Barnabas and Paul returned to Antioch, taking along with them John Mark, Barnabas's cousin (Acts 12:25).

Ministry in Asia Minor and Syria.

First Missionary Journey. Beginning with chapter 13, the Book of Acts focuses almost exclusively on the missionary work of Paul. Under direct divine guidance, the church in Antioch sent him and Barnabas, with Mark as helper, to spread the gospel abroad. Sailing from the port city of Seleucia, they traveled to Cyprus, Barnabas' home country. When they reached the city of Paphos, a significant event took place: the proconsul

Sergius Paulus, after witnessing the miraculous blinding of a sorcerer, responded to the preaching of the gospel. It is at this point in the narrative (Acts 13:9) that Luke tells us for the first time that Saul was also called Paul. Some have thought that Paul adopted this name as a result of this incident and in honor of the proconsul Sergius Paulus, but Luke certainly does not say that, and it seems unlikely anyway (Paul would almost surely have been given a Roman name at birth.)

The significance of this information should be tied to the fact that, while up to this point Luke has referred to the party as "Barnabas and Saul," from now on he uses the expression "Paul and his companions" (v 13) or "Paul and Barnabas" (v 43, etc.; the only real exception is 15:12). There appears to have been, therefore, not merely a name change, but a shift of leadership, and possibly a change in the party's missionary strategy. It has been suggested, with good reason, that the conversion of Sergius Paulus signaled a fundamentally new development. Prior to this incident, the reception of Gentiles into the church seems to have been limited to "God-fearers," that is, individuals who already had a point of contact with Jewish tradition. Quite possibly, the proconsul's conversion was the first instance of a Gentile who was received as part of God's people *without the intermediary role of the synagogue*.

This seems so natural to modern Christians that it is difficult to appreciate how shocking it must have sounded to Jewish ears. Indeed, it may well be that this *theological* problem (and not merely homesickness!) is what led Mark to abandon the missionary party and return to Jerusalem (Acts 13:13; this would also help to explain why Paul was so adamantly opposed to taking Mark again at a later point, 15:36–40). Whether this interpretation of the evidence is valid or not, the fact is that Paul plays a prominent role in the subsequent narrative, and that the distinctiveness of his ministry lay in his vigorous presentation of the gospel to Gentiles in spite of Jewish opposition.

An immediate example of this is in connection with the party's arrival in Antioch of Pisidia (inland in Asia Minor). Paul and Barnabas preached the gospel in the Jewish synagogue there and received a positive response (Acts 13:42, 43), but their success led to Jewish enmity and a word of judgment had to be pronounced: "We had to speak the word of God to you first. Since you reject it and do not consider yourselves worthy of eternal life, we now turn to the Gentiles" (v 46). Great success among the Gentiles led to further and more vigorous persecution and so they moved on to Iconium, where the same pattern developed. After visiting two other nearby cities (Lystra and Derbe), they retraced their steps, strengthening and encouraging the believers. Eventually they returned to their "headquarters" in Antioch of Syria, where they stayed for "a long time" (Acts 14:28).

The Apostolic Council. Chapter 15 of Acts plays a key role in the narrative, since it relates what was perhaps the most important event in early church history, the great Apostolic Council in Jerusalem (A.D. 49). Some of the Jewish Christians who were quite unhappy with the way in which Gentiles were being freely received as believers traveled to Antioch of Syria and demanded that they become Jews by submitting to circumcision (v 1). This led to intense debate and the church, no doubt deeply troubled, commissioned Paul and Barnabas to visit Jerusalem and discuss the matter with the apostles and elders there.

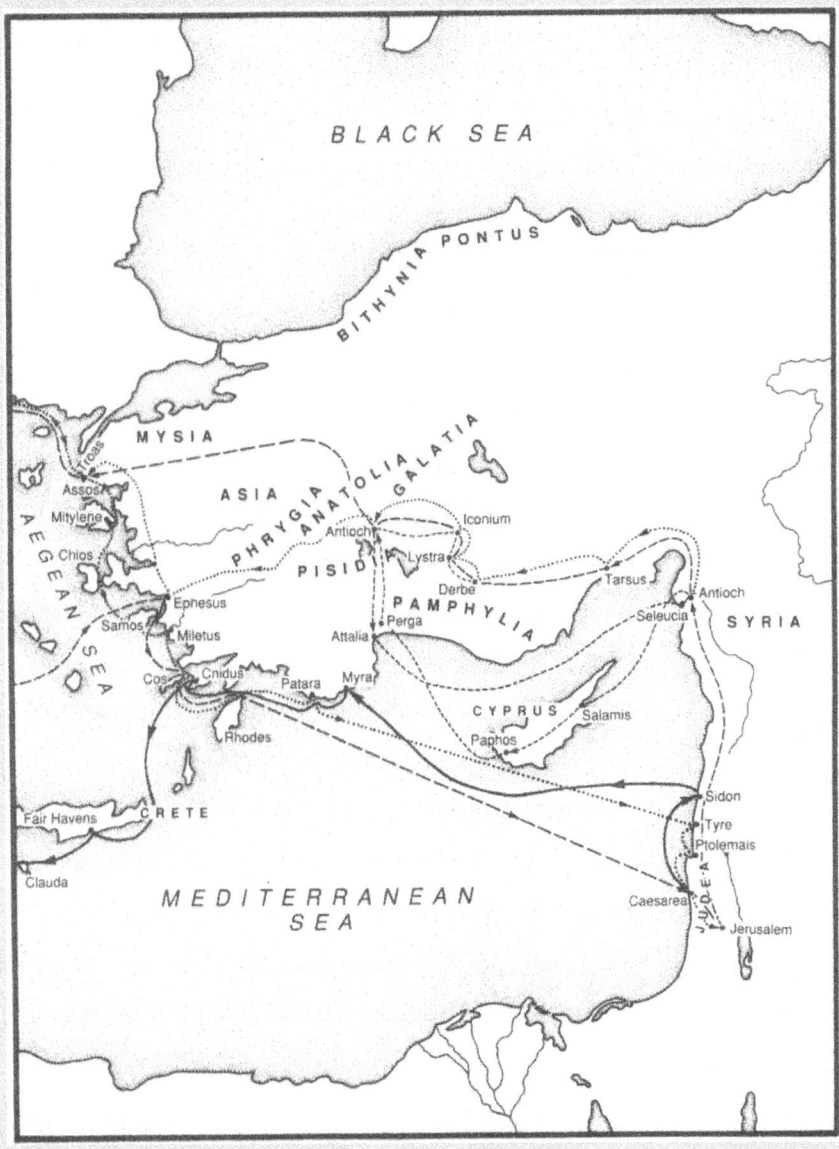

An apparently formal meeting was called and the missionaries reported on their activities. This report led to a lengthy discussion on the question whether Gentiles should be expected to become Jewish. If this is the same meeting to which Paul refers in Galatians 2:1–10, the Gentile Titus became a test case, with the Judaizers arguing that he ought to be circumcised. Paul's description in that passage suggests that the great "apostles of the circumcision," James, Peter, and John, may have at first been impressed by the Judaizers' arguments. Finally, however, Peter stood up and, reflecting on his experience with Cornelius, argued that the Gentiles' salvation comes through grace and not by fulfilling the Jewish ceremonies (Acts 15:7–11). At that point Barnabas and Paul gave further testimony to the mighty works of God among the Gentiles (that Barnabas is mentioned first in v 12 may reflect his prominence in that particular setting).

Having no doubt perceived a growing sense of unanimity in the council, James (who was apparently regarded as the leader of the Jerusalem church) appealed to a prophecy regarding the Gentiles in Amos 9:11, 12 and concluded that no unnecessary obstacles should be placed before believing Gentiles (Acts 15:13–21). The council drafted a letter that was taken to Antioch by Paul and Barnabas along with two men from Jerusalem, Judas Barsabbas and Silas. The letter in effect rejected the Judaizers' view that Gentiles must be circumcised; instead, it simply requested that gentile Christians abstain from certain practices that were offensive to the Jews. This decision was a source of great joy and encouragement for the believers in Antioch (vv 22–30).

It is difficult to grasp fully what a magnanimous decision this was and what a fundamental role it played in the development of early church history. The churches in Jerusalem and Judea were under great pressure to do nothing that might infuriate the unbelieving Jews; indeed, to accept Gentiles as part of the church could easily be interpreted as apostasy. Nevertheless, they were willing to suffer the consequences of their action for the sake of preserving the great principle of salvation by grace.

This great event had a major significance therefore for Paul's ministry. His concern to preach a gospel of freedom now received the support of "the pillars of the church," who gave him and Barnabas the right hand of fellowship and commended them to preach among the Gentiles (Gal 2:7–9). However, the Judaizers who were so soundly defeated at the Council of Jerusalem were not all necessarily submissive to this decision. Eventually they would take more positive steps to undermine the work of the apostle.

Conflict in Antioch. It should also be noted that in spite of the significant agreement reached at the council, not all of the leaders saw the issues as clearly as Paul did. Evidence for this appears in an incident that perhaps took place soon after the council (though scholars are not agreed on this matter). According to Galatians 2:11–14, Peter visited Antioch and took it upon himself to eat with the Christian Gentiles. It could be argued that this move went beyond what the council had required. The council's decision seemed to suggest that Christian Jews would continue practicing their customs and that Gentiles need not follow them. It did not address the question of table fellowship, however. If a Jew wanted to preserve Jewish practices, he would not be able to have this kind of fellowship with Gentiles; on the other hand, refusing to commune in this way with them implied a lack of acceptance. Accordingly, Peter chose the more generous option.

Unfortunately, when certain strict Jews from Jerusalem came to Antioch, it seems that Peter felt ashamed of how they might interpret his actions and therefore withdrew from the Gentiles. This decision influenced other believers, even Barnabas himself. Paul, however, saw clearly that this turn of events was a blatant denial of the very principle upon which the council had agreed. By their actions, Peter and the others were in effect telling the Gentiles that they must become Jews—otherwise they would always remain second-class citizens. Not surprisingly, the apostle proceeded to rebuke Peter publicly. There is possibly a summary of the contents of Paul's rebuke in Galatians 2:15–21. Here Paul affirms that the Law itself, by its teachings and effects, leads us to die to the Law so that we might live to God by faith in Christ. If we suggest in any way that the righteousness required by God can be obtained by our own obedience to the Law, then we are in effect saying that Christ died in vain.

Asia Minor Revisited. What is usually called Paul's "second missionary journey" began perhaps a few months after the Council of Jerusalem. After the dispute with Barnabas over the advisability of taking along Mark, Paul chose as his new companion Silas, who no doubt had strongly supported the council's decision. Traveling on land, the party went through Cilicia, surely visiting Tarsus, then on to the cities of Derbe and Lystra, where churches had been established earlier. In Lystra, Paul was apparently impressed with a young man named Timothy who had never been circumcised even though his mother was Jewish. Paul wanted to take him along and, in order to avoid unnecessary conflicts with Jews (who might consider Timothy an apostate), he had Timothy circumcised (Acts 16:1–3). Luke makes a point of telling about this, perhaps to make clear that Paul had no objections whatever to a Jew retaining his cultural identity; he also states, for example, that some years later Paul himself took on a Jewish vow (18:18).

Ministry in Macedonia and Achaia.

Philippi. Paul's travels eventually took him to the port city of Troas, on the western coast of Asia Minor. Here he had the well-known vision of a Macedonian asking him, "Come over to Macedonia and help us" (16:9). At this point in the narrative the author of Acts begins to refer to the missionary party, not as "Paul and his companions," but rather as "we" (v 10). It appears therefore that Luke joined the party in Troas (indeed, some speculate that he was the Macedonian who appeared in Paul's vision) and that he accompanied them to Philippi, Paul's first major stop in what is now called Europe.

Since the author drops the "we" in describing Paul's departure from Philippi, it may well be that Luke was left in charge of the new Christian congregation in that city. That congregation consisted of Lydia and other influential women (such as Euodia and Syntyche, Phil 4:2, 3), and their faithful support of the apostle's labor stands as one of the most beautiful examples of Christian commitment in the pages of the NT (cf. 2 Cor 8:1–5; Phil 4:14–19).

Paul's stay in Philippi was cut short on account of his having exorcised a divining spirit from a slave girl. The girl's owners had profited considerably from her fortune-telling, so when they "realized that their hope of making money was gone" they accused Paul and Silas of "throwing our city into an uproar by advocating customs unlawful for us Romans to accept or practice" (Acts 16:19–21). The two men were severely flogged, put in prison, and fastened in the stocks.

Miraculously, about midnight, while they were singing hymns, an earthquake shook the prison, the doors were opened, and all the chains came loose. When the jailer woke up, he assumed that the prisoners had escaped and, to save his honor, prepared to kill himself. Paul assured him, however, that no one had escaped. The jailer, acknowledging the evidence of God's work in the ministry of the apostle, asked how he could be saved. "Believe in the Lord Jesus," they replied, "and you will be saved—you and your household" (Acts 16:31).

Thessalonica, Beroea, Athens. The next morning the city officials decided to release Paul and Silas, but now Paul accused them of punishing Roman citizens without due process. Alarmed, the officials apologized and requested them to leave. Soon after that they traveled west to the capital of Macedonia, Thessalonica. Following the usual pattern, Paul spoke powerfully to the Jews, some of whom were persuaded by his preaching. The majority, however, were angered and started a riot. They accused Paul and Silas of political sedition against Caesar (Acts 17:6, 7), precipitating their flight south to Beroea. As soon as the Thessalonian Jews heard of this they went to Beroea as well. The agitation was such that the believers took Paul to the coast, boarded a ship with him, and headed for Athens.

According to 1 Thessalonians 3:1, 2, Timothy must have joined Paul in Athens soon after this. The apostle, however, was intensely concerned about the welfare of the Thessalonians, whom he had left after only a few weeks of ministry (1 Thes 2:17-20; cf. Acts 17:2). Unfortunately, as he says, Satan prevented him from returning to the church, a remark that may allude to some recurrent physical ailment. (cf. 2 Cor 12:7, 8; Gal 4:13-15. On the slim basis of Acts 23:1-5 and Gal 6:11, some have argued that Paul suffered from an eye disease. Perhaps better is the suggestion that he contracted malaria when he reached Asia Minor in his first journey, but this too is speculative.) At any rate, Paul decided to send Timothy back to Thessalonica. His form of expression in 1 Thessalonians 2:17-3:10 suggests strongly that this was a period of great loneliness and stress for him (note also 1 Cor 2:3, in which Paul tells the church in Corinth that he first came to them, right after his experiences in Athens, "in weakness and fear, and with much trembling").

All that Luke says in his narrative of Acts 17:16-34 is that Paul was distressed to witness the idolatry of the city, preached to both Jews and God-fearers, and began to dispute with the city's philosophers. Their interest piqued, the philosophers brought Paul to a formal meeting of the Areopagus, where he challenged their idolatry and proclaimed the only God as the one who commands people to repent, because he will judge everyone through Jesus, whom he raised from the dead (vv 22-31). Paul's reference to the resurrection was more than they could take, however, and they dismissed him, some courteously, others mockingly.

Corinth. During this time Paul had been anxiously waiting for Timothy's return and for news of the situation in Thessalonica. Perhaps discouraged, he left Athens and traveled to Corinth, a very busy commercial center in the province of Achaia. Some time later Timothy and Silas joined Paul in Corinth.

Timothy's report was very encouraging. The Thessalonians, in spite of many trials, had remained strong in their faith. At the same time, it appears that some opponents of Paul had accused him of being a charlatan, a flyby-night philosopher who had stayed in Thessalonica just long enough to cause trouble and make a profit. In addition, some of the believers, having misunderstood Paul's teaching concerning the return of Christ, were very depressed that friends and relatives had died prior to this great event. They wondered if this meant they were lost. Others in the congregation, sure that Jesus' return was near, thought it unnecessary to continue working and were making themselves a burden.

Immediately, Paul sat down to write a letter to these believers. It is quite likely that 1 Thessalonians is the earliest of Paul's letters (many prominent scholars, however, believe that Galatians is even earlier). The thrust of this letter is generally positive. He does however defend himself against the apparent charges of dishonesty (cf. 2:1–12). He encourages them in their difficult times of trial (2:13–16; 3:2–10), reminds them of their need for sanctification (4:1–12), and clarifies the doctrines associated with the second coming of Christ (4:13–5:11).

Soon after, while Paul was still in Corinth, he found it necessary to write a second letter to the Thessalonians. Perhaps some of the believers had further misunderstood Paul's teaching; perhaps a false letter had been circulated (2 Thess 2:2). In any case, 2 Thessalonians gives further instruction regarding the end times as well as more severe warnings to those who remain idle (2 Thess 3:6–15).

Although Luke says nothing about this correspondence, he does give some interesting information regarding Paul's ministry in Corinth, which lasted more than 18 months (Acts 8:11, 18). With the support of an influential Christian couple, Aquila and Priscilla, Paul preached in the synagogue until, as usual, Jewish opposition forced him to focus his ministry on Gentiles. It seems clear that the Christian congregation in Corinth, composed of both Jews and Gentiles, flourished dramatically (cf. vv 8–10). Luke also mentions that at one point the Jews brought Paul to trial.

Nothing came of this, but the incident is of some importance because Luke identifies the proconsul as Gallio (vv 12–17), whose name is otherwise attested. According to an inscription, Gallio served as proconsul of the province of Achaia beginning in the year 51 (possibly 52), and thus Paul's second missionary journey can be dated with relative precision as covering the years 50–52 (it began no earlier than 49 and it ended no later than 53), that is, when Paul was in his early 40s.

Third Missionary Journey.

Ministry in Ephesus. On his way back to Antioch, Paul stopped to visit the great port city of Ephesus, on the southwestern coast of Asia Minor. The apostle was no doubt impressed with the potential of this metropolitan center for the spread of the gospel and he determined to return (Acts 18:18–21). It is not know how long it was before Paul set out on his third missionary journey (Luke merely tells us that he spent "some time in Antioch," v 23). For this trip Paul appears to have followed the same route he had traveled on the previous journey, except instead of heading northwest to Troas he went to Ephesus, as he had planned (18:23; 19:1).

His stay in Ephesus was long, productive, and stormy. As usual, he began to preach in the synagogue; as usual, opposition drove him away (19:8, 9). His ministry lasted for more than two years and the gospel spread throughout the large province of Asia (v 10). Luke also relates two major incidents: an exorcism that led to many conversions (vv 13-17) and a riot provoked by craftsmen (vv 23-40). The latter, who fashioned shrines for the goddess Artemis, were losing money as a result of Paul's success. Paul was not directly affected by the uproar. Luke may have emphasized the incident as evidence that officials could find nothing legally wrong with Paul's activities.

The Corinthian Problem. Some important events took place, however, that Luke does not mention at all. Paul had sent, perhaps at the beginning of this journey, a letter to the Corinthian Christians in which he warned them of associating with disobedient believers (1 Cor 5:9). He had also mentioned to this church that he was raising a collection for the poor in Jerusalem (1 Cor 16:1). While in Ephesus, however, Paul received reports that the church in Corinth was experiencing severe problems, particularly divisions within the congregation (1 Cor 1:11, 12). Immorality, disruptions in the worship services, confusions about the resurrection, and several other evils threatened the spiritual life of this church. Moreover, the church itself had written a letter to Paul requesting instruction about such matters as marriage and divorce, meat offered to idols, spiritual gifts, and the method Paul was using for his collection (1 Cor 7:1; 8:1; 12:1; 16:1).

The apostle was confronted with a massive task, and his long first letter to the Corinthians was his attempt to deal with the problem. It appears that the church as a whole did not respond positively to this letter. Encouraged by a certain false apostle who opposed Paul, the members resisted the apostle's authority. Paul found it necessary to pay a "painful visit" to Corinth (not recorded in Acts, but alluded to in 2 Cor 2:1; cf. 13:1). This too was unsuccessful, so Paul sent Titus as his representative. It is probable that Titus carried with him a written ultimatum (the "sorrowful letter" mentioned in 2 Cor 2:4 and 7:8, though some scholars believe these verses refer to 1 Cor). In any case, Paul instructed Titus to attempt to resolve the problem and to meet him in Troas (cf. 2 Cor 2:12, 13).

The Galatian Problem. During this difficult time in Ephesus, Paul was also facing one of the most serious challenges to his ministry. Reports from the churches in Galatia (Iconium, Lystra, Derbe) indicated that Judaizers had visited these Christians and largely persuaded them that Paul, who had received his teaching and authority from the Jerusalem apostles (James, Peter, John), was a renegade who could not be trusted. Quite impressed by the Judaizers' arguments, the Galatians listened to their claim that Gentiles ought to be circumcised and observe the Jewish rites.

Paul, deeply disturbed by these reports, feared that the Galatian churches were at the point of committing apostasy: adopting the Judaizers' position meant abandoning the freedom of the gospel, salvation by grace (Gal 1:6–9; 2:15–21; 3:1–5; 4:8–11; 5:2–4). Accordingly, his Letter to the Galatians is full of polemics, with some very harsh statements against the false teachers (esp. 5:7–12). In it he denies absolutely that he received his gospel from the other apostles, for it came to him as a revelation from God himself (1:11–17); he also argues very carefully that the true heirs of Abraham are not those who are his physical descendants but those who, whether Jews or Gentiles, believe in God's promise as Abraham himself believed (3:7–29). Unfortunately, there is no evidence of how these churches responded to Paul's letter, though the apostle's expression of confidence (e.g., 5:10) indicates that they would have recognized the truth of his message.

(It should be pointed out that many conservative scholars do not think it possible that the Letter to the Galatians could have been written as late as the third missionary journey. In their opinion, the letter was written many years earlier, prior to the Apostolic Council of Jerusalem, usually dated in the year 49. If this early date is correct, there is reason to believe that the Galatians did repent of their error, for Paul continued to visit those churches in his subsequent journeys.)

Travel to Corinth. When Paul finally left Ephesus he went to Troas and was distressed not to find Titus there (2 Cor 2:12, 13). Concerned that perhaps Titus had met more trouble in Corinth, Paul continued on to Macedonia, probably to the city of Philippi (cf. Acts 20:1). There he did meet Titus, who reported with great joy that the Corinthians had finally come around (2 Cor. 7:5–7, 13–16). To be sure, not everything was in order. There seemed to be some hesitation, for example, with regard to supporting the collection Paul was raising. More seriously, a few individuals in the church continued to resist Paul's authority, and their opposition had to be dealt with.

Inscribed sherds from Corinth, where Paul stayed 3 months and founded a church.

In preparation for his upcoming visit to Corinth, therefore, Paul wrote 2 Corinthians from Macedonia. In this letter he expresses considerable joy at the response of the church, explains the nature of his ministry (3:1–5:21), encourages the congregation to give generously for the poor in Jerusalem (chs 8, 9), and argues vigorously against the "super-apostles" who oppose him (chs 10–13). All indications are that the response to 2 Corinthians was positive. Later Paul mentioned, for example, that the believers in Achaia (the province where Corinth was located) "were pleased to make a contribution for the poor among the saints in Jerusalem" (Rom 15:26). Another indirect piece of evidence is that during his three-month stay in Corinth (cf. Acts 20:2, 3) Paul wrote the great Letter to the Romans. The character of this letter—it is the lengthiest and the most carefully reasoned—out of his writings—suggests strongly that Paul enjoyed a period of relative calm in which he was able to formulate in coherent fashion his most important theological concerns.

The Letter to the Romans. The fact that Romans is so clearly theological in character has led most interpreters to ignore the historical occasion of the letter. It is important to remember, however, that during the third journey Paul had been dealing in a painful and personal way with the very issues that Romans carefully expounds. Moreover, the letter itself indicates that the apostle was anticipating controversy in the near future, upon his arrival at Jerusalem. In 15:30–32 Paul urges the believers in Rome to "struggle" in prayer with regard to this visit to Jerusalem. Paul was concerned not only about the unbelieving Jews, but also about Jewish believers who might question or even oppose his work among the Gentiles and who therefore might be reluctant to accept the offering he was bringing to them.

The apostle realized that when he met the Jerusalem church he would be faced with the same objections that had been thrown at him by the Judaizers during his third journey. The calm that he was enjoying in Corinth provided him with the opportunity to gather his thoughts and to formulate in a clear and organized way his answer to those objections. Under divine inspiration, therefore, he wrote a letter that may be viewed as a systematic response to the criticisms raised by Jews against what he called *his* gospel, that is, his distinctive presentation to the Gentiles.

After emphasizing the sin of both Jews and Gentiles (1:18–3:20), Paul states briefly the essence of his preaching in 3:21–24—free justification, apart from the Law, to those who believe in Jesus Christ. But a Jew might object that this renders God unjust: how can a just God simply acquit the guilty? Paul's answer is that God has not overlooked sin but condemned it by offering Christ as the atoning sacrifice (vv 25, 26). Again, it may be objected that God revealed his salvation to Abraham and that obedience to the sign of circumcision was part of the divine covenant. But Paul responds that Abraham was accounted righteous when he *believed*, and this happened while Abraham was still uncircumcised (4:9–12). Similarly, the charge that Paul's preaching encouraged sinful behavior ("if obedience to the law is not necessary for salvation, Gentiles will conclude that they might as well continue sinning") is one that the apostle answers with a three-chapter-long discussion of sanctification: those who have been justified freely have also been sanctified, they have broken their bond to sin and walk according to the Spirit (6:1–4, 15–18; 7:4–6; 8:1–8).

Most important is Paul's handling of the unbelief of Israel in chapters 9–11. Though many view this section of the letter as parenthetical or otherwise unrelated to the previous chapters, it is more likely the very heart of the letter, for no Jewish objection to the gospel was so powerful as their claim that, if Paul's preaching were true, then surely God's own people would recognize it as such. The fact that the Jewish nation as a whole rejected the gospel, they claimed, could only mean one of two things: either the gospel is not true or else God's promise has failed and his people have been rejected. Yet the apostle gives us a third option. God's word has *not* failed—it is simply that being a descendant of Abraham does not make one automatically part of God's people (Rom 9:6). Earlier in the letter he had affirmed that a true Jew is one who is circumcised, not in the flesh, but in the heart (2:28, 29); and that the true child of Abraham is one who, whether circumcised or not, follows in the steps of Abraham's faith (4:11, 12; note the earlier discussion of Gal). Chapter 9 picks up this emphasis, relating it to God's purpose of election (v 11), the OT concept of the remnant (v 27), the sin of the Israelites (10:16), and God's future plans (11:25–36).

If Paul, by writing this letter, was rehearsing his upcoming "defense" in Jerusalem, why would he send the letter to Rome? Paul had for some time wanted to visit Rome, the capital of the Roman Empire (cf. Acts 19:21). He intended to fulfill those wishes as soon as he had delivered the offering to the saints in Judea (Rom 15:23–25, 28, 32). It is likely, however, that the church in Rome had some awareness of the criticisms that had been raised against Paul. In fact, this church too was experiencing some Jewish—Gentile tensions of its own (cf. Rom 11:13–21 and the debate over eating meat in ch 14). Therefore, the best way for Paul to introduce himself to the Roman Christians was by giving them a clear exposition of "his" gospel (cf. 2:16) in the context of the controversies that surrounded him.

Travel to Jerusalem. Picking up the Acts narrative at 20:3, Paul left Corinth and retraced his steps through Macedonia. He and those accompanying him stopped in Troas for a week (20:6-11), then sailed on to the island of Miletus, where the elders from nearby Ephesus came to hear a farewell from the apostle (vv 13-38). To them he mentioned that the Holy Spirit had warned him of hardships he would have to face in Jerusalem (v 23). Indeed, as the party landed in Palestine, some of the brethren in Tyre pleaded with Paul not to go to Jerusalem; the scene repeated itself in Caesarea after the prophet Agabus prophesied that Paul would be imprisoned (Acts 21:4, 10-12). Paul was persuaded, however, that he must fulfill his mission, and he was more than ready to suffer in the name of Christ (v 13).

Upon his arrival in Jerusalem, he was met by James and the elders, who informed Paul that thousands of Jewish believers had questions about his methods and wondered whether in fact Paul was leading Jews to abandon Judaism. They suggested that Paul give evidence of his own obedience to the Law by joining four men who had made a vow and by paying for the expenses involved (21:17-24). Paul was quite willing to do this. Unfortunately, some Jews from the area around Ephesus recognized Paul and incited the crowds in the temple to riot (vv 27-30). When the Roman troops arrived on the scene, Paul was given the opportunity to speak to the crowds. He gave a ringing affirmation of his Christian faith, but as soon as he mentioned that God had commissioned him to go to the Gentiles (22:21) the crowds became unruly again.

Imprisonment and Death.

Caesarea. The next day Paul was brought before the Jewish Sanhedrin; on this occasion he made an issue of his belief in the resurrection, and as a result members of the Sanhedrin began to argue vigorously among themselves. (The Sadducees opposed this doctrine while the Pharisees accepted it.) The dispute led to violence and Paul was taken to the barracks (23:6-10); the following night, having been apprised of a Jewish plot to kill Paul, the commander dispatched him to Caesarea, the official residence of the Roman governor, Felix (23:12-35).

Within a week Felix gave audience to the Jewish accusers and listened both to their complaints and to Paul's defense, but he refused to make a judgment in the hopes of receiving a bribe. As a result Paul remained imprisoned in Caesarea for two years, until the governor was replaced by Porcius Festus (24:1-27). The most likely date for this change in administration is the year 59. Paul's imprisonment in Caesarea, therefore, is usually dated about 57-59; this means that the third missionary journey would have spanned the period from 53 to 57.

Soon after Festus became governor, the Jews urged him to send Paul to Jerusalem to be tried. Paul protested, however, and, exercising his right as a Roman citizen, demanded to be tried by the emperor himself (Acts 25:1–12). Festus consulted with King Agrippa, who asked to hear Paul. Luke records a lengthy defense by Paul in chapter 26; Agrippa's judgment was that "this man could have been set free, if he had not appealed to Caesar" (v 32).

To Rome. Luke also documents quite carefully the trip to Rome, including the shipwreck and the stay on the island of Malta (27:1–28:10). Upon his arrival in Rome, Paul asked to see the Jewish leaders, to whom he gave an account of his situation. They were at first receptive and Paul presented the gospel to them. While some believed, most apparently objected, for the apostle reminded them of Isaiah's mission to blind the eyes of the people and then concluded, "Therefore I want you to know that God's salvation has been sent to the Gentiles and they will listen!" (28:17–28). The Book of Acts somewhat abruptly comes to an end with the information that Paul stayed under house arrest for two years and that he continued to preach boldly and without hindrance (vv 30, 31).

Traditionally, this two-year period is regarded as the setting for the so-called prison letters—Ephesians, Philippians, Colossians, and Philemon. Many modern scholars question this opinion and prefer to view either Caesarea or Ephesus as the place from which these letters (some or all of them) were written. It is doubtful if a definitive solution to this problem will ever be reached, but there is no compelling reason to abandon the traditional view.

Apart from Philemon, which was written to deal with the very specific problem of the runaway slave Onesimus, the prison letters are characterized by an emphasis on the *present* enjoyment of heavenly blessings ("realized eschatology"; see esp. Eph 1:3, 13, 14; 2:4–7; Phil 1:6; 3:20; Col 3:1–4). In addition, Ephesians and Colossians are similar in their treatment of the unity of the church as the body of Christ (Eph 1:22, 23; 4:15, 16; Col 1:18, 24; 2:19). Philippians, perhaps best known for its "Christ-hymn" (2:6–11), is an important source for Paul's teaching on joy, suffering, and sanctification (1:9–11, 21, 27–30; 2:12, 13; 3:12–14; 4:4–9).

Last Years. The evidence gathered from outside of Acts is not at all clear as to whether or not Paul was released from his imprisonment. If the Letter to the Philippians was written during this period, it can be inferred that Paul had some concern that he might be executed (cf. Phil 1:19–24; 2:17). On the other hand, he sounds rather confident that he will be released and will be able to see the Philippians again (1:25, 26; cf. also Phlm 22).

Conservative scholars have argued that Paul was indeed released after two years, since the charges against him were groundless; that he possibly traveled to Spain as he had hoped (Rom 15:24, 28); that he returned to the east, visiting Crete (Ti 1:5), Ephesus and Macedonia (1 Tm 1:3), Miletus and Corinth (2 Tm 4:20), Troas (2 Tm 4:13), and Nicopolis (on the western coast of the Greek mainland, Ti 3:12); that he wrote 1 Timothy and Titus during this period of freedom; that finally he was imprisoned again after a.d. 64 (the year of the great fire in Rome, which led to the Neronian persecution of Christians); that he wrote 2 Timothy during this second imprisonment in Rome; and that he was decapitated under Nero between the years 65 and 67. Most likely, Paul was not yet 60 years old when he became a martyr for the faith.

This reconstruction of events is somewhat speculative, but it seems to account for the data more clearly than other suggestions. However, even if Paul was indeed released after the imprisonment described in Acts 28, it must be emphasized that almost nothing is known about his activities after such a release. In other words, the real significance of Paul's ministry must be deduced from the material actually found in the Book of Acts and in the major Pauline letters. God in his wisdom had determined that Paul would be "my chosen instrument to carry my name before the Gentiles and their kings and before the people of Israel. I will show him how much he must suffer for my name" (Acts 9:15, 16). The evidence is clear: Paul was obedient to the heavenly vision (26:19), and his ministry made possible the spread of the gospel to the ends of the earth.

Mamertine prison in Rome, where, according to tradition, both Paul and Peter were imprisoned.[2]

MOISÉS SILVA

---

[2] Walter A. Elwell and Barry J. Beitzel, Baker Encyclopedia of the Bible (Grand Rapids, MI: Baker Book House, 1988), 1621–1634.

CHAPTER I His Place In History

Paragraphs 1–12.

1, 2.   The Man Needed by the Time.

3, 4.   A Type of Christian Character.

5, 6.   The Thinker of Christianity.

9–12.   The Missionary of the Gentiles.

1. There are some men whose lives it is impossible to study without receiving the impression that they were expressly sent into the world to do a work required by the juncture of history on which they fell. The story of the Reformation, for example, cannot be read by a devout mind without wonder at the providence by which such great men as Luther, Zwingli, Calvin, and Knox were simultaneously raised up in different parts of Europe to break the yoke of the papacy and republish the gospel of grace. When the Evangelical Revival, after blessing England, was about to break into Scotland and end the dreary reign of Moderatism, there was raised up in Thomas Chalmers a mind of such capacity as completely to absorb the new movement into itself, and of such sympathy and influence as to diffuse it to every corner of his native land.

2. This impression is produced by no life more than by that of the apostle Paul. He was given to Christianity when it was in its most rudimentary beginnings. It was not indeed feeble, nor can any mortal man be spoken of as indispensable to it; for it contained within itself the vigor of a divine and immortal existence, which could not but have unfolded itself in the course of time. But if we recognize that God makes use of means which commend themselves even to our eyes as suited to the ends he has in view, then we must say that the Christian movement at the moment when Paul appeared upon the stage was in the utmost need of a man of extraordinary endowments, who, becoming possessed with its genius, should incorporate it with the general history of the world; and in Paul it found the man it needed.

3. Christianity obtained in Paul an incomparable type of Christian character. It already indeed possessed the perfect model of human character in the person of its Founder. However, he was not as other men, because from the beginning he had no sinful imperfections to struggle with; and Christianity still required to show what it could make of imperfect human nature. Paul supplied the opportunity of exhibiting this. He was naturally of immense mental stature and force. He would have been a remarkable man even if he had never become a Christian. The other apostles would have lived and died in the obscurity of Galilee if

they had not been lifted into prominence by the Christian movement; but the name of Saul of Tarsus would have been remembered still in some character or other even if Christianity had never existed. Christianity got the opportunity in him of showing the world the whole force that was in it. Paul was aware of this himself, though he expressed it with perfect modesty, when he said, "For this cause I obtained mercy, that in me as chief might Jesus Christ show forth all his long-suffering for an ensample of them who should hereafter believe on him to everlasting life."

4. His conversion proved the power of Christianity to overcome the strongest prejudices and to stamp its own type on a large nature by a revolution both instantaneous and permanent. Paul's was a personality so strong and original that no other man could have been less expected to sink himself in another; but from the moment when he came into contact with Christ he was so overmastered with His influence that ever afterwards his ruling desire was to be the mere echo and reflection of Him to the world. But if Christianity showed its strength in making so complete a conquest of Paul, it showed its worth no less in the kind of man it made of him when he had given himself up to its influence. It satisfied the needs of a peculiarly hungry nature, and never to the close of his life did he betray the slightest sense that this satisfaction was abating. His constitution was originally compounded of fine materials, but the spirit of Christ passing into them raised them to a pitch of excellence altogether unique. Nor was it ever doubtful either to himself or to others that it was the influence of Christ which made him what he was. The truest motto for his life would be his own saying, "I live; yet not I, but Christ liveth in me." Indeed, so perfectly was Christ formed in him that we can study Christ's character in his, and beginners may perhaps learn even more of Christ from studying Paul's life than from studying Christ's own. In Christ himself there was a blending and softening of all the excellences which make his greatness elude the glance of the beginner, just as the very perfection of Raphael's painting makes it disappointing to an untrained eye; whereas in Paul a few of the greatest elements of Christian character were exhibited with a decisiveness which no one can mistake, just as the most prominent characteristics of the painting of Rubens can be appreciated by every spectator.

5. Christianity obtained in Paul, secondly, a great thinker. This it specially needed at the moment. Christ had departed from the world, and those whom he had left to represent him were unlettered fishermen, and for the most part men of no intellectual mark. In one sense this fact reflects a peculiar glory on Christianity, for it shows that it did not owe its place as one of the great influences of the world to the abilities of its human representatives: not by might nor by power, but by the Spirit of God, was Christianity established in the earth. Yet, as we look back now,

we can clearly see how essential it was that an apostle of a different stamp and training should arise.

6. Christ had manifested forth the glory of the Father once for all and completed his atoning work. But this was not enough. It was necessary that the meaning of his appearance should be explained to the world. Who was he who had been here? What precisely had he done? To these questions the original apostles could give brief popular answers; but none of them had the intellectual reach or the educational training necessary to put the answers into a form to satisfy the intellect of the world. Happily it is not essential to salvation to be able to answer such questions with scientific accuracy. There are many who know and believe that Jesus was the Son of God and died to take away sin, and, trusting to him as their Saviour, are purified by faith, but who could not explain these statements at any length without falling into mistakes in almost every sentence. Yet if Christianity was to make an intellectual as well as a moral conquest of the world, it was necessary for the church to have accurately explained to her the full glory of her Lord and the meaning of his saving work. Of course Jesus himself had in his mind a comprehension both of what he was and of what he was doing which was luminous as the sun. But it was one of the most pathetic aspects of his earthly ministry that he could not tell all his mind to his followers. They were not able to bear it; they were too rude and limited to take it in. He had to carry his deepest thoughts out of the world with him unuttered, trusting with a sublime faith that the Holy Ghost would lead his church to grasp them in the course of its subsequent development. Even what he did utter was very imperfectly understood. There was one mind, it is true, in the original apostolic circle of the finest quality and capable of soaring into the rarest altitudes of speculation. The words of Christ sank into the mind of John, and, after lying there for half a century, grew up into the wonderful forms we inherit in his Gospel and Epistles. But even the mind of John was not equal to the exigency of the church; it was too fine, mystical, unusual. His thoughts to this day remain the property only of the few finest minds. There was needed a thinker of broader and more massive make to sketch the first outlines of Christian doctrine; and he was found in Paul.

7. Paul was a born thinker. His mind was of majestic breadth and force. It was restlessly busy, never able to leave any object with which it had to deal until it had pursued it back to its remotest causes and forward into all its consequences. It was not enough for him to know that Christ was the Son of God; he had to unfold this statement into its elements and understand precisely what it meant. It was not enough for him to believe that Christ died for sin; he had to go farther and inquire why it was necessary that He should do so and how His death took sin away. But not

only had he from nature this speculative gift; his talent was trained by education. The other apostles were unlettered men, but he enjoyed the fullest scholastic advantages of the period. In the rabbinical school he learned how to arrange and state and defend his ideas. We have the issue of all this in his Epistles, which contain the best explanation of Christianity possessed by the world. The right way to look at them is to regard them as the continuation of Christ's own teaching. They contain the thoughts which Christ carried away from the earth with him unuttered. Of course Jesus would have uttered them differently and far better. Paul's thoughts have everywhere the coloring of his own mental peculiarities. But the substance of them is what Christ's must have been if he had himself given them expression.

8. There was one great subject especially which Christ had to leave unexplained—his own death. He could not explain it before it had taken place. This became the leading topic of Paul's thinking—to show why it was needed and what were its blessed results. But indeed there was no aspect of the appearance of Christ into which his restlessly inquiring mind did not penetrate. His thirteen Epistles, when arranged in chronological order, show that his mind was constantly getting deeper and deeper into the subject. The progress of his thinking was determined partly by the natural progress of his own experience in the knowledge of Christ, for he always wrote straight out of his own experience; and partly by the various forms of error which he had at successive periods to encounter, and which became a providential means of stimulating and developing his apprehension of the truth, just as ever since in the Christian church the rise of error has been the means of calling forth the clearest statements of doctrine. The ruling impulse, however, of his thinking, as of his life, was ever Christ, and it was his lifelong devotion to this exhaustless theme that made him the thinker of Christianity.

9. Christianity obtained in Paul, thirdly, the missionary of the Gentiles. It is rare to find the highest speculative power united with great practical activity; but they were united in him. He was not only the church's greatest thinker, but the very foremost worker she has ever possessed. We have been considering the speculative task which was awaiting him when he joined the Christian community; but there was a no less stupendous practical task awaiting him too. This was the evangelization of the Gentile world.

10. One of the great objects of the appearance of Christ was to break down the wall of separation between Jew and Gentile and make the blessings of salvation the property of all men, without distinction of race or language. But he was not himself permitted to carry this change into practical realization. It was one of the strange limitations of his earthly life

that he was sent only to the lost sheep of the house of Israel. It can easily be imagined how congenial a task it would have been to his intensely human heart to carry the gospel beyond the limits of Palestine and make it known to nation after nation; and—if it be not too bold to say so—this would certainly have been his chosen career had he been spared. But he was cut off in the midst of his days and had to leave this task to his followers.

11. Before the appearance of Paul on the scene the execution of this task had been begun. Jewish prejudice had been partially broken down, the universal character of Christianity had been in some measure realized, and Peter had admitted the first Gentiles into the church by baptism. But none of the original apostles was equal to the emergency. None of them was large-minded enough to grasp the idea of the perfect equality of Jew and Gentile and apply it without flinching in all its practical consequences; and none of them had the combination of gifts necessary to attempt the conversion of the Gentile world on a large scale. They were Galilean fishermen, fit enough to teach and preach within the bounds of their native Palestine. But beyond Palestine lay the great world of Greece and Rome—the world of vast populations, of power and culture, of pleasure and business. It needed a man of unlimited versatility, of education, of immense human sympathy and breadth, to go out there with the gospel message; a man who could not only be a Jew to the Jews, but a Greek to the Greeks, a Roman to the Romans, a barbarian to the barbarians; a man who could encounter not only rabbis in their synagogues, but proud magistrates in their courts and philosophers in the haunts of learning; a man who could face travel by land and by sea, who could exhibit presence of mind in every variety of circumstances, and would be cowed by no difficulties. No man of this size belonged to the original apostolic circle; but Christianity needed such a one, and he was found in Paul.

12. Originally attached more strictly than any of the other apostles to the peculiarities and prejudices of Jewish exclusiveness, he cut his way out of the jungle of these prepossessions, accepted the equality of all men in Christ, and applied this principle relentlessly in all its issues. He gave his heart to the Gentile mission, and the history of his life is the history of how true he was to his vocation. There was never such singleness of eye and wholeness of heart. There was never such superhuman and untiring energy. There was never such an accumulation of difficulties victoriously met and of sufferings cheerfully borne for any cause. In him Jesus Christ went forth to evangelize the world, making use of his hands and feet, his tongue and brain and heart, for doing the work which in His own bodily presence He had not been permitted by the limits of His mission to accomplish.

CHAPTER II His Unconscious Preparation for His Work

Paragraphs 13–36.

14–16.   Date and Place of Birth.

His love of Cities.

17, 18.   Home.

19–26.   Education.

19. Roman Citizenship; 20. Tent-making; 21, 22. Knowledge of Greek Literature; 23–26. Rabbinical Teaching. Gamaliel. Knowledge of Old Testament.

27–30.   Moral and Religious Development.

28. The Law; 29, 30. Departure from and Return to Jerusalem.

31–33.   State of the Christian Church. Stephen.

34–36.   The Persecutor.

13. Persons whose conversion takes place after they are grown up are wont to look back upon the period of their life which has preceded this event with sorrow and shame, and to wish that an obliterating hand might blot the record of it out of existence. St. Paul felt this sentiment strongly; to the end of his days he was haunted by the spectres of his lost years, and was wont to say that he was the least of all the apostles, who was not worthy to be called an apostle, because he had persecuted the church of God. But these sombre sentiments are only partially justifiable. God's purposes are very deep, and even in those who know him not he may be sowing seeds which will only ripen and bear their fruit long after their godless career is over. Paul would never have been the man he became or have done the work he did, if he had not in the years preceding his conversion gone through a course of preparation designed to fit him for his subsequent career. He knew not what he was being prepared for; his own intentions about his future were different from God's; but there is a divinity which shapes our ends, and it was making him a polished shaft for God's quiver, though he knew it not.

14. The date of Paul's birth is not exactly known, but it can be settled with a closeness of approximation which is sufficient for practical purposes. When in the year 33 A. D. those who stoned Stephen laid down their clothes at Paul's feet, he was "a young man." This term has,

indeed, in Greek as much latitude as in English, and may indicate any age from something under twenty to something over thirty. In this case it probably touched the latter rather than the former limit; for there is reason to believe that at this time, or very soon after, he was a member of the Sanhedrin—an office which no one could hold who was under thirty years of age; and the commission he received from the Sanhedrin immediately afterwards to persecute the Christians would scarcely have been entrusted to a very young man. About thirty years after playing this sad part in Stephen's murder, in the year 62 A. D., he was lying in a prison in Rome awaiting sentence of death for the same cause for which Stephen had suffered, and, writing one of the last of his Epistles, that to Philemon, he called himself an old man. This term also is one of great latitude, and a man who had gone through so many hardships might well be old before his time; yet he could scarcely have taken the name of "Paul the aged" before sixty years of age. These calculations lead us to the conclusion that he was born about the same time as Jesus. When the boy Jesus was playing in the streets of Nazareth the boy Paul was playing in the streets of his native town, away on the other side of the ridges of Lebanon. They seemed likely to have totally diverse careers. Yet by the mysterious arrangement of Providence these two lives, like streams flowing from opposite watersheds, were one day, as river and tributary, to mingle together.

15. The place of his birth was Tarsus, the capital of the province of Cilicia, in the southeast of Asia Minor. It stood a few miles from the coast, in the midst of a fertile plain, and was built upon both banks of the river Cydnus, which descended to it from the neighboring Taurus Mountains, on whose snowy peaks the inhabitants of the town were wont, in the summer evenings, to watch from the flat roofs of their houses the glow of the sunset. Not far above the town the river poured over the rocks in a vast cataract, but below this it became navigable, and within the town its banks were lined with wharves, on which was piled the merchandise of many countries, while sailors and merchants, dressed in the costumes and speaking the languages of different races, were constantly to be seen in the streets. The town enjoyed an extensive trade in timber, with which the province abounded, and in the long fine hair of the goats kept in thousands on the neighboring mountains, which was made into a coarse kind of cloth and manufactured into various articles, among which tents, such as Paul was afterwards employed in sewing, formed an extensive article of merchandise all along the shores of the Mediterranean. Tarsus was also the centre of a large transport trade; for behind the town a famous pass, called the Cilician Gates, led up through the mountains to the central countries of Asia Minor; and Tarsus was the dépôt to which the products of these countries were brought down to be distributed over

the east and the west. The inhabitants of the city were numerous and wealthy. The majority of them were native Cilicians, but the wealthiest merchants were Greeks. The province was under the sway of the Romans, the signs of whose sovereignty could not be absent from the capital, although Tarsus itself enjoyed the privilege of self-government. The number and variety of the inhabitants were still further increased by the fact that, like our own Glasgow, Tarsus was not only a centre of commerce, but also a seat of learning. It was one of the three principal university cities of the period, the other two being Athens and Alexandria; and it was said to surpass its rivals in intellectual eminence. Students from many countries were seen in its streets, a sight which could not but awaken thoughts in youthful minds about the value and the aims of learning.

16. Who does not see how fit a place this was for the apostle of the Gentiles to be born in? As he grew up he was being unawares prepared to encounter men of every class and race, to sympathize with human nature in all its varieties, and to look with tolerance upon the most diverse habits and customs. In after life he was always a lover of cities. Whereas his Master avoided Jerusalem and loved to teach on the mountain-side or the shore of the lake, Paul was constantly moving from one great city to another. Antioch, Ephesus, Athens, Corinth, Rome, the capitals of the ancient world, were the scenes of his activity. The words of Jesus are redolent of the country and teem with pictures of its still beauty or homely toil—the lilies of the field, the sheep following the shepherd, the sower in the furrow, the fishermen drawing their nets. But the language of Paul is impregnated with the atmosphere of the city and alive with the tramp and hurry of the streets. His imagery is borrowed from scenes of human energy and monuments of cultivated life—the soldier in full armor, the athlete in the arena, the building of houses and temples, the triumphal procession of the victorious general. So lasting are the associations of the boy in the life of the man.

17. Paul had a certain pride in the place of his birth, as he showed by boasting on one occasion that he was a citizen of no mean city. He had a heart formed by nature to feel the warmest glow of patriotism. Yet it was not for Cilicia and Tarsus that this fire burned. He was an alien in the land of his birth. His father was one of those numerous Jews who were scattered in that age over the cities of the Gentile world, engaged in trade and commerce. They had left the Holy Land, but they did not forget it. They never coalesced with the populations among which they dwelt, but, in dress, food, religion, and many other particulars, remained a peculiar people. As a rule, indeed, they were less rigid in their religious views and more tolerant of foreign customs than those Jews who remained in Palestine. But Paul's father was not one who had given way to laxity. He

belonged to the straitest sect of his religion. It is probable that he had not left Palestine long before his son's birth, for Paul calls himself a Hebrew of the Hebrews—a name which seems to have belonged only to the Palestinian Jews and to those whose connection with Palestine had continued very close. Of his mother we hear absolutely nothing, but everything seems to indicate that the home in which he was brought up was one of those out of which nearly all eminent religious teachers have sprung—a home of piety, of character, perhaps of somewhat stern principle, and of strong attachment to the peculiarities of a religious people. He was imbued with its spirit. Although he could not but receive innumerable and imperishable impressions from the city he was born in, the land and the city of his heart were Palestine and Jerusalem; and the heroes of his young imagination were not Curtius and Horatius, Hercules and Achilles, but Abraham and Joseph, Moses and David and Ezra. As he looked back on the past it was not over the confused annals of Cilicia that he cast his eyes, but he gazed up the clear stream of Jewish history to its sources in Ur of the Chaldees; and when he thought of the future, the vision which rose on him was the kingdom of the Messiah enthroned in Jerusalem and ruling the nations with a rod of iron.

18. The feeling of belonging to a spiritual aristocracy, elevated above the majority of those among whom he lived, would be deepened in him by what he saw of the religion of the surrounding population. Tarsus was the centre of a species of Baal-worship of an imposing but unspeakably degrading character, and at certain seasons sons of the year it was the scene of festivals, which were frequented by the whole population of the neighboring regions, and were accompanied with orgies of a degree of moral abominableness happily beyond the reach even of our imaginations. Of course a boy could not see the depths of this mystery of iniquity, but he could see enough to make him turn from idolatry with the scorn peculiar to his nation, and to make him regard the little synagogue where his family worshipped the Holy One of Israel as far more glorious than the gorgeous temples of the heathen; and perhaps to these early experiences we may trace back in some degree those convictions of the depths to which human nature can fall and its need of an omnipotent redeeming force which afterwards formed so fundamental a part of his theology and gave such a stimulus to his work.

19. The time at length arrived for deciding what occupation the boy was to follow—a momentous crisis in every life; and in this case much was involved in the decision. Perhaps the most natural career for him would have been that of a merchant; for his father was engaged in trade, the busy city offered splendid prizes to mercantile ambition, and the boy's own energy would have guaranteed success. Besides, his father had an advantage to give him specially useful to a merchant: though a Jew, he

was a Roman citizen, and this right would have given his son protection, into whatever part of the Roman world he might have had occasion to travel. How the father got this right we cannot tell; it might be bought, or won by distinguished service to the state, or acquired in several other ways; at all events his son was free-born. It was a valuable privilege, and one which was to prove of great use to Paul, though not in the way in which his father might have been expected to desire him to make use of it. But it was decided that he was not to be a merchant. The decision may have been due to his father's strong religious views, or his mother's pious ambition, or his own predilections; but it was resolved that he should go to college and become a rabbi—that is, a minister, a teacher, and a lawyer all in one. It was a wise decision in view of the boy's spirit and capabilities, and it turned out to be of infinite moment for the future of mankind.

20. But although he thus escaped the chances which seemed likely to drift him into a secular calling, yet before going away to prepare for the sacred profession he was to get some insight into business life; for it was a rule among the Jews that every boy, whatever might be the profession he was to follow, should learn a trade as a resource in time of need. This was a rule with wisdom in it; for it gave the young employment at an age when too much leisure is dangerous, and acquainted the wealthy and the learned in some degree with the feelings of those who have to earn their bread with the sweat of their brow. The trade which he was put to was the commonest one in Tarsus—the making of tents from the goat's-hair cloth for which the district was celebrated. Little did he or his father think, when he began to handle the disagreeable material, of what importance this handicraft was to be to him in subsequent years; it became the means of his support during his missionary journeys, and, at a time when it was essential that the propagators of Christianity should be above the suspicion of selfish motives, enabled him to maintain himself in a position of noble independence.

21. It is a question natural to ask, whether, before leaving home to go and get his training as a rabbi, Paul attended the University of Tarsus. Did he drink at the wells of wisdom which flow from Mt. Helicon before he went to sit by those which spring from Mt. Zion? From the fact that he makes two or three quotations from the Greek poets it has been inferred that he was acquainted with the whole literature of Greece. But on the other hand, it has been pointed out that his quotations are brief and commonplace, such as any man who spoke Greek would pick up and use occasionally; and the style and vocabulary of his Epistles are not those of the models of Greek literature, but of the Septuagint, the Greek version of the Hebrew Scriptures, which was then in universal use among the Jews of the Dispersion. Probably his father would have considered it sinful to

allow his son to attend a heathen university. Yet it is not likely that he grew up in a great seat of learning without receiving any influence from the academic tone of the place. His speech at Athens shows that he was able, when he chose, to wield a style much more stately than that of his writings, and so keen a mind was not likely to remain in total ignorance of the great monuments of the language which he spoke.

22. There were other impressions too which the learned Tarsus probably made upon him. Its university was famous for those petty disputes and rivalries, which sometimes ruffle the calm of academical retreats; and it is possible that the murmur of these may have given the first impulse to that scorn for the tricks of the rhetorician and the windy disputations of the sophist which forms so marked a feature in some of his writings. The glances of young eyes are clear and sure, and even as a boy he may have perceived how small may be the souls of men and how mean their lives when their mouths are filled with the finest phraseology.

23. The college for the education of Jewish rabbis was in Jerusalem, and thither Paul was sent about the age of thirteen. His arrival in the Holy City may have happened in the same year in which Jesus, at the age of twelve, first visited it, and the overpowering emotions of the boy from Nazareth at the first sight of the capital of his race may be taken as an index of the unrecorded experience of the boy from Tarsus. To every Jewish child of a religious disposition Jerusalem was the centre of all things; the footsteps of prophets and kings echoed in its streets; memories sacred and sublime clung to its walls and buildings; and it shone in the glamour of illimitable hopes.

24. It chanced that at this time the college of Jerusalem was presided over by one of the most noted teachers the Jews have ever possessed. This was Gamaliel, at whose feet Paul tells us he was brought up. He was called by his contemporaries the Beauty of the Law, and is still remembered among the Jews as the Great Rabbi. He was a man of lofty character and enlightened mind, a Pharisee strongly attached to the traditions of the fathers, yet not intolerant or hostile to Greek culture, as some of the narrower Pharisees were. The influence of such a man on an open mind like Paul's must have been very great; and although for a time the pupil became an intolerant zealot, yet the master's example may have had something to do with the conquest he finally won over prejudice.

25. The course of instruction which a rabbi had to undergo was lengthened and peculiar. It consisted entirely of the study of the Scriptures and the comments of the sages and masters upon them. The words of Scripture and the sayings of the wise were committed to memory; discussions were carried on about disputed points; and by a rapid fire of questions, which the scholars were allowed to put as well as the masters,

the wits of the students were sharpened and their views enlarged. The outstanding qualities of Paul's intellect which were conspicuous in his subsequent life—his marvellous memory, the keenness of his logic, the super-abundance of his ideas, and his original way of taking up every subject—first displayed themselves in this school, and excited, we may believe, the warm interest of his teacher.

26. He himself learned much here which was of great moment in his subsequent career. Although he was to be specially the missionary of the Gentiles, he was also a great missionary to his own people. In every city he visited where there were Jews he made his first public appearance in the synagogue. There his training as a rabbi secured him an opportunity of speaking, and his familiarity with Jewish modes of thought and reasoning enabled him to address his audiences in the way best fitted to secure their attention. His knowledge of the Scriptures enabled him to adduce proofs from an authority which his hearers acknowledged to be supreme. Besides, he was destined to be the great theologian of Christianity and the principal writer of the New Testament. Now the New grew out of the Old; the one is in all its parts the prophecy and the other the fulfilment. But it required a mind saturated not only with Christianity, but with the Old Testament, to bring this out; and, at the age when the memory is most retentive, Paul acquired such a knowledge of the Old Testament that everything it contains was at his command: its phraseology became the language of his thinking; he literally writes in quotations, and he quotes from all parts with equal facility—from the Law, the Prophets, and the Psalms. Thus was the warrior equipped with the armor and the weapons of the Spirit before he knew in what cause he was to use them.

27. Meantime what was his moral and religious state? He was learning to be a religious teacher; was he himself religious? Not all who are sent to college by their parents to prepare for the sacred office are so, and in every city of the world the path of youth is beset with temptations which may ruin life at its very commencement. Some of the greatest teachers of the church, such as St. Augustine, have had to look back on half their life blotted and scarred with vice or crime. No such fall defaced Paul's early years. Whatever struggles with passion may have raged in his own breast, his conduct was always pure. Jerusalem was no very favorable place in that age for virtue. It was the Jerusalem against whose external sanctity, but internal depravity, our Lord a few years afterwards hurled such withering invectives; it was the very seat of hypocrisy, where an able youth might easily have learned how to win the rewards of religion while escaping its burdens. But Paul was preserved amid these perils, and could afterwards claim that he had lived in Jerusalem from the first in all good conscience.

28. He had brought with him from home the conviction, which forms the basis of a religious life, that the one prize that makes life worth living is the love and favor of God. This conviction grew into a passionate longing as he advanced in years, and he asked his teachers how the prize was to be won. Their answer was ready—By the keeping of the law. It was a terrible answer; for the law meant not only what we understand by the term, but also the ceremonial law of Moses and the thousand and one rules added to it by the Jewish teachers, whose observance made life a kind of purgatory to a tender conscience. But Paul was not the man to shrink from difficulties. He had set his heart upon winning God's favor, without which this life appeared to him a blank and eternity the blackness of darkness; and if this was the way to the goal, he was willing to tread it. Not only, however, were his personal hopes involved in this, the hopes of his nation depended on it too; for it was the universal belief of his people that the Messiah would only come to a nation keeping the law, and it was even said that if one man kept it perfectly for a single day, his merit would bring to the earth the King for whom they were waiting. Paul's rabbinical training, then, culminated in the desire to win this prize of righteousness, and he left the halls of sacred learning with this as the purpose of his life. The lonely student's resolution was momentous for the world; for he was first to prove amid secret agonies that this way of salvation was false, and then to teach his discovery to mankind.

29. We cannot tell in what year Paul's education at the college of Jerusalem was finished or where he went immediately afterwards. The young rabbis, after completing their studies, scattered in the same way as our own divinity students do, and began practical work in different parts of the Jewish world. He may have gone back to his native Cilicia and held office in some synagogue there. At all events, he was for some years at a distance from Jerusalem and Palestine; for these were the very years in which fell the movement of John the Baptist and the ministry of Jesus, and it is certain that Paul could not have been in the vicinity without being involved in both of these movements either as a friend or as a foe.

30. But before long he returned to Jerusalem. It was as natural for the highest rabbinical talent to gravitate in those times to Jerusalem as it is for the highest literary and commercial talent to gravitate in our times to London. He arrived in the capital of Judaism very soon after the death of Jesus; and we can easily imagine the representations of that event and of the career thereby terminated which he would receive from his Pharisaic friends. We have no reason to suppose that as yet he had any doubts about his own religion. We gather, indeed, from his writings that he had already passed through severe mental conflicts. Although the conviction stood fast in his mind that the blessedness of life was attainable only in the favor of God, yet his efforts to reach this coveted position by the

observance of the law had not satisfied him. On the contrary, the more he strove to keep the law the more active became the motions of sin within him; his conscience was becoming more oppressed with the sense of guilt, and the peace of a soul at rest in God was a prize which eluded his grasp. Still he did not question the teaching of the synagogue. To him as yet this was of one piece with the history of the Old Testament, whence looked down on him the figures of the saints and prophets, which were a guarantee that the system they represented must be divine, and behind which he saw the God of Israel revealing himself in the giving of the law. The reason why he had not attained to peace and fellowship with God was, he believed, because he had not struggled enough with the evil of his nature or honored enough the precepts of the law. Was there no service by which he could make up for all deficiencies and win that grace at last in which the great of old had stood? This was the temper of mind in which he returned to Jerusalem and learned with astonishment and indignation of the rise of a sect which believed that Jesus who had been crucified was the Messiah of the Jewish people.

31. Christianity was as yet only two or three years old, and was growing very quietly in Jerusalem. Although those who had heard it preached at Pentecost had carried the news of it to their homes in many quarters, its public representatives had not yet left the city of its birth. As first the authorities had been inclined to persecute it and checked its teachers when they appeared in public. But they had changed their minds and, acting under the advice of Gamaliel, resolved to neglect it, believing that it would die out if let alone. The Christians, on the other hand, gave as little offence as possible; in the externals of religion they continued to be strict Jews and zealous of the law, attending the temple worship, observing the Jewish ceremonies, and respecting the ecclesiastical authorities. It was a kind of truce which allowed Christianity a little space for secret growth. In their upper rooms the brethren met to break bread and pray to their ascended Lord. It was a most beautiful spectacle. The new faith had alighted among them like an angel, and was shedding purity on their souls from its wings and breathing over their humble gatherings the spirit of peace. Their love to each other was unbounded; they were filled with the inspiring sense of discovery; and as often as they met their invisible Lord was in their midst. It was like heaven upon earth. While Jerusalem around them was going on in its ordinary course of worldliness and ecclesiastical asperity, these few humble souls were felicitating themselves with a secret which they knew to contain within it the blessedness of mankind and the future of the world.

32. But the truce could not last, and these scenes of peace were soon to be invaded with terror and bloodshed. Christianity could not keep such a truce, for there is in it a world-conquering force which impels it at

all risks to propagate itself, and the fermentation of the new wine of gospel liberty was sure sooner or later to burst the forms of the Jewish law. At length a man arose in the church in whom these aggressive tendencies embodied themselves. This was Stephen, one of the seven deacons who had been appointed to watch over the temporal affairs of the Christian society. He was a man full of the Holy Ghost and possessed of capabilities which the brevity of his career only permitted to suggest, but not to develop themselves. He went from synagogue to synagogue, preaching the Messiahship of Jesus and announcing the advent of freedom from the yoke of the law. Champions of Jewish orthodoxy encountered him, but were not able to withstand his eloquence and holy zeal. Foiled in argument, they grasped at other weapons, stirring up the authorities and the populace to murderous fanaticism.

33. One of the synagogues in which these disputations took place was that of the Cilicians, the countrymen of Paul. May he have been a rabbi in this synagogue and one of Stephen's opponents in argument? At all events, when the argument of logic was exchanged for that of violence, he was in the front. When the witnesses who cast the first stones at Stephen were stripping for their work, they laid down their garments at his feet. There, on the margin of that wild scene, in the field of judicial murder, we see his figure standing a little apart and sharply outlined against the mass of persecutors unknown to fame—the pile of many-colored robes at his feet and his eyes bent upon the holy martyr, who is kneeling in the article of death and praying, "Lord, lay not this sin to their charge."

34. His zeal on this occasion brought Paul prominently under the notice of the authorities. It probably procured him a seat in the Sanhedrin, where we find him soon afterwards giving his vote against the Christians. At all events, it led to his being entrusted with the work of utterly uprooting Christianity, which the authorities now resolved upon. He accepted their proposal; for he believed it to be God's work. He saw more clearly than any one else what was the drift of Christianity; and it seemed to him destined, if unchecked, to overturn all that he considered most sacred. The repeal of the law was in his eyes the obliteration of the one way of salvation, and faith in a crucified Messiah blasphemy against the divinest hope of Israel. Besides, he had a deep personal interest in the task. Hitherto he had been striving to please God, but always felt his services to come short; here was a chance of making up for all arrears by one splendid act of service. This was the iron of agony in his soul which gave edge and energy to his zeal. In any case he was not a man to do things by halves; and he flung himself headlong into his task.

35. Terrible were the scenes which ensued. He flew from synagogue to synagogue and from house to house, dragging forth men and women, who were cast into prison and punished. Some appear to have been put to death, and, darkest trait of all, others were compelled to blaspheme the name of the Saviour. The church at Jerusalem was broken in pieces and its members who escaped the rage of the persecutor were scattered over the neighboring provinces and countries.

36. It may seem too venturesome to call this the last stage of Paul's unconscious preparation for his apostolic career. But so indeed it was. In entering on the career of a persecutor he was going on straight in the line of the creed in which he had been brought up; and this was its reduction to absurdity. Besides, through the gracious working of Him whose highest glory it is out of evil still to bring forth good, there sprang out of these sad doings in the mind of Paul an intensity of humility, a willingness to serve even the least of the brethren of those whom he had abused, and a zeal to redeem lost time by the parsimonious use of what was left, which became permanent spurs to action in his subsequent career.

CHAPTER III His Conversion

Paragraphs 37–50.

37, 38.   Severity of the Persecution.

39–42.   Kicking against the Goad.

43, 44.   The Vision of Christ.

45–48.   Effect of his Conversion on his Thinking.

49, 50.   Its Effect on his Destiny.

37. It was the persecutor's hope utterly to exterminate Christianity. But little did he understand its genius. It thrives on persecution. Prosperity has often been fatal to it, persecution never. "They that were scattered abroad went everywhere preaching the word." Hitherto the church had been confined within the walls of Jerusalem; but now all over Judæa and Samaria, and in distant Phœnicia and Syria, the beacon of the gospel began in many a town and village to twinkle through the darkness, and twos and threes met together in upper rooms to impart to each other their joy in the Holy Ghost.

38. We can imagine with what rage the tidings of these outbreaks of the fanaticism which he had hoped to stamp out would fill the persecutor. But he was not the person to be balked, and he resolved to hunt up the objects of his hatred even in their most obscure and distant hiding-places. In one strange city after another he accordingly appeared, armed with the apparatus of the inquisitor, to carry his sanguinary purpose out. Having heard that Damascus, the capital of Syria, was one of the places where the fugitives had taken refuge, and that they were carrying on their propaganda among the numerous Jews of that city, he went to the high priest, who had jurisdiction over the Jews outside as well as inside Palestine, and got letters empowering him to seize and bind and bring to Jerusalem all of the new way of thinking whom he might find there.

39. As we see him start on this journey, which was to be so momentous, we naturally ask, What was the state of his mind? His was a noble nature and a tender heart; but the work he was engaged in might be supposed to be congenial only to the most brutal of mankind. Had his mind then been visited with no compunctions? Apparently not. We are told that, as he was ranging through strange cities in pursuit of his victims, he was exceedingly mad against them; and as he was setting out to Damascus he was still breathing out threatenings and slaughter. He was sheltered against doubt by his reverence for the objects which the heresy

imperilled; and if he had to outrage his natural feelings in the bloody work was not his merit all the greater?

40. But on this journey doubt at last invaded his mind. It was a long journey of over a hundred and sixty miles; with the slow means of locomotion then available it would occupy at least six days; and a considerable portion of it lay across a desert, where there was nothing to distract the mind from its own reflections. In this enforced leisure doubts arose. What else can be meant by the word with which the Lord saluted him, "It is hard for thee to kick against the goad"? The figure of speech is borrowed from a custom of Eastern countries: the ox-driver wields a long pole, at the end of which is fixed a piece of sharpened iron, with which he urges the animal to go on or stand still or change its course; and if it is refractory it kicks against the goad, injuring and infuriating itself with the wounds it receives. This is a vivid picture of a man wounded and tortured by compunctions of conscience. There was something in him rebelling against the course of inhumanity on which he was embarked and suggesting that he was fighting against God.

41. It is not difficult to conceive whence these doubts arose. He was the scholar of Gamaliel, the advocate of humanity and tolerance, who had counselled the Sanhedrin to leave the Christians alone. He was himself too young yet to have hardened his heart to all the disagreeables of such ghastly work. Highly strung as was his religious zeal, nature could not but speak out at last. But probably his compunctions were chiefly awakened by the character and behavior of the Christians. He had heard the noble defense of Stephen and seen his face in the council-chamber shining like that of an angel. He had seen him kneeling on the field of execution and praying for his murderers. Doubtless in the course of the persecution he had witnessed many similar scenes. Did these people look like enemies of God? As he entered their homes to drag them forth to prison he got glimpses of their social life. Could such spectacles of purity and love be products of the powers of darkness? Did not the serenity with which his victims went to meet their fate look like the very peace which he had long been sighing for in vain? Their arguments too must have told on a mind like his. He had heard Stephen proving from the Scriptures that it behooved the Messiah to suffer; and the general tenor of the earliest Christian apologetic assures us that many of the accused must on their trial have appealed to passages like the fifty-third of Isaiah, where a career is predicted for the Messiah startlingly like that of Jesus of Nazareth. He heard incidents of Christ's life from their lips which betokened a personage very different from the picture sketched for him by his Pharisaic informants; and the sayings of their Master which the Christians quoted did not sound like the utterances of the fanatic he conceived Jesus to have been.

42. Such may have been some of the reflections which agitated the traveller as he moved onward sunk in gloomy thought. But might not these be mere suggestions of temptation—the morbid fancies of a wearied mind or the whispers of a wicked spirit attempting to draw him off from the service of Jehovah? The sight of Damascus shining out like a gem in the heart of the desert restored him to himself. There, in the company of sympathetic rabbis and in the excitement of effort, he would dispel from his mind these fancies bred of solitude. So onward he pressed, and the sun of noonday, from which all but the most impatient travelers in the East take refuge in a long siesta, looked down upon him still urging forward his course towards the city gate.

43. The news of Saul's coming had arrived at Damascus before him; and the little flock of Christ was praying that, if it were possible, the progress of the wolf who was on his way to spoil the fold might be arrested. Nearer and nearer however he drew; he had reached the last stage of his journey, and at the sight of the place which contained his victims his appetite grew keener for the prey. But the Good Shepherd had heard the cries of the trembling flock and went forth to face the wolf on their behalf. Suddenly at midday, as Paul and his company were riding forward beneath the blaze of the Syrian sun, a light which dimmed even that fierce glare shone round about them, a shock vibrated through the atmosphere, and in a moment they found themselves prostrate upon the ground. The rest was for Paul alone: a voice sounded in his ears, "Saul, Saul, why persecutest thou Me?" and as he looked up and asked the radiant Figure that had spoken, "Who art thou, Lord?" the answer was, "I am Jesus, whom thou art persecuting."

44. The language in which he ever afterwards spoke of this event forbids us to think that it was a mere vision of Jesus he saw. He ranks it as the last of the appearances of the risen Savior to his disciples, and places it on the same level as the appearances to Peter, to James, to the eleven, and to the five hundred. It was, in fact, Christ Jesus in the vesture of his glorified humanity, who for once had left the spot, wherever it may be in the spaces of the universe, where now he sits on his mediatorial throne, in order to show himself to this elect disciple; and the light which outshone the sun was no other than the glory in which his humanity is there enveloped. An incidental evidence of this was supplied in the words which were addressed to Paul. They were spoken in the Hebrew, or rather the Aramaic tongue—the same language in which Jesus had been wont to address the multitudes by the lake and converse with his disciples in the desert solitudes; and, as in the days of his flesh he was wont to open his mouth in parables, so now he clothed his rebuke in a striking metaphor, "It is hard for thee to kick against the goad."

45. It would be impossible to exaggerate what took place in the mind of Paul in this single instant. It is but a clumsy way we have of dividing time by the revolution of the clock into minutes and hours, days and years, as if each portion so measured were of the same size as another of equal length. This may suit well enough for the common ends of life, but there are finer measurements for which it is quite misleading. The real size of any space of time is to be measured by the amount it contains of the soul's experience; no one hour is exactly equal to another, and there are single hours which are larger than months. So measured, this one moment of Paul's life was perhaps larger than all his previous years. The glare of revelation was so intense that it might well have scorched the eye of reason or burned out life itself, as the external light dazzled the eyes of his body into blindness. When his companions recovered themselves and turned to their leader they discovered that he had lost his sight, and they had to take him by the hand and lead him into the city. What a change was there! Instead of the proud Pharisee riding through the streets with the pomp of an inquisitor, a stricken man, trembling, groping, clinging to the hand of his guide, arrives at the house of entertainment amid the consternation of those who receive him, and, getting hastily to a room where he can ask them to leave him alone, sinks down there in the darkness.

46. But though it was dark without it was bright within. The blindness had been sent for the purpose of secluding him from outward distractions and enabling him to concentrate himself on the objects presented to the inner eye. For the same reason he neither ate nor drank for three days. He was too absorbed in the thoughts which crowded on him thick and fast.

47. In these three days, it may be said with confidence, he got at least a partial hold of all the truths he afterwards proclaimed to the world, for his whole theology is nothing but the explication of his own conversion. First of all, his whole previous life fell down in fragments at his feet. It had been of one piece and wonderfully complete. It had appeared to himself to be a consistent deduction from the highest revelation he knew, and, in spite of its imperfections, to lie in the line of the will of God. But, instead of this, it had been rushing in diametrical opposition against the will and revelation of God, and had now been brought to a stop and broken in pieces by the collision. That which had appeared to him the perfection of service and obedience had involved his soul in the guilt of blasphemy and innocent blood. Such had been the issue of seeking righteousness by the works of the law. At the very moment when his righteousness seemed at last to be turning to the whiteness so long desired, it was caught in the blaze of this revelation and whirled away in shreds of shriveled blackness. It had been a mistake then

from first to last. Righteousness was not to be obtained by the law, but only guilt and doom. This was the unmistakable conclusion, and it became the one pole of Paul's theology.

48. But while his theory of life thus fell in pieces with a crash that might by itself have shaken his reason, in the same moment an opposite experience befell him. Not in wrath and vengeance did Jesus of Nazareth appear to him, as He might have been expected to appear to the deadly enemy of his cause. His first word might have been a demand for retribution, and his first might have been his last. But instead of this, his face had been full of divine benignity and his words full of considerateness for his persecutor. In the very moment when the divine strength cast him down on the ground he felt himself encompassed by the divine love. This was the prize he had all his lifetime been struggling for in vain, and now he grasped it in the very moment in which he discovered that his struggles had been fightings against God; he was lifted up from his fall in the arms of God's love; he was reconciled and accepted for ever. As time went on he was more and more assured of this. In Christ he found without effort of his own the peace and the moral strength he had striven for in vain. And this became the other pole of his theology—that righteousness and strength are found in Christ without man's works by mere trust in God's grace and acceptance of His gift. There were a hundred other things involved in these two which it required time to work out; but within these two poles the system of Paul's thinking ever afterwards revolved.

49. The three dark days were not done before he knew one thing more—that his life was to be devoted to the proclamation of these discoveries. In any case this must have been. Paul was a born propagandist and could not have become the possessor of such revolutionary truth without spreading it. Besides, he had a warm heart, that could be deeply moved with gratitude; and when Jesus, whom he had blasphemed and tried to blot out of the memory of the world, treated him with such divine benignity, giving him back his forfeited life and placing him in that position which had always appeared to him the prize of life, he could not but put himself at His service with all his powers. He was an ardent patriot, and the hope of the Messiah had long occupied for him the whole horizon of the future; and when he knew that Jesus of Nazareth was the Messiah of his people and the Saviour of the world, it followed as a matter of course that he must spend his life in making this known.

50. But this destiny was also clearly announced to him from the outside. Ananias, probably the leading man in the small Christian community at Damascus, was informed in a vision of the change which

had happened to Paul and sent to restore his sight and admit him into the Christian Church by baptism. Nothing could be more beautiful than the way in which this servant of God approached the man who had come to the city to take his life. As soon as he learned the state of the case he forgave and forgot all the crimes of the enemy and sprang to clasp him in the arms of Christian love. Certain as may have been the assurance of forgiveness which in the inner world of the mind Paul had in those three days received, it must have been to him a most welcome reassurance when, on opening his eyes again upon the external world, he was met with no contradiction of the visions he had been looking on, but the first object he saw was a human face bending over him with looks of forgiveness and trustful love. He learned from Ananias the future the Savior had appointed him: he had been apprehended by Christ in order to be a vessel to bear His name to Gentiles and kings and to the children of Israel. He accepted the mission with limitless devotion; and from that hour to the hour of his death he had but one ambition—to apprehend that for which he had been apprehended of Christ Jesus.

CHAPTER IV His Gospel

Paragraphs 51–67.

51–53.   Sojourn in Arabia.

54–58.   Failure of Man's Righteousness.

56. Failure of the Gentiles.

57. Failure of the Jews.

58. The Fall the ultimate Cause of Failure.

59–65.   The Righteousness of God.

   The New Adam. The New Man.

66, 67.   Leading Peculiarities of the Pauline Gospel

51. When a man has been suddenly converted, as Paul was, he is generally driven by a strong impulse to make known what has happened to him. Such testimony is very impressive; for it is that of a soul which is receiving its first glimpses of the realities of the unseen world, and there is a vividness about the report it gives of them which produces an irresistible sense of reality. Whether Paul yielded at once to this impulse or not we cannot say with certainty. The language of the book of Acts, where it is said that "straightway he preached Christ in the synagogues," would lead us to suppose so. But we learn from his own writings that there was another powerful impulse influencing him at the same time; and it is uncertain which of the two he obeyed first. This other impulse was the wish to retreat into solitude and think out the meaning and issues of that which had befallen him. It cannot be wondered at that he felt this to be a necessity. He had believed his former creed intensely and staked everything on it; to see it suddenly shattered in pieces must have shaken him severely. The new truth which had been flashed upon him was so far-reaching and revolutionary that it could not be taken in at once in all its bearings. Paul was a born thinker; it was not enough for him to experience anything; he required to comprehend it and fit it into the structure of his convictions. Immediately, therefore, after his conversion he went away, he tells us, into Arabia. He does not indeed say for what purpose he went; but as there is no record of his preaching in that region and this statement occurs in the midst of a vehement defence of the originality of his gospel, we may conclude with considerable certainty that he went into retirement for the purpose of grasping in thought the details and the bearings of the revelation he had been put in possession of. In lonely contemplation he worked them out; and when he returned to mankind he was in possession of that view of Christianity which was

peculiar to himself and formed the burden of his preaching during the subsequent years.

52. There is some doubt as to the precise place of his retirement, because Arabia is a word of vague and variable significance. But most probably it denotes the Arabia of the Wanderings, whose principal feature was Mt. Sinai. This was a spot hallowed by great memories and by the presence of other great men of revelation. Here Moses had seen the burning bush and communed with God on the top of the mountain. Here Elijah had roamed in his season of despair and drunk anew at the wells of inspiration. What place could be more appropriate for the meditations of this successor of these men of God? In the valleys where the manna fell and under the shadow of the peaks which had burned beneath the feet of Jehovah he pondered the problem of his life. It is a great example. Originality in the preaching of the truth depends on the solitary intuition of it. Paul enjoyed the special inspiration of the Holy Ghost; but this did not render the concentrated activity of his own thinking unnecessary, but only lent it peculiar intensity; and the clearness and certainty of his gospel were due to these months of sequestered thought. His retirement may have lasted a year or more; for between his conversion and his final departure from Damascus, to which he returned from Arabia, three years intervened; and one of them at least was spent in this way.

53. We have no detailed record of what the outlines of his gospel were till a period long subsequent to this; but as these, when first they are traceable, are a mere cast of the features of his conversion, and as his mind was working so long and powerfully on the interpretation of this event at this period, there can be no doubt that the gospel sketched in the Epistles to the Romans and the Galatians was substantially the same as he preached from the first; and we are safe in inferring from these writings our account of his Arabian meditations.

54. The starting-point of Paul's thinking was still the conviction, inherited from pious generations, that the true end and felicity of man lay in the enjoyment of the favor of God. This was to be attained through righteousness: only the righteous could God be at peace with and favor with his love. To attain righteousness must therefore be the chief end of man.

55. But man had failed to attain righteousness and had therefore come short of the favor of God and exposed himself to His wrath. Paul proves this by taking a vast survey of the history of mankind in pre-Christian times in its two great sections—the Gentile and the Jewish.

56. The Gentiles failed. It might, indeed, be supposed that they had not the preliminary conditions for entering on the pursuit of righteousness

at all, because they did not enjoy the advantage of a special revelation. But Paul holds that even the heathen know enough of God to be aware of the obligation to follow after righteousness. There is a natural revelation of God in his works and in the human conscience sufficient to enlighten men as to this duty. But the heathen, instead of making use of this light, wantonly extinguished it. They were not willing to retain God in their knowledge and to fetter themselves with the restraints which a pure knowledge of him imposed. They corrupted the idea of God in order to feel at ease in an immoral life. The revenge of nature came upon them in the darkening and confusion of their intellects. They fell into such insensate folly as to change the glorious and incorruptible nature of God into the images of men and beasts, birds and reptiles. This intellectual degeneracy was followed by still deeper moral degeneracy. God, when they forsook him, let them go; and when his restraining grace was removed, down they rushed into the depths of moral putridity. Lust and passion got the mastery of them, and their life became a mass of moral disease. In the end of the first chapter of Romans the features of their condition are sketched in colors that might be borrowed from the abode of devils, but were literally taken, as is too plainly proved by the pages even of Gentile historians, from the condition of the cultured heathen nations at that time. This, then, was the history of one half of mankind: it had utterly fallen from righteousness and exposed itself to the wrath of God, which is revealed from heaven against all unrighteousness of men.

57. The Jews were the other half of the world. Had they succeeded where the Gentiles had failed? They enjoyed, indeed, great advantages over the heathen; for they possessed the oracles of God, in which the divine nature was exhibited in a form which rendered it inaccessible to human perversion, and the divine law was written with equal plainness in the same form. But had they profited by these advantages? It is one thing to know the law and another thing to do it; but it is doing, not knowing, which is righteousness. Had they, then, fulfilled the will of God which they knew? Paul had lived in the same Jerusalem in which Jesus assailed the corruption and hypocrisy of scribes and Pharisees; he had looked closely at the lives of the representative men of his nation; and he does not hesitate to charge the Jews in mass with the very same sins as the Gentiles; nay, he says that through them the name of God was blasphemed among the Gentiles. They boasted of their knowledge and were the bearers of the torch of truth whose fierce blaze exposed the sins of the heathen. But their religion was a bitter criticism of the conduct of others. They forgot to examine their own conduct by the same light; and while they were repeating, Do not steal, Do not commit adultery, and a multitude of other commandments, they were indulging in these sins themselves. What good in these circumstances did their knowledge do

them? It only condemned them the more; for their sin was against light. While the heathen knew so little that their sins were comparatively innocent, the sins of the Jews were conscious and presumptuous. Their boasted superiority was therefore inferiority. They were more deeply condemned than the Gentiles they despised, and exposed to a heavier curse.

58. The truth is, Gentiles and Jews had both failed for the same reason. Trace these two streams of human life back to their sources and you come at last to a point where they are not two streams but one; and before the bifurcation took place something had happened which predetermined the failure of both. In Adam all fell, and from him all, both Gentiles and Jews, inherited a nature too weak for the arduous attainment of righteousness; human nature is carnal now, not spiritual, and therefore unequal to this supreme spiritual achievement. The law could not alter this; it had no creative power to make the carnal spiritual. On the contrary, it aggravated the evil. It actually multiplied offences; for its clear and full description of sins, which would have been an incomparable guide to a sound nature, turned into temptation for a morbid one. The very knowledge of sin tempts to its commission; the very command not to do anything is a reason to a diseased nature for doing it. This was the effect of the law: it multiplied and aggravated transgressions. And this was God's intention. Not that He was the author of sin; but, like a skilful physician, who has sometimes to use appliances to bring a sore to a head before he heals it, He allowed the heathen to go their own way and gave the Jews the law, that the sin of human nature might exhibit all its inherent qualities before he intervened to heal it. The healing, however, was His real purpose all the time: He concluded all under sin that He might have mercy upon all.

59. Man's extremity was God's opportunity; not, indeed, in the sense that, one way of salvation having failed, God devised another. The law had never, in His intention, been a way of salvation. It was only a means of illustrating the need of salvation. But the moment when this demonstration was complete was the signal for God to produce his method, which he had kept locked in his counsel through the generations of human probation. It had never been his intention to permit man to fail of his true end. Only he allowed time to prove that fallen man could never reach righteousness by his own efforts; and when the righteousness of man had been demonstrated to be a failure, he brought forth his secret—the righteousness of God. This was Christianity; this was the sum and issue of the mission of Christ—the conferring upon man, as a free gift, of that which is indispensable to his blessedness, but which he had failed himself to attain. It is a divine act; it is grace; and man obtains it by acknowledging that he has failed himself to attain it and by accepting it

from God; it is got by faith only. It is "the righteousness of God, by the faith of Jesus Christ, unto all and upon all them that believe."

60. Those who thus receive it enter at once into that position of peace and favor with God in which human felicity consists and which was the goal aimed at by Paul when he was striving for righteousness by the law. "Being justified by faith, we have peace with God through our Lord Jesus Christ, by whom also we have access by faith into this grace wherein we stand, and rejoice in hope of the glory of God." It is a sunny life of joy, peace, and hope which those lead who have come to know this gospel. There may be trials in it; but when a man's life is reposing in the attainment of its true end, trials are light and all things work together for good.

61. This righteousness of God is for all the children of men—not for the Jews only, but for the Gentiles also. The demonstration of man's inability to attain righteousness was made, in accordance with the divine purpose, in both sections of the human race; and its completion was the signal for the exhibition of God's grace to both alike. The work of Christ was not for the children of Abraham, but for the children of Adam. "As in Adam all died, so in Christ shall all be made alive." The Gentiles did not need to undergo circumcision and to keep the law in order to obtain salvation; for the law was no part of salvation; it belonged entirely to the preliminary demonstration of man's failure; and when it had accomplished this service it was ready to vanish away. The only human condition of obtaining God's righteousness is faith; and this is as easy for Gentile as Jew. This was an inference from Paul's own experience. It was not as a Jew, but as a man, that he had been dealt with in his conversion. No Gentile could have been less entitled to obtain salvation by merit than he had been. So far from the law raising him a single step towards salvation, it had removed him to a greater distance from God than any Gentile and cast him into a deeper condemnation. How, then, could it profit the Gentiles to be placed in this position? In obtaining the righteousness in which he was now rejoicing he had done nothing which was not within the power of any human being.

62. It was this universal love of God revealed in the gospel which inspired Paul with unbounded admiration for Christianity. His sympathies had been cribbed, cabined, and confined in a narrow conception of God; the new faith uncaged his heart and let it forth into the free and sunny air. God became a new God to him. He calls his discovery the mystery which had been hidden from ages and generations, but had been revealed to him and his fellow-apostles. It seemed to him to be the secret of the ages and to be destined to usher in a new era, far better than any the world had ever seen What kings and prophets had not known had been

revealed to him. It had burst on him like the dawn of a new creation. God was now offering to every man the supreme felicity of life—that righteousness which had been the vain endeavor of the past ages.

63. This secret of the new epoch had not, indeed, been entirely unanticipated in the past. It had been "witnessed by the law and the prophets." The law could bear witness to it only negatively by demonstrating its necessity. But the prophets anticipated it more positively. David, for example, described "the blessedness of the man unto whom God imputed righteousness without works." Still more clearly had Abraham anticipated it. He was a justified man; and it was by faith, not by works, that he was justified: "he believed God, and it was imputed unto him for righteousness." The law had nothing to do with his justification, for it was not in existence for four centuries afterwards. Nor had circumcision anything to do with it, for he was justified before this rite was instituted. In short, it was as a man, not as a Jew, that he was dealt with by God, and God might deal with any human being in the same way. It had once made the thorny road of legal righteousness sacred to Paul to think that Abraham and the prophets had trodden it before him; but now he knew that their life of religious joy and psalms of holy calm were inspired by quite different experiences, which were now diffusing the peace of heaven through his heart also. But only the first streaks of dawn had been descried by them; the perfect day had broken in his own time.

64. Paul's discovery of this way of salvation was an actual experience; he simply knew that Christ, in the moment when He met him, had placed him in that position of peace and favor with God which he had long sighed for in vain; and as time went on he felt more and more that in this position he was enjoying the true blessedness of life. His mission henceforth would be to herald this discovery in its simple and concrete reality under the name of the Righteousness of God. But a mind like his could not help inquiring how it was that the possession of Christ did so much for him. In the Arabian wilderness he pondered over this question, and the gospel he subsequently preached contained a luminous answer to it.

65. From Adam his children derive a sad double heritage—a debt of guilt, which they cannot reduce, but are constantly increasing, and a carnal nature, which is incapable of righteousness. These are the two features of the religious condition of fallen man, and they are the double source of all his woes. But Christ is a new Adam, a new Head of humanity, and those who are connected with him by faith become heirs of a double heritage of a precisely opposite kind. On the one hand, just as through our birth in the first Adam's line we get inevitably entangled in

guilt, like a child born into a family which is drowned in debt, so through our birth in the line of the second Adam we get involved in a boundless heritage of merit, which Christ, as the Head of his family, makes the common property of its members. This extinguishes the debt of our guilt and makes us rich in Christ's righteousness. "As by one man's disobedience many were made sinners, so by the obedience of one shall many be made righteous." On the other hand, just as Adam transmitted to his posterity a carnal nature, alien to God and unfit for righteousness, so the new Adam imparts to the race of which he is the Head a spiritual nature, akin to God and delighting in righteousness. The nature of man, according to Paul, normally consists of three sections—body, soul, and spirit. In his original constitution these occupied definite relations of superiority and subordination to one another, the spirit being supreme, the body undermost, and the soul occupying the middle position. But the fall disarranged this order, and all sin consists in the usurpation by the body or the soul of the place of the spirit. In fallen man these two inferior sections of human nature, which together form what Paul calls the flesh, or that side of human nature which looks towards the world and time, have taken possession of the throne and completely rule the life, while the spirit, the side of man which looks towards God and eternity, has been dethroned and reduced to a condition of inefficiency and death. Christ restores the lost predominance of the spirit of man by taking possession of it by his own Spirit. His Spirit dwells in the human spirit, vivifying it and sustaining it in such growing strength that it becomes more and more the sovereign part of the human constitution. The man ceases to be carnal and becomes spiritual; he is led by the Spirit of God and becomes more and more harmonious with all that is holy and divine. The flesh does not, indeed, easily submit to the loss of supremacy. It clogs and obstructs the spirit and fights to regain possession of the throne. Paul has described this struggle in sentences of terrible vividness, in which all generations of Christians have recognized the features of their deepest experience. But the issue of the struggle is not doubtful. Sin shall not again have dominion over those in whom Christ's Spirit dwells, or dislodge them from their standing in the favor of God.

66. Such are the bare outlines of the gospel which Paul brought back with him from the Arabian solitudes and afterwards preached with unwearied enthusiasm. It could not but be mixed up in his mind and in his writings with the peculiarities of his own experience as a Jew, and these make it difficult for us to grasp his system in some of its details. The belief in which he was brought up, that no man could be saved without becoming a Jew, and the notions about the law from which he had to cut himself free, lie very distant from our modern sympathies; yet his theology could not shape itself in his mind except in contrast to these

misconceptions. This became subsequently still more inevitable when his own old errors met him as the watchwords of a party within the Christian Church itself, against which he had to wage a long and relentless war. Though this conflict forced his views into the clearest expression, it encumbered them with references to feelings and beliefs which are now dead to the interest of mankind. But, in spite of these drawbacks the gospel of Paul remains a possession of incalculable value to the human race. Its searching investigation of the failure and the wants of human nature, its wonderful unfolding of the wisdom of God in the education of the pre-Christian world, and its exhibition of the depth and universality of the divine love are among the profoundest elements of revelation.

67. But it is in its conception of Christ that Paul's gospel wears its imperishable crown. The evangelists sketched in a hundred traits of simple and affecting beauty the fashion of the earthly life of the man Christ Jesus, and in these the model of human conduct will always have to be sought; but to Paul was reserved the task of making known, in its heights and depths, the work which the Son of God accomplished as the Saviour of the race. He scarcely ever refers to the incidents of Christ's earthly life, although here and there he betrays that he knew them well. To him Christ was ever the glorious Being, shining with the splendor of heaven, who appeared to him on the way to Damascus, and the Saviour who caught him up into the heavenly peace and joy of a new life. When the Church of Christ thinks of her Head as the deliverer of the soul from sin and death, as a spiritualizing presence ever with her and at work in every believer, and as the Lord over all things who will come again without sin unto salvation, it is in forms of thought given her by the Holy Ghost through the instrumentality of this apostle.

CHAPTER V The Work Awaiting the Worker

Paragraphs 68–78.

68–70. Eight Years of Comparative Inactivity at Tarsus. Gentiles admitted to Christian Church.

71, 72. Paul discovered by Barnabas and brought to Antioch. His Work there.

73–78. The Known World of that Period.

75. The Greeks; 76. The Romans; 77. The Jews;

78. Barbarians and Slaves.

68. Paul was now in possession of his gospel and was aware that it was to be the mission of his life to preach it to the Gentiles; but he had still to wait a long time before his peculiar career commenced. We hear scarcely anything of him for other seven or eight years; and yet we can only guess what may have been the reasons of Providence for imposing on His servant so long a time of waiting.

69. There may have been personal reasons for it connected with Paul's own spiritual history, because waiting is a common instrument of providential discipline for those to whom exceptional work has been appointed. A public reason may have been that he was too obnoxious to the Jewish authorities to be tolerated yet in those scenes where Christian activity commanded any notice. He had attempted to preach in Damascus, where his conversion had taken place, but was immediately forced to flee from the fury of the Jews; and, going thence to Jerusalem and beginning to testify as a Christian, he found the place in two or three weeks too hot to hold him. No wonder; how could the Jews be expected to allow the man who had so lately been the chief champion of their religion to preach the faith which they had employed him to destroy? When he fled from Jerusalem he bent his steps to his native Tarsus, where for years he remained in obscurity. No doubt he testified for Christ there to his own family, and there are some indications that he carried on evangelistic operations in his native province of Cilicia; but, if he did so, his work may be said to have been that of a man in hiding, for it was not in the central or even in a visible stream of the new religious movement.

70. These are but conjectural reasons for the obscurity of these years. But there was one undoubted reason for the delay of Paul's career of the greatest possible importance. In this interval took place that revolution— one of the most momentous in the history of mankind—by which the

Gentiles were admitted to equal privileges with the Jews in the church of Christ. This change proceeded from the original circle of apostles in Jerusalem, and Peter, the chief of the apostles, was the instrument of it. By the vision of the sheet of clean and unclean beasts, which he saw at Joppa, he was prepared for the part he was to play in this transaction, and he admitted the Gentile Cornelius, of Cæsarea, and his family to the church by baptism without circumcision. This was an innovation involving boundless consequences. It was a necessary preliminary to Paul's mission work, and subsequent events were to show how wise was the divine arrangement that the first Gentile entrants into the church should be admitted by the hands of Peter rather than by those of Paul.

71. As soon as this event had taken place the arena was clear for Paul's career, and a door was immediately opened for his entrance upon it. Almost simultaneously with the baptism of the Gentile family at Cæsarea a great revival broke out among the Gentiles of the city of Antioch, the capital of Syria. The movement had been begun by fugitives driven by persecution from Jerusalem, and it was carried on with the sanction of the apostles, who sent Barnabas, one of their trusted coadjutors, from Jerusalem to superintend it. This man knew Paul. When the latter first came to Jerusalem after his conversion and assayed to join himself to the Christians there, they were all afraid of him, suspecting the teeth and claws of the wolf beneath the fleece of the sheep. But Barnabas rose superior to these fears and suspicions, and, having taken the new convert and heard his story, believed him and persuaded the rest to receive him. The intercourse thus begun only lasted a week or two at that time, as Paul had to leave Jerusalem; but Barnabas had received a profound impression of his personality and did not forget him. When he was sent down to superintend the revival at Antioch, he soon found himself embarrassed with its magnitude and in need of assistance; and the idea occurred to him that Paul was the man he wanted. Tarsus was not far off, and thither he went to seek him. Paul accepted his invitation and returned with him to Antioch.

72. The hour he had been waiting for had struck, and he threw himself into the work of evangelizing the Gentiles with the enthusiasm of a great nature that found itself at last in its proper sphere. The movement at once responded to the pressure of such a hand; the disciples became so numerous and prominent that the heathen gave them a new name—that name of "Christians," which has ever since continued to be the badge of faith in Christ; and Antioch, a city of half a million inhabitants, became the headquarters of Christianity instead of Jerusalem. Soon a large church was formed, and one of the manifestations of the zeal with which it was pervaded was a proposal, which gradually shaped itself into an

enthusiastic resolution, to send forth a mission to the heathen. As a matter of course, Paul was designated for this service.

73. As we see him thus brought at length face to face with the task of his life, let us pause to take a brief survey of the world which he was setting out to conquer. Nothing less was what he aimed at. In Paul's time the known world was so small a place that it did not seem impossible even for a single man to make a spiritual conquest of it; and it had been wonderfully prepared for the new force which was about to assail it.

74. It consisted of a narrow disk of land surrounding the Mediterranean Sea. The sea deserved at that time the name it bears, for the world's center of gravity, which has since shifted to other latitudes, was in it. The interest of human life was concentrated in the southern countries of Europe, the portion of western Asia, and the strip of northern Africa which form its shores. In this little world there were three cities which divided between them the interest of those ages. These were Rome, Athens, and Jerusalem, the capitals of the three races—the Romans, the Greeks, and the Jews—which in every sense ruled that old world. It was not that each of them had mastered a third part of the circle of civilization, but each of them had in turn diffused itself over the whole of it, and either still held its grip or at least had left imperishable traces of its presence.

75. The Greeks were the first to take possession of the world. They were the people of cleverness and genius, the perfect masters of commerce, literature, and art. In very early ages they displayed the instinct for colonization and sent forth their sons to find new abodes on the east and the west, far from their native home. At length there arose among them one who concentrated in himself the strongest tendencies of the race and by force of arms extended the dominion of Greece to the borders of India. The vast empire of Alexander the Great split into pieces at his death; but a deposit of Greek life and influence remained in all the countries over which the deluge of his conquering armies had swept. Greek cities, such as Antioch in Syria and Alexandria in Egypt, flourished all over the East; Greek merchants abounded in every centre of trade; Greek teachers taught the literature of their country in many lands; and—what was most important of all—the Greek language became the general vehicle for the communication of the more serious thought between nation and nation. Even the Jews in New Testament times read their own Scriptures in a Greek version, the original Hebrew having become a dead language. Perhaps the Greek is the most perfect tongue the world has known, and there was a special providence in its universal diffusion before Christianity needed a medium of international communication. The New Testament was written in Greek, and wherever the apostles of

Christianity travelled they were able to make themselves understood in this language.

76. The turn of the Romans came next to obtain possession of the world. Originally a small clan in the neighborhood of the city from which they derived their name, they gradually extended and strengthened themselves and acquired such skill in the arts of war and government that they became irresistible conquerors and marched forth in every direction to make themselves masters of the globe. They subdued Greece itself and, flowing eastward, seized upon the countries, which Alexander and his successors had ruled. The whole known world, indeed, became theirs from the Straits of Gibraltar to the utmost East. They did not possess the genius or geniality of the Greeks; their qualities were strength and justice; their arts were not those of the poet and the thinker, but those of the soldier and the judge. They broke down the divisions between the tribes of men and compelled them to be friendly towards each other, because they were all alike prostrate beneath one iron rule. They pierced the countries with roads, which connected them with Rome and were such solid triumphs of engineering skill that some of them remain to this day. Along these highways the message of the gospel ran. Thus the Romans also proved to be pioneers for Christianity, for their authority in so many countries afforded to its first publishers facility of movement and protection from the caprices and injustice of local tribunals.

77. Meanwhile the third nation of antiquity had also completed its conquest of the world. Not by force of arms did the Jews diffuse themselves, as the Greeks and Romans had done. For centuries, indeed, they had dreamed of the coming of a warlike hero, whose prowess should outshine that of the most celebrated Gentile conquerors. But he never came; and their occupation of the centres of civilization had to take place in a more silent way. There is no change in the habits of any nation more striking than that which passed over the Jewish race in that interval of four centuries between Malachi and Matthew of which we have no record in the sacred Scriptures. In the Old Testament we see the Jews pent within the narrow limits of Palestine, engaged mainly in agricultural pursuits and jealously guarding themselves from intermingling with foreign nations. In the New Testament we find them still, indeed, clinging with a desperate tenacity to Jerusalem and to the idea of their own separateness; but their habits and abodes have been completely changed: they have given up agriculture and betaken themselves with extraordinary eagerness and success to commerce; and with this object in view they have diffused themselves everywhere—over Africa, Asia, Europe—and there is not a city of any importance where they are not to be found. By what steps this extraordinary change came about it were hard to tell and long to trace. But it had taken place; and this turned out to be a

circumstance of extreme importance for the early history of Christianity. Wherever the Jews were settled they had their synagogues, their sacred Scriptures, their uncompromising belief in the One true God. Not only so; their synagogues everywhere attracted proselytes from the surrounding Gentile populations. The heathen religions were at that period in a state of utter collapse. The smaller nations had lost faith in their deities, because they had not been able to defend them from the victorious Greeks and Romans. But the conquerors had for other reasons equally lost faith in their own gods. It was an age of skepticism, religious decay, and moral corruption. But there are always natures which must possess a faith in which they can trust. These were in search of a religion, and many of them found refuge from the coarse and incredible myths of the gods of polytheism in the purity and monotheism of the Jewish creed. The fundamental ideas of this creed are also the foundations of the Christian faith. Wherever the messengers of Christianity travelled, they met with people with whom they had many religious conceptions in common. Their first sermons were delivered in synagogues, their first converts were Jews and proselytes. The synagogue was the bridge by which Christianity crossed over to the heathen.

78. Such, then, was the world which Paul was setting out to conquer. It was a world everywhere pervaded with these three influences. But there were two other elements of population which require to be kept in mind, as both of them supplied numerous converts to the early preachers: there were the original inhabitants of the various countries; and there were the slaves, who were either captives taken in war or their descendants, and were liable to be shifted from place to place, being sold according to the necessities or caprices of their masters. A religion whose chief boast it was to preach glad tidings to the poor could not neglect these down-trodden classes, and although the conflict of Christianity with the forces of the time which had possession of the fate of the world naturally attracts attention, it must not be forgotten that its best triumph has always consisted in the sweetening and brightening of the lot of the humble.

CHAPTER VI His Missionary Travels

Paragraphs 79–114.

79–88.   The First Journey.

79, 80.   His Companions.

81. Cyprus. Change of his Name.

82–87.   The Mainland of Asia Minor.

83. Desertion of Mark; 84. Antioch-in-Pisidia and Iconium; 85–87. Lystra and Derbe; 88. Return.

89–108.   The Second Journey.

90, 91.   Separation from Barnabas.

92, 93.   Unrecorded Half of the Journey.

94–96.   Crossing to Europe.

97–108.   Greece.

97–101.   Macedonia.

99. Women and the Gospel; 100. Liberality of Churches.

102–108.   Achaia.

103–105.   Athens; 106–108. Corinth.

109–114.   The Third Journey.

Ephesus; Polemic against Superstition.

The First Journey

79. From the beginning it had been the wont of the preachers of Christianity not to go alone on their expeditions, but two and two. Paul improved on this practice by going generally with two companions, one of them being a younger man, who perhaps took charge of the travelling arrangements. On his first journey his comrades were Barnabas and John Mark the nephew of Barnabas.

80. We have already seen that Barnabas may be called the discoverer of Paul; and when they set out on this journey together he was probably in a position to act as Paul's patron, for he enjoyed much consideration in the Christian community. Converted apparently on the day of Pentecost, he had played a leading part in the subsequent events. He was a man of high social position, a landed proprietor in the island of Cyprus; and he

sacrificed all to the new movement into which he had been drawn. In the outburst of enthusiasm which led the first Christians to share their property with one another, he sold his estate and laid the money at the apostles' feet. He was constantly employed thereafter in the work of preaching, and he had so remarkable a gift of eloquence that he was called the Son of Exhortation. An incident which occurred at a later stage of this journey gives us a glimpse of the appearance of the two men. When the inhabitants of Lystra mistook them for gods, they called Barnabas Jupiter and Paul Mercury. Now in ancient art Jupiter was always represented as a tall, majestic, and benignant figure, while Mercury was the small, swift messenger of the father of gods and men. Probably it appeared, therefore, that the large, gracious, paternal Barnabas was the head and director of the expedition, while Paul, little and eager, was the subordinate. The direction in which they set out, too, was the one which Barnabas might naturally have been expected to choose. They went first to Cyprus, the island where his property had been and many of his friends still were. It lay eighty miles to the southwest of Seleucia, the seaport of Antioch, and they might reach it on the very day they left their headquarters.

81. But although Barnabas appeared to be the leader, the good man probably knew already that the humble words of the Baptist might be used by himself with reference to his companion, "He must increase, but I must decrease." At all events, as soon as their work commenced in earnest this was shown to be the relation between them. After going through the length of the island, from east to west, evangelizing, they arrived at Paphos, its chief town, and there the problems they had come out to face met them in the most concentrated form. Paphos was the seat of the worship of Venus, the goddess of love, who was said to have been born of the foam of the sea at this very spot; and her worship was carried on with the wildest licentiousness. It was a picture in miniature of Greece sunk in moral decay. Paphos was also the seat of the Roman Government, and in the proconsular chair sat a man, Sergius Paulus, whose noble character but utter lack of certain faith formed a companion picture of the inability of Rome at that epoch to meet the deepest necessities of her best sons. In the proconsular court, playing upon the inquirer's credulity, a Jewish sorcerer and quack, named Elymas, was flourishing, whose arts were a picture of the lowest depths to which the Jewish character could sink. The whole scene was a kind of miniature of the world whose evils the missionaries had set forth to cure. In the presence of these exigencies Paul unfolded for the first time the mighty powers which lay in him. An access of the Spirit seized him and enabled him to overcome all obstacles. He covered the Jewish magician with disgrace, converted the Roman Governor, and founded in the town a

Christian church in opposition to the Greek shrine. From that hour Barnabas sank into the second place and Paul took his natural position as the head of the mission. We no longer read, as heretofore, of "Barnabas and Saul," but always of "Paul and Barnabas." The subordinate had become the leader; and, as if to mark that he had become a new man and taken a new place, he was no longer called by the Jewish name of Saul, which up to this point he had borne, but by the name of Paul, which has ever since been his designation among Christians.

82. The next move was as obviously the choice of the new leader as the first one had been due to Barnabas. They struck across the sea to Perga, a town near the middle of the southern coast of Asia Minor, then right up, a hundred miles, into the mainland, and thence eastward to a point almost straight north of Tarsus. This route carried them in a kind of half circuit through the districts of Pamphylia, Pisidia, and Lycaonia, which border to the west and north on Cilicia, Paul's native province; so that, if it be the case that he had evangelized Cilicia already, he was now merely extending his labors to the nearest surrounding regions.

83. At Perga, the starting-point of this second half of the journey, a misfortune befell the expedition: John Mark deserted his companions and sailed for home. It may be that the new position assumed by Paul had given him offence, though his generous uncle felt no such grudge at that which was the ordinance of nature and of God. But it is more likely that the cause of his withdrawal was dismay at the dangers upon which they were about to enter. These were such as might well strike terror even into resolute hearts. Behind Perga rose the snow-clad peaks of the Taurus Mountains, which had to be penetrated through narrow passes, where crazy bridges spanned the rushing torrents, and the castles of robbers, who watched for passing travellers to pounce upon, were hidden in positions so inaccessible that even the Roman arms had not been able to exterminate them. When these preliminary dangers were surmounted, the prospect beyond was anything but inviting; the country to the north of the Taurus was a vast table-land, more elevated than the summits of the highest mountains of England, and scattered over with solitary lakes, irregular mountain masses, and tracts of desert, where the population was rude and spoke an almost endless variety of dialects. These things terrified Mark, and he drew back. But his companions took their lives in their hand and went forward. To them it was enough that there were multitudes of perishing souls there needing the salvation of which they were the heralds; and Paul knew that there were scattered handfuls of his own people in these remote regions of the heathen.

84. Can we conceive what their procedure was like in the towns they visited? It is difficult, indeed, to picture it to ourselves. As we try to

see them with the mind's eye entering any place, we naturally think of them as the most important personages in it; to us their entry is as august as if they had been carried on a car of victory. Very different, however, was the reality. They entered a town as quietly and unnoticed as any two strangers who may walk into one of our towns any morning. Their first care was to get a lodging; and then they had to seek for employment, for they worked at their trade wherever they went. Nothing could be more commonplace. Who could dream that this travel-stained man, going from one tentmaker's door to another, seeking for work, was carrying the future of the world beneath his robe! When the Sabbath came round they would cease from toil, like the other Jews in the place, and repair to the synagogue. They joined in the psalms and prayers with the other worshippen and listened to the reading of the Scriptures. After this the presiding elder might ask if any one present had a word of exhortation to deliver. This was Paul's opportunity. He would rise and, with outstretched hand, begin to speak. At once the audience recognized the accents of the cultivated rabbi; and the strange voice won their attention. Taking up the passages which had been read, he would soon be moving forward on the stream of Jewish history, till he led up to the astounding announcement that the Messiah hoped for by their fathers and promised by their prophets had come, and he had been sent among them as His apostle. Then would follow the story of Jesus: it was true, he had been rejected by the authorities of Jerusalem and crucified, but this could be shown to have taken place in accordance with prophecy; and his resurrection from the dead was an infallible proof that he had been sent of God; now he was exalted a Prince and a Saviour to give repentance unto Israel and the remission of sins. We can easily imagine the sensation produced by such a sermon from such a preacher, and the buzz of conversation which would arise among the congregation after the dismission of the snyagogue. During the week it would become the talk of the town; and Paul was willing to converse at his work or in the leisure of the evening with any who might desire further information. Next Sabbath the synagogue would be crowded, not with Jews only, but Gentiles also, who were curious to see the strangers; and Paul now unfolded the secret that salvation by Jesus Christ was as free to Gentiles as to Jews. This was generally the signal for the Jews to contradict and blaspheme; and, turning his back on them, Paul addressed himself to the Gentiles. But meantime the fanaticism of the Jews was roused, and they either stirred up the mob or secured the interest of the authorities against the strangers; and in a storm of popular tumult or by the breath of authority the messengers of the gospel were swept out of the town. This was what happened at Antioch-in-Pisidia, their first halting-place in the interior of Asia Minor; and it was repeated in a hundred instances in Paul's subsequent life.

85. Sometimes they did not get off so easily. At Lystra, for example, they found themselves in a population of rude heathens, who were at first so charmed with Paul's winning words and impressed with the appearance of the preachers that they took them for gods and were on the point of offering sacrifice to them. This filled the missionaries with horror, and they rejected the intentions of the crowd with unceremonious haste. A sudden revolution in the popular sentiment ensued, and Paul was stoned and cast out of the city apparently dead.

86. Such were the scenes of excitement and peril through which they had to pass in this remote region. But their enthusiasm never flagged; they never thought of turning back, but, when they were driven out of one city, moved forward to another. And total as their discomfiture sometimes appeared, they quitted no city without leaving behind them a little band of converts—perhaps a few Jews, a few more proselytes, and a number of Gentiles. The gospel found those for whom it was intended—penitents burdened with sin, souls dissatisfied with the world and their ancestral religion, hearts yearning for divine sympathy and love; "as many as were ordained to eternal life believed;" and these formed in every city the nucleus of a Christian church. Even at Lystra, where the defeat seemed so utter, a little group of faithful hearts gathered round the mangled body of the apostle outside the city gates; Eunice and Lois were there with tender womanly ministrations; and young Timothy, as he looked down on the pale and bleeding face, felt his heart for ever knit to the hero who had courage to suffer to the death for his faith.

87. In the intense love of such hearts Paul received compensation for suffering and injustice. If, as some suppose, the people of this region formed part of the Galatian churches, we see from his Epistle to them the kind of love they gave him. They received him, he says, as an angel of God, nay, as Jesus Christ himself; they were ready to have plucked out their eyes and given them to him. They were people of rude kindness and headlong impulses; their native religion was one of excitement and demonstrativeness, and they carried these characteristics into the new faith they had adopted. They were filled with joy and the Holy Ghost, and the revival spread on every hand with great rapidity, till the word, sounding out from the little Christian communities, was heard all along the slopes of Taurus and down the glens of the Cestrus and Halys. Paul's warm heart could not but enjoy such an outburst of affection. He responded to it by giving in return his own deep love. The towns mentioned in their itinerary are the Pisidian Antioch, Iconium, Lystra, and Derbe; but when at the last of them he had finished his course and the way lay open to him to descend by the Cilician Gates to Tarsus and thence get back to Antioch, he preferred to return by the way he had come. In spite of the most imminent danger he revisited all these places,

to see his dear converts again and cheer them in face of persecution; and he ordained elders in every city to watch over the churches in his absence.

88. At length the missionaries descended again from these uplands to the southern coast and sailed back to Antioch, from which they had set out. Worn with toil and suffering, but flushed with the joy of success, they appeared among those who had sent them forth and had doubtless been following them with their prayers; and, like discoverers returned from the finding of a new world, they related the miracles of grace they had witnessed in the strange world of the heathen.

The Second Journey

89. In his first journey Paul may be said to have been only trying his wings; for his course, adventurous though it was, only swept in a limited circle round his native province. In his second journey he performed a far more distant and perilous flight. Indeed, this journey was not only the greatest he achieved, but perhaps the most momentous recorded in the annals of the human race. In its issues it far outrivalled the expedition of Alexander the Great when he carried the arms and civilization of Greece into the heart of Asia, or that of Cæsar when he landed on the shores of Britain, or even the voyage of Columbus when he discovered a new world. Yet, when he set out on it, he had no idea of the magnitude which it was to assume or even the direction which it was to take. After enjoying a short rest at the close of the first journey, he said to his fellow-missionary, "Let us go again and visit our brethren in every city where we have preached the word of the Lord and see how they do." It was the parental longing to see his spiritual children which was drawing him; but God had far more extensive designs, which opened up before him as he went forward.

90. Unfortunately the beginning of this journey was marred by a dispute between the two friends who meant to perform it together. The occasion of their difference was the offer of John Mark to accompany them. No doubt when this young man saw Paul and Barnabas returning safe and sound from the undertaking which he had deserted, he recognized what a mistake he had made; and he now wished to retrieve his error by rejoining them. Barnabas naturally wished to take his nephew, but Paul absolutely refused. The one missionary, a man of easy kindliness, urged the duty of forgiveness and the effect which a rebuff might have on a beginner; while the other, full of zeal for God, represented the danger of making so sacred a work in any way dependent on one who could not be relied upon, for "confidence in an unfaithful man in time of trouble is like a broken tooth or a foot out of joint." We cannot now tell which of them was in the right or if both were partly

wrong. Both of them, at all events, suffered for it: Paul had to part in anger from the man to whom he probably owed more than to any other human being; and Barnabas was separated from the grandest spirit of the age.

91. They never met again. This was not due, however, to an unchristian continuation of their quarrel; the heat of passion soon cooled down and the old love returned. Paul mentions Barnabas with honor in his writings, and in the very last of his Epistles he sends for Mark to come to him at Rome, expressly adding that he is profitable to him for ministry—the very thing he had disbelieved about him before. In the meantime, however, their difference separated them. They agreed to divide between them the region they had evangelized together. Barnabas and Mark went away to Cyprus; and Paul undertook to visit the churches on the mainland. As companion he took with him Silas or Silvanus, in the place of Barnabas; and he had not proceeded far on his new journey when he met with one to take the place of Mark. This was Timothy, a convert he had made at Lystra in his first journey; he was youthful and gentle; and he continued a faithful companion and a constant comfort to the apostle to the end of his life.

92. In pursuance of the purpose with which he had set out, Paul commenced this journey by revisiting the churches in whose founding he had taken part. Beginning at Antioch and proceeding in a northwesterly direction, he did this work in Syria, Cilicia, and other parts, till he reached the centre of Asia Minor, where the primary object of his journey was completed. But when a man is on the right road, all sorts of opportunities open up before him. When he had passed through the provinces which he had visited before, new desires to penetrate still farther began to fire his mind, and Providence opened up the way. He still went forward in the same direction through Phrygia and Galatia. Bithynia, a large province lying along the shore of the Black Sea, and Asia, a densely populated province in the west of Asia Minor, seemed to invite him and he wished to enter them. But the Spirit who guided his footsteps indicated, by some means unknown to us, that these provinces were shut to him in the meantime; and, pushing onward in the direction in which his divine Guide permitted him to go, he found himself at Troas, a town on the northwest coast of Asia Minor.

93. Thus he had travelled from Antioch in the southeast to Troas in the northwest of Asia Minor, a distance as far as from Land's End to John o' Groat's, evangelizing all the way. It must have taken months, perhaps even years. Yet of this long, laborious period we possess no details whatever except such features of his intercourse with the Galatians as may be gathered from the Epistle to that church. The truth is that, thrilling as

are the notices of Paul's career given in the Acts, this record is a very meagre and imperfect one, and his life was far fuller of adventure, of labors and sufferings for Christ, than even Luke's narrative would lead us to suppose. The plan of the Acts is to tell only what was most novel and characteristic in each journey, while it passes over, for instance, all his repeated visits to the same scenes. There are thus great blanks in the history, which were in reality as full of interest as the portions of his life which are fully described. There is a startling proof of this in an Epistle which he wrote within the period covered by the Acts of the Apostles. His argument calling upon him to enumerate some of his outstanding adventures, "Are they ministers of Christ?" he asks, "I am more; in labors more abundant, in stripes above measure, in prisons more frequent, in deaths oft. Of the Jews five times received I forty stripes save one. Thrice was I beaten with rods. Once was I stoned. Thrice I suffered shipwreck. A night and a day have I been in the deep. In journeyings often, in perils of waters, in perils of robbers, in perils by mine own countrymen, in perils by the heathen, in perils in the city, in perils in the wilderness, in perils in the sea, in perils among false brethren; in weariness and painfulness, in watchings often, in hunger and thirst, in fastings often, in cold and nakedness." Now, of the items of this extraordinary catalogue the book of Acts mentions very few: of the five Jewish scourgings it notices not one, of the three Roman beatings only one; the one stoning it records, but not one of the three shipwrecks, for the shipwreck so fully detailed in the Acts happened later. It was no part of the design of Luke to exaggerate the figure of the hero he was painting; his brief and modest narrative comes far short even of the reality; and, as we pass over the few simple words into which he condenses the story of months or years, our imagination requires to be busy, filling up the outline with toils and pains at least equal to those whose memory he has preserved.

94. It would appear that Paul reached Troas under the direction of the guiding Spirit without being aware whither his steps were next to be turned. But could he doubt what the divine intention was when, gazing across the silver streak of the Hellespont, he beheld the shores of Europe on the other side? He was now within the charmed circle where for ages civilization had had her home; and he could not be entirely ignorant of those stories of war and enterprise and those legends of love and valor which have made it for ever bright and dear to the heart of mankind. At only four miles' distance lay the Plain of Troy, where Europe and Asia encountered each other in the struggle celebrated in Homer's immortal song. Not far off Xerxes, sitting on a marble throne, reviewed the three millions of Asiatics with which he meant to bring Europe to his feet. On the other side of that narrow strait lay Greece and Rome, the centres from which issued the learning, the commerce, and the armies which

governed the world. Could his heart, so ambitious for the glory of Christ, fail to be fired with the desire to cast himself upon these strongholds, or could he doubt that the Spirit was leading him forward to this enterprise? He knew that Greece, with all her wisdom, lacked that knowledge which makes wise unto salvation, and that the Romans, though they were the conquerors of this world, did not know the way of winning an inheritance in the world that is to come; but in his breast he carried the secret which they both required.

95. It may have been such thoughts, dimly moving in his mind, that projected themselves into the vision which he saw at Troas; or was it the vision which first awakened the idea of crossing to Europe? As he lay asleep, with the murmur of the Ægean in his ears, he saw a man standing on the opposite coast, on which he had been looking before he went to rest, beckoning and crying, "Come over into Macedonia and help us." That figure represented Europe, and its cry for help Europe's need of Christ. Paul recognized in it a divine summons; and the very next sunset which bathed the Hellespont in its golden light shone upon his figure seated on the deck of a ship whose prow was moving towards the shore of Macedonia.

96. In this passage of Paul from Asia to Europe a great providential decision was taking effect, of which, as children of the West, we cannot think without the profoundest thankfulness. Christianity arose in Asia and among an Oriental people; and it might have been expected to spread first among those races to which the Jews were most akin. Instead of coming west, it might have gone eastward. It might have penetrated into Arabia and taken possession of those regions where the faith of the False Prophet now holds sway. It might have visited the wandering tribes of Central Asia, and, piercing its way down through the passes of the Himalayas, reared its temples on the banks of the Ganges, the Indus, and the Godavery. It might have travelled farther east to deliver the swarming millions of China from the cold secularism of Confucius. Had it done so, missionaries from India and Japan might have been coming to England at the present day to tell the story of the Cross. But Providence conferred on Europe a blessed priority, and the fate of our continent was decided when Paul crossed the Ægean.

97. As Greece lay nearer than Rome to the shore of Asia, its conquest for Christ was the great achievement of this second missionary journey. Like the rest of the world, it was at that time under the sway of Rome, and the Romans had divided it into two provinces—Macedonia in the north and Achaia in the south. Macedonia was therefore the first scene of Paul's Greek mission. It was traversed from east to west by a great Roman

road, along which the missionary moved, and the places where we have accounts of his labors are Philippi, Thessalonica, and Berœa.

98. The Greek character in this northern province was much less corrupted than in the more polished society of the south. In the Macedonian population there still lingered something of the vigor and courage which four centuries before had made its soldiers the conquerors of the world. The churches which Paul founded here gave him more comfort than any he established elsewhere. There are none of his Epistles more cheerful and cordial than those to the Thessalonians and Philippians; and as he wrote the latter late in life, their perseverance in adhering to the gospel must have been as remarkable as the welcome they gave it at the first. At Berœa he even met with a generous and open-minded synagogue of Jews—the rarest occurrence in his experience.

99. A prominent feature of the work in Macedonia was the part taken in it by women. Amid the general decay of religions throughout the world at this period, many women everywhere sought satisfaction for their religious instincts in the pure faith of the synagogue. In Macedonia, perhaps on account of its sound morality, these female proselytes were more numerous than elsewhere; and they pressed in large numbers into the Christian Church. This was a good omen; it was a prophecy of the happy change in the lot of woman which Christianity was to produce in the nations of the West. If man owes much to Christ, woman owes still more. He has delivered her from the degradation of being man's slave and plaything and raised her to be his friend and his equal before heaven; while, on the other hand, a new glory has been added to Christ's religion by the fineness and dignity with which it is invested when embodied in the female character. These things were vividly illustrated in the earliest footsteps of Christianity on the European continent. The first convert was a woman; at the first Christian service held on European soil the heart of Lydia was opened to receive the truth; and the change which passed upon her prefigured what woman in Europe was to become under the influence of Christianity. In the same town of Philippi there was seen too at the same time an equally representative image of the condition of woman in Europe before the gospel reached it, in a poor girl, possessed of a spirit of divination and held in slavery by men who were making gain out of her misfortune, whom Paul restored to sanity. Her misery and degradation were a symbol of the disfiguration, as Lydia's sweet and benevolent Christian character was of the transfiguration, of womanhood.

100. Another feature which prominently marked the Macedonian churches was the spirit of liberality. They insisted on supplying the bodily wants of the missionaries; and, even after Paul had left them, they sent gifts to meet his necessities in other towns. Long afterwards, when he was

a prisoner at Rome, they deputed Epaphroditus, one of their teachers, to carry thither similar gifts to him and to act as his attendant. Paul accepted the generosity of these loyal hearts, though in other places he would work his fingers to the bone and forego his natural rest rather than accept of similar favors. Nor was their willingness to give due to superior wealth. On the contrary, they gave out of deep poverty. They were poor to begin with, and they were made poorer by the persecutions which they had to endure. These were very severe after Paul left, and they lasted long. Of course they had broken first of all on Paul himself. Though he was so successful in Macedonia, he was swept out of every town at last like the off-scourings of all things. It was generally by the Jews that this was brought about. They either fanaticized the mob against him, or accused him before the Roman authorities of introducing a new religion or disturbing the peace or proclaiming a king who would be a rival to Cæsar. They would neither go into the kingdom of heaven themselves nor suffer others to enter.

101. But God protected his servant. At Philippi he delivered him from prison by a physical miracle and by a miracle of grace still more marvellous wrought upon his cruel jailer; and in other towns He saved him by more natural means. In spite of bitter opposition, churches were founded in city after city, and from these the glad tidings sounded out over the whole province of Macedonia.

102. When, leaving Macedonia, Paul proceeded south into Achaia, he entered the real Greece—the paradise of genius and renown. The memorials of the country's greatness rose around him on his journey. As he quitted Berœa, he could see behind him the snowy peaks of Mt. Olympus, where the deities of Greece had been supposed to dwell. Soon he was sailing past Thermopylæ, where the immortal Three Hundred stood against the barbarian myriads; and, as his voyage neared its close, he saw before him the island of Salamis, where again the existence of Greece was saved from extinction by the valor of her sons.

103. His destination was Athens, the capital of the country. As he entered the city he could not be insensible to the great memories which clung to its streets and monuments. Here the human mind had blazed forth with a splendor it has never exhibited elsewhere. In the golden age of its history Athens possessed more men of the very highest genius than have ever lived in any other city. To this day their names invest hers with glory. Yet even in Paul's day the living Athens was a thing of the past. Four hundred years had elapsed since its golden age, and in the course of these centuries, it had experienced a sad decline. Philosophy had degenerated into sophistry, art into dilettanteism, oratory into rhetoric, poetry into verse-making. It was a city living on its past. Yet it still had a

great name and was full of culture and learning of a kind. It swarmed with so-called philosophers of different schools, and with teachers and professors of every variety of knowledge; and thousands of strangers of the wealthy class, collected from all parts of the world, lived there for study or the gratification of their mental tastes. It still represented to an intelligent visitor one of the great factors in the life of the world.

104. With the amazing versatility which enabled him to be all things to all men, Paul adapted himself to this population also. In the marketplace, the lounge of the learned, he entered into conversation with students and philosophers, as Socrates had been wont to do on the same spot five centuries before. But he found even less appetite for the truth than the wisest of the Greeks had met with. Instead of the love of truth, an insatiable intellectual curiosity possessed the inhabitants. This made them willing enough to tolerate the advances of any one bringing before them a new doctrine; and as long as Paul was merely developing the speculative part of his message they listened to him with pleasure. Their interest seemed to deepen, and at last a multitude of them conveyed him to Mars' Hill, in the very centre of the splendors of their city, and requested a full statement of his faith. He complied with their wishes, and in the magnificent speech he made them there gratified their peculiar tastes to the full as in sentences of the noblest eloquence he unfolded the great truths of the unity of God and the unity of man which lie at the foundation of Christianity. But when he advanced from these preliminaries to touch the consciences of his audience and address them about their own salvation, they departed in a body and left him talking.

105. He quitted Athens and never returned to it. Nowhere else had he so completely failed. He had been accustomed to endure the most violent persecution and to rally from it with a light heart. But there is something worse than persecution to a fiery faith like his, and he had to encounter it here: his message roused neither interest nor opposition. The Athenians never thought of persecuting him; they simply did not care what the babbler said; and this cold disdain cut him more deeply than the stones of the mob or the lictors' rods. Never perhaps was he so much depressed. When he left Athens he moved on to Corinth, the other great city of Achaia; and he tells us himself that he arrived there in weakness and in fear and in much trembling.

106. There was in Corinth enough of the spirit of Athens to prevent these feelings from being easily assuaged. Corinth was to Athens very much what Glasgow is to Edinburgh. The one was the commercial, the other the intellectual capital of the country. Even the situations of the two places in Greece resembled in some respects those of these two cities in Scotland. But the Corinthians also were full of disputatious curiosity and

intellectual hauteur. Paul dreaded the same kind of reception as he had met with in Athens. Could it be that these were people for whom the gospel had no message? This was the staggering question which was making him tremble. There seemed to be nothing in them on which the gospel could take hold: they appeared to feel no wants which it could satisfy.

107. There were other elements of discouragement in Corinth. It was the Paris of ancient times—a city rich and luxurious, wholly abandoned to sensuality. Vice displayed itself without shame in forms which struck deadly despair into Paul's pure Jewish mind. Could men be rescued from the grasp of such monstrous vices? Besides, the opposition of the Jews rose here to unusual virulence. He was compelled at length to depart from the synagogue altogether, and did so with expressions of strong feeling. Was the soldier of Christ going to be driven off the field and forced to confess that the gospel was not suited for cultured Greece? It looked like it.

108. But the tide turned. At the critical moment Paul was visited with one of those visions which were wont to be vouchsafed to him at the most trying and decisive crises of his history. The Lord appeared to him in the night, saying, "Be not afraid, but speak, and hold not thy peace; for I am with thee, and no man shall set on thee to hurt thee; for I have much people in this city." The apostle took courage again, and the causes of discouragement began to clear away. The opposition of the Jews was broken, when they hurried him with mob violence before the Roman governor, Gallio, but were dismissed from his tribunal with ignominy and disdain. The very president of the synagogue became a Christian, and conversions multiplied among the native Corinthians. Paul enjoyed the solace of living under the roof of two leal-hearted friends of his own race and his own occupation, Aquila and Priscilla. He remained a year and a half in the city and founded one of the most interesting of his churches, thus planting the standard of the cross in Achaia also and proving that the gospel was the power of God unto salvation even in the headquarters of the world's wisdom.

The Third Journey

109. It must have been a thrilling story Paul had to tell at Jerusalem and Antioch when he returned from his second journey; but he had no disposition to rest on his laurels, and it was not long before he set out on his third journey.

110. It might have been expected that, having in his second journey planted the gospel in Greece, he would in his third journey have made

Rome his aim. But if the map be referred to, it will be observed that, in the midst, between the regions of Asia Minor which he evangelized during his first journey and the provinces of Greece in which he planted churches in his second journey, there was a hiatus—the populous province of Asia, in the west of Asia Minor. It was on this region he descended in his third journey. Staying for no less than three years in Ephesus, its capital, he effectively filled up the gap and connected together the conquests of his former campaigns. This journey included, indeed, at its beginning, a visitation of all the churches formerly founded in Asia Minor, and, at its close, a flying visit to the churches of Greece; but, true to his plan of dwelling only on what was new in each journey, the author of the Acts has supplied us only with the details relating to Ephesus.

111. This city was at that time the Liverpool of the Mediterranean. It possessed a splendid harbor, in which was concentrated the traffic of the sea which was then the highway of the nations; and as Liverpool has behind her the great towns of Lancashire, so had Ephesus behind and around her such cities as those mentioned along with her in the epistles to the churches in the book of Revelation—Smyrna, Pergamos, Thyatira, Sardis, Philadelphia, and Laodicea. It was a city of vast wealth, and it was given over to every kind of pleasure, the fame of its theatre and racecourse being world-wide.

112. But Ephesus was still more famous as a sacred city. It was a seat of the worship of the goddess Diana, whose temple was one of the most celebrated shrines of the ancient world. This temple was enormously rich and harbored great numbers of priests. It was a resort at certain seasons of the year of flocks of pilgrims from the surrounding regions; and the inhabitants of the town flourished by ministering in various ways to this superstition. The goldsmiths drove a trade in little silver models of the image of the goddess which the temple contained and which was said to have fallen from heaven. Copies of the mystic characters engraven on this ancient relic were sold as charms. The city swarmed with wizards, fortune-tellers, interpreters of dreams, and other gentry of the like kind, who traded on the mariners, merchants, and pilgrims who frequented the port.

113. Paul's work had therefore to assume the form of a polemic against superstition. He wrought such astonishing miracles in the name of Jesus that some of the Jewish palterers with the invisible world attempted to cast out devils by invoking the same name; but the attempt issued in their signal discomfiture. Other professors of magical arts were converted to the Christian faith and burned their books. The venders of superstitious objects saw their trade slipping through their fingers. To such an extent did this go at one of the festivals of the goddess that the silversmiths,

whose traffic in little images had been specially smitten, organized a riot against Paul, which took place in the theatre and was so successful that he was forced to quit the city.

114. But he did not go before Christianity was firmly established in Ephesus, and the beacon of the gospel was twinkling brightly on the Asian coast in response to that which was shining from the shores of Greece on the other side of the Ægean. We have a monument of his success in the churches lying all around Ephesus which St. John addressed a few years afterwards in the Apocalypse; for they were probably the indirect fruit of Paul's labors. But we have a far more astonishing monument of it in the Epistle to the Ephesians. This is perhaps the profoundest book in existence; yet its author evidently expected the Ephesians to understand it. If the orations of Demosthenes, with their closely packed arguments, between whose articulations even a knife cannot be thrust, be a monument of the intellectual greatness of the Greece which listened to them with pleasure; if the plays of Shakespeare, with their deep views of life and their obscure and complex language, be a testimony to the strength of mind of the Elizabethan Age, which could enjoy such solid fare in a place of entertainment; then the Epistle to the Ephesians, which sounds the lowest depths of Christian doctrine and scales the loftiest heights of Christian experience, is a testimony to the proficiency which Paul's converts had attained under his preaching at Ephesus.

CHAPTER VII His Writings and His Character

Paragraphs 115–127.

115–119.   His Writings.

115, 116.   Principal Literary Period.

117.   Form of his Writings.

118.   His Style.

119.   Inspiration.

120–127.   His Character.

121.   Combination of Natural and Spiritual.

122–127.   Characteristics.

122.   Physique; 123. Enterprise; 124. Influence over Men; 125. Unselfishness; 126. Sense of having a Mission; 127. Personal Devotion to Christ

115. It has been mentioned that the third missionary journey closed with a flying visit to the churches of Greece. This visit lasted several months; but in the Acts it is passed over in two or three verses. Probably it was little marked with those exciting incidents which naturally tempt the biographer into detail. Yet we know from other sources that it was nearly the most important part of Paul's life; for during this half-year he wrote the greatest of all his Epistles, that to the Romans, and two others only less important, that to the Galatians and the second to the Corinthians.

116. We have thus alighted on the portion of his life most signalized by literary work. Overpowering as is the impression of the remarkableness of this man produced by following him, as we have been doing, as he hurries from province to province, from continent to continent, over land and sea, in pursuit of the object to which he was devoted, this impression is immensely deepened when we remember that he was at the same time the greatest thinker of his age, if not of any age, and, in the midst of his outward labors, was producing writings which have ever since been among the mightiest intellectual forces of the world, and are still growing in their influence. In this respect he rises sheer above all other evangelists and missionaries. Some of them may have approached him in certain respects—Xavier or Livingstone in the world-conquering instinct, St. Bernard or Whitefield in earnestness and activity.

But few of these men added a single new idea to the world's stock of beliefs, whereas Paul, while at least equalling them in their own special line, gave to mankind a new world of thought. If his Epistles could perish, the loss to literature would be the greatest possible with only one exception—that of the Gospels which record the life, the sayings, and the death of our Lord. They have quickened the mind of the church as no other writings have done, and scattered in the soil of the world hundreds of seeds whose fruit is now the general possession of mankind. Out of them have been brought the watchwords of progress in every reformation which the church has experienced. When Luther awoke Europe from the slumber of centuries, it was a word of Paul which he uttered with his mighty voice; and when, one hundred years ago, our own country was revived from almost universal spiritual death, she was called by the voices of men who had re-discovered the truth for themselves in the pages of Paul.

117. Yet in penning his Epistles Paul may himself have had little idea of the part they were to play in the future. They were drawn out of him simply by the exigencies of his work. In the truest sense of the word they were letters, written to meet particular occasions, not formal writings, carefully designed and executed with a view to fame or to futurity. Letters of the right kind are, before everything else, products of the heart; and it was the eager heart of Paul, yearning for the weal of his spiritual children or alarmed by the dangers to which they were exposed, that produced all his writings. They were part of his day's work. Just as he flew over sea and land to revisit his converts, or sent Timothy or Titus to carry them his counsels and bring news of how they fared, so, when these means were not available, he would send a letter with the same design.

118. This may seem to detract from the value of these writings. We may be inclined to wish that, instead of having the course of his thinking determined by the exigencies of so many special occasions and his attention distracted by so many minute particulars, he had been able to concentrate the force of his mind on one perfect book and expound his views on the high subjects which occupied his thoughts in a systematic form. It cannot be maintained that Paul's Epistles are models of style. They were written far too hurriedly for this; and the last thing he thought of was to polish his periods. Often, indeed, his ideas, by the mere virtue of their fineness and beauty, run into forms of exquisite language, or there is in them such a sustained throb of emotion that they shape themselves spontaneously into sentences of noble eloquence. But oftener his language is rugged and formless; no doubt it was the first that came to hand for expressing what he had to say. He begins sentences and omits to finish them; he goes off into digressions and forgets to pick up the line of thought he has dropped; he throws out his ideas in lumps instead of

fusing them into mutual coherence. Nowhere perhaps will there be found so exact a parallel to the style of Paul as in the letters and speeches of Oliver Cromwell. In the Protector's brain there lay the best and truest thoughts about England and her complicated affairs which existed at the time among Englishmen; but when he tried to express them in speech or letter there issued from his mind the most extraordinary mixture of exclamations, questions, arguments soon losing themselves in the sands of words, unwieldy parentheses, and morsels of beautiful pathos or subduing eloquence. Yet, as you read these amazing utterances, you come by degrees to feel that you are getting to see the very heart and soul of the Puritan Era, and that you would rather be beside this man than any other representative of the period. You see the events and ideas of the time in the very process of birth. Perhaps, indeed, a certain formlessness is a natural accompaniment of the very highest originality. The perfect expression and orderly arrangement of ideas is a later process; but when great thoughts are for the first time coming forth there is a kind of primordial roughness about them, as if the earth out of which they are arising were still clinging to them: the polishing of the gold comes late and has to be preceded by the heaving of the ore out of the bowels of nature. Paul in his writings is hurling forth the original ore of truth. We owe to him hundreds of ideas which were never uttered before. After the original man has got his idea out, the most commonplace scribe may be able to express it for others better than he, though he could never have originated it. So throughout the writings of Paul there are materials which others may combine into systems of theology and ethics, and it is the duty of the church to do so. But his Epistles permit us to see revelation in the very process of birth. As we read them closely we seem to be witnessing the creation of a world of truth, as the angels wondered to see the firmament evolving itself out of chaos and the multitudinous earth spreading itself forth in the light. Minute as are the details he has often to deal with, the whole of his vast view of the truth is recalled in his treatment of every one of them, as the whole sky is mirrored in a single drop of dew. What could be a more impressive proof of the fecundity of his mind than the fact that, amid the innumerable distractions of a second visit to his Greek converts, he should have written in half a year three such books as Romans, Galatians, and Second Corinthians?

119. It was God by his Spirit who communicated this revelation of truth to Paul. Its own greatness and divineness supply the best proof that it could have had no other origin. But none the less did it break in upon Paul with the joy and pain of original thought; it came to him through his experience; it drenched and dyed every fibre of his mind and heart; and the expression which it found in his writings was in accordance with his peculiar genius and circumstances.

120. It would be easy to suggest compensations in the form of Paul's writings for the literary qualities they lack. But one of these so outweighs all others that it is sufficient by itself to justify in this case the ways of God. In no other literary form could we, to the same extent, in the writings have got the man. Letters are the most personal form of literature. A man may write a treatise or a history or even a poem and hide his personality behind it. But letters are valueless unless the writer shows himself. Paul is constantly visible in his letters. You can feel his heart throbbing in every chapter he ever wrote. He has painted his own portrait—not only that of the outward man, but of his innermost feelings—as no one else could have painted it. It is not from Luke, admirable as is the picture drawn in the Acts of the Apostles, that we learn what the true Paul was, but from Paul himself. The truths he reveals are all seen embodied in the man. As there are some preachers who are greater than their sermons, and the principal gain of their hearers in listening to them is obtained in the inspiring glimpses they get of a great and sanctified personality, so the best thing in the writings of Paul is Paul himself, or rather the grace of God in him.

121. His character presented a wonderful combination of the natural and the spiritual. From nature he had received a strongly marked individuality; but the change which Christianity produces was no less obvious in him. In no saved man's character is it possible to separate nicely what is due to nature and what to grace; for nature and grace blend sweetly in the redeemed life. In Paul the union of the two was singularly complete; yet it was always clear that there were two elements in him of diverse origin; and this is indeed the key to a successful estimate of his character.

122. To begin with what was most simply natural: his physique was an important condition of his career. As want of ear may make a musical career impossible or a failure of eyesight stop the progress of a painter, so the missionary life is impossible without a certain degree of physical stamina. To any one reading by itself the catalogue of Paul's sufferings, and observing the elasticity with which he rallied from the severest of them and resumed his labors, it would naturally occur that he must have been a person of Herculean mould. On the contrary, he appears to have been little of stature, and his bodily presence was weak. This weakness seems to have been sometimes aggravated by disfiguring disease; and he felt keenly the disappointment which he knew his bodily presence would excite among strangers; for every preacher who loves his work would like to preach the gospel with all the graces which conciliate the favor of hearers to an orator. God, however, used his very weakness, beyond his hopes, to draw out the tenderness of his converts; and so, when he was weak, then he was strong, and he was able to glory even in his infirmities.

There is a theory, which has obtained extensive currency, that the disease he suffered from was violent ophthalmia, causing disagreeable redness of the eyelids. But its grounds are very slender. He seems, on the contrary, to have had a remarkable power of fascinating and cowing an enemy with the keenness of his glance, as in the story of Elymas the sorcerer, which reminds us of the tradition about Luther, that his eyes sometimes so glowed and sparkled that bystanders could scarcely look on them. There is no foundation whatever for an idea of some recent biographers of Paul that his bodily constitution was excessively fragile and chronically afflicted with shattering nervous disease. No one could have gone through his labors or suffered the stoning, the scourgings, and other tortures he endured without having an exceptionally tough and sound constitution. It is true that he was sometimes worn out with illness and torn down by the acts of violence to which he was exposed; but the rapidity of his recovery on such occasions proves what a large fund of bodily force he had to draw upon. And who can doubt that, when his face was melted with tender love in beseeching men to be reconciled to God or lighted up with enthusiasm in the delivery of his message, it must have possessed a noble beauty far above mere regularity of feature?

123. There was a good deal that was natural in another element of his character on which much depended—his spirit of enterprise. There are many men who like to grow where they are born; to have to change into new circumstances and make acquaintance with new people is intolerable to them. But there are others who have a kind of vagabondism in the blood; they are the persons intended by nature for emigrants and pioneers; and, if they take to the work of the ministry, they make the best missionaries. In modern times no missionary has had this consecrated spirit of adventure in the same degree as our lamented hero, David Livingstone. When he first went to Africa he found the missionaries clustered in the south of the continent, just within the fringe of heathenism; they had their houses and gardens, their families, their small congregations of natives; and they were content. But he moved at once away beyond the rest into the heart of heathenism, and dreams of more distant regions never ceased to haunt him, till at length he commenced his extraordinary tramps over thousands of miles where no missionary had ever been before; and when death overtook him he was still pressing forward. Paul's was a nature of the same stamp, full of courage and adventure. The unknown in the distance, instead of dismaying, drew him on. He could not bear to build on other men's foundations, but was constantly hastening to virgin soil, leaving churches behind for others to build up. He believed that, if he lit the lamp of the gospel here and there over vast areas, the light would spread in his absence by its own virtue. He liked to count the leagues he had left behind him, but his watchword

was ever forward. In his dreams he saw men beckoning him to new countries; he had always a long unfulfilled programme in his mind; and as death approached he was still thinking of journeys into the remotest corners of the known world.

124. Another element of his character near akin to the one just mentioned was his influence over men. There are those to whom it is painful to have to accost a stranger even on pressing business; and most men are only quite at home in their own set—among men of the same class or profession as themselves. But the life he had chosen brought Paul into contact with men of every kind, and he had constantly to be introducing to strangers the business with which he was charged. He might be addressing a king or a consul the one hour and a roomful of slaves or common soldiers the next. One day he had to speak in the synagogue of the Jews, another among a crowd of Athenian philosophers, another to the inhabitants of some provincial town far from the seats of culture. But he could adapt himself to every man and every audience. To the Jews he spoke as a rabbi out of the Old Testament Scriptures; to the Greeks he quoted the words of their own poets; and to the barbarians he talked of the God who giveth rain from heaven and fruitful seasons, filling our hearts with food and gladness. When a weak or insincere man attempts to be all things to all men, he ends by being nothing to anybody. But, living on this principle, Paul found entrance for the gospel everywhere, and at the same time won for himself the esteem and love of those to whom he stooped. If he was bitterly hated by enemies, there was never a man more intensely loved by his friends. They received him as an angel of God, or even as Jesus Christ himself, and were ready to pluck out their eyes and give them to him. One church was jealous of another getting too much of him. When he was not able to pay a visit at the time he had promised, they were angry, as if he had done them a wrong. When he was parting from them, they wept sore and fell on his neck and kissed him. Numbers of young men were continually about him, ready to go on his messages. It was the largeness of his manhood which was the secret of this fascination; for to a big nature all resort, feeling that in its neighborhood it is well with them.

125. This popularity was partly, however, due to another quality which shone conspicuously in his character—the spirit of unselfishness. This is the rarest quality in human nature, and it is the most powerful of all in its influence on others, where it exists in purity and strength. Most men are so absorbed in their own interests and so naturally expect others to be the same that, if they see any one who appears to have no interests of his own to serve, but is willing to do as much for the sake of others as the generality do for themselves, they are at first incredulous, suspecting that he is only hiding his designs beneath the cloak of benevolence; but if

he stand the test and his unselfishness prove to be genuine, there is no limit to the homage they are prepared to pay him. As Paul appeared in country after country and city after city, he was at first a complete enigma to those whom he approached. They formed all sorts of conjectures as to his real design. Was it money he was seeking, or power, or something darker and less pure? His enemies never ceased to throw out such insinuations. But those who got near him and saw the man as he was, who knew that he refused money and worked with his hands day and night to keep himself above the suspicion of mercenary motives, who heard him pleading with them one by one in their homes and exhorting them with tears to a holy life, who saw the sustained personal interest he took in every one of them—these could not resist the proofs of his disinterestedness or deny him their affection. There never was a man more unselfish; he had literally no interest of his own to live for. Without family ties, he poured all the affections of his big nature, which might have been given to wife and children, into the channels of his work. He compares his tenderness to his converts to that of a nursing mother to her children; he pleads with them to remember that he is their father who has begotten them in the gospel. They are his glory and crown, his hope and joy and crown of rejoicing. Eager as he was for new conquests, he never lost his hold upon those he had won. He could assure his churches that he prayed and gave thanks for them night and day, and he remembered his converts by name at the throne of grace. How could human nature resist disinterestedness like this? If Paul was a conqueror of the world, he conquered it by the power of love.

126. The two most distinctively Christian features of his character have still to be mentioned. One of them was the sense of having a divine mission to preach Christ, which he was bound to fulfil. Most men merely drift through life, and the work they do is determined by a hundred indifferent circumstances; they might as well be doing anything else, or they would prefer, if they could afford it, to be doing nothing at all. But, from the time when he became a Christian, Paul knew that he had a definite work to do; and the call he had received to it never ceased to ring like a tocsin in his soul. "Woe is unto me if I preach not the gospel:" this was the impulse which drove him on. He felt that he had a world of new truths to utter and that the salvation of mankind depended on their utterance. He knew himself called to make Christ known to as many of his fellow-creatures as his utmost exertions could enable him to reach. It was this which made him so impetuous in his movements, so blind to danger, so contemptuous of suffering. "None of these things move me, neither count I my life dear unto myself, so that I might finish my course with joy, and the ministry which I have received of the Lord Jesus, to testify the gospel of the grace of God." He lived with the account which

he would have to give at the judgment-seat of Christ ever in his eye, and his heart was revived in every hour of discouragement by the vision of the crown of life which, if he proved faithful, the Lord, the righteous Judge, would place upon his head.

127. The other peculiarly Christian quality which shaped his career was personal devotion to Christ. This was the supreme characteristic of the man and from first to last the mainspring of his activities. From the moment of his first meeting with Christ he had but one passion; his love to his Saviour burned with more and more brightness to the end. He delighted to call himself the slave of Christ, and had no ambition except to be the propagator of His ideas and the continuer of His influence. He took up this idea of being Christ's representative with startling boldness. He says the heart of Christ is beating in his bosom towards his converts; he says the mind of Christ is thinking in his brain; he says that he is continuing the work of Christ and filling up that which was lacking in His sufferings; he says the wounds of Christ are reproduced in the scars upon his body; he says he is dying that others may live, as Christ died for the life of the world. But it was in reality the deepest humility which lay beneath these bold expressions. He had the sense that Christ had done everything for him; He had entered into him, casting out the old Paul and ending the old life, and had begotten a new man, with new designs, feelings, and activities. And it was his deepest longing that this process should go on and become complete—that his old self should vanish quite away, and that the new self, which Christ had created in his own image and still sustained, should become so predominant that, when the thoughts of his mind were Christ's thoughts, the words on his lips Christ's words, the deeds he did Christ's deeds, and the character he wore Christ's character, he might be able to say, "I live; yet not I, but Christ liveth in me."

CHAPTER VIII Picture of a Pauling Church

Paragraphs 128–144.

128, 129.   The Exterior and the Interior View of History

130–143.   A Christian Church in a Heathen City.

131.   The Place of Meeting.

132, 133.   The Persons Present.

134–137.   The Services.

138–143.   Abuses and Irregularities.

139, 140.   Of Domestic Life.

141–143.   Inside the Church.

144.   Inferences.

128. A holiday visitor to a foreign city walks through the streets, guide-book in hand, looking at monuments, churches, public buildings, and the outsides of the houses, and in this way is supposed to be made acquainted with the town; but, on reflection, he will find that he has scarcely learned anything about it, because he has not been inside the houses. He does not know how the people live—not even what kind of furniture they have or what kind of food they eat—not to speak of far deeper matters, such as how they love, what they admire and pursue, and whether they are content with their lot. In reading history one is often at a loss in the same way. It is only the outside of life that is made visible. It is as if the eyes were carried along the external surface of a tree, instead of seeing a cross section of its substance. The pomp and glitter of the court, the wars waged, and the victories won, the changes in the constitution and the rise and fall of administrations, are faithfully recorded. But the reader feels that he would learn far more of the real history of the time if he could see for one hour what was happening beneath the roofs of the peasant, the shopkeeper, the clergyman, and the noble. Even in Scripture history there is the same difficulty. In the narrative of the Acts of the Apostles we receive thrilling accounts of the external details of Paul's history; we are carried rapidly from city to city, and informed of the incidents which accompanied the founding of the various churches. But we cannot help wishing sometimes to stop and learn what one of these churches was like inside. In Paphos or Iconium, in Thessalonica or Berœa or Corinth, how did things go on after Paul left? What were the Christians like, and what was the aspect of their worship?

129. Happily it is possible to obtain this interior view of things. As Luke's narrative describes the outside of Paul's career, so Paul's own Epistles permit us to see its deeper aspects. They rewrite the history on a different plane. This is especially the case with those Epistles written at the close of his third journey, which cast a flood of light back upon the period covered by all his journeys. In addition to the three Epistles already mentioned as having been written at this time, there is another belonging to the same part of his life—the first to the Corinthians—which may be said to transport us, as on a magician's mantle, back over two thousand years, and stationing us in mid-air above a great Greek city, in which there was a Christian church, to take the roof off the meeting-house of the Christians and permit us to see what was going on within.

130. It is a strange spectacle we witness from this coigne of vantage. It is Sabbath evening, but of course the heathen city knows of no Sabbath. The day's work at the busy seaport is over, and the streets are thronged with gay revellers intent on a night of pleasure, for it is the wickedest city of that wicked ancient world. Hundreds of merchants and sailors from foreign parts are lounging about. The gay young Roman, who has come across to this Paris for a bout of dissipation, drives his light chariot through the streets. If it is near the time of the annual games, there are groups of boxers, runners, charioteers, and wrestlers, surrounded by their admirers and discussing their chances of winning the coveted crowns. In the warm genial climate old and young are out of doors enjoying the evening hour, while the sun, going down over the Adriatic, is casting its golden light upon the palaces and temples of the wealthy city.

131. Meantime the little company of Christians has been gathering from all directions to their place of worship; for it is the hour of their stated assembly. The place of meeting itself does not rise very clearly before our view. But at all events it is no gorgeous temple like those by which it is surrounded; it has not even the pretensions of the neighboring synagogue. It may be a large room in a private house or the wareroom of some Christian merchant cleared for the occasion.

132. Glance round the benches and look at the faces. You at once discern one marked distinction among them; some have the peculiar facial contour of the Jew, while the rest are Gentiles of various nationalities; and the latter are the majority. But look closer still and you notice another distinction: some wear the ring which denotes that they are free, while others are slaves; and the latter preponderate. Here and there among the Gentile members there is one with the regular features of the born Greek, perhaps shaded with the pale thoughtfulness of the philosopher or distinguished with the self-confidence of wealth; but not many great, not many mighty, not many noble, are there; the majority

belong to what in this pretentious city would be reckoned the foolish, the weak, the base, the despised things of this world; they are slaves, whose ancestors did not breathe the pellucid air of Greece, but roamed in savage hordes on the banks of the Danube or the Don.

133. But observe one thing besides on all the faces present—the terrible traces of their past life. In a modern Christian congregation one sees in the faces on every hand that peculiar cast of feature which Christian nurture, inherited through many centuries, has produced; and it is only here and there that a face may be seen in whose lines the tale is written of debauchery or crime. But in this Corinthian congregation these awful hieroglyphics are everywhere. "Know ye not," Paul writes to them, "that the unrighteous shall not inherit the kingdom of God? Be not deceived: neither fornicators nor idolaters nor adulterers nor effeminate nor abusers of themselves with mankind nor thieves nor covetous nor extortioners shall inherit the kingdom of God. And such were some of you." Look at that tall, sallow-faced Greek; he has wallowed in the mire of Circe's swine-pens. Look at that low-browed Scythian slave; he has been a pickpocket and a jail-bird. Look at that thin-nosed, sharp-eyed Jew; he has been a Shylock, cutting his pound of flesh from the gilded youth of Corinth. Yet there has been a great change. Another story besides the tale of sin is written on these countenances: "But ye are washed, but ye are sanctified, but ye are justified in the name of the Lord Jesus and by the Spirit of our God." Listen, they are singing; it is the fortieth Psalm: "He took me from the fearful pit and from the miry clay." What pathos they throw into the words, what joy overspreads their faces! They know themselves to be monuments of free grace and dying love.

134. But suppose them now all gathered; how does their worship proceed? There was this difference between their services and most of ours, that instead of one man conducting them—offering the prayers, preaching, and giving out the psalms—all the men present were at liberty to contribute their part. There may have been a leader or chairman; but one member might read a portion of Scripture, another offer prayer, a third deliver an address, a fourth raise a hymn, and so on. Nor does there seem to have been any fixed order in which the different parts of the service occurred; any member might rise and lead away the company into praise or prayer or meditation, as he felt prompted.

135. This peculiarity was due to another great difference between them and us: the members were endowed with very extraordinary gifts. Some of them had the power of working miracles, such as the healing of the sick. Others possessed a strange gift called the gift of tongues. It is not quite clear what it was; but it seems to have been a kind of tranced utterance, in which the speaker poured out an impassioned rhapsody by

which his religious feeling received both expression and exaltation. Some of those who possessed this gift were not able to tell others the meaning of what they were saying, while others had this additional power; and there were those who, though not speaking with tongues themselves, were able to interpret what the inspired speakers were saying. Then again, there were members who possessed the gift of prophecy—a very valuable endowment. It was not the power of predicting future events, but a gift of impassioned eloquence, whose effects were sometimes marvelous: when an unbeliever entered the assembly and listened to the prophets, he was seized with uncontrollable emotion, the sins of his past life rose up before him, and, falling on his face, he confessed that God was among them of a truth. Other members exercised gifts more like those we are ourselves acquainted with, such as the gift of teaching or the gift of management. But in all cases there appears to have been a kind of immediate inspiration, so that what they did was not the effect of calculation or preparation, but of a strong present impulse.

136. These phenomena are so remarkable that, if narrated in a history, they would put a severe strain on Christian faith. But the evidence for them is incontrovertible: no man, writing to people about their own condition, invents a mythical description of their circumstances; and besides, Paul was writing to restrain rather than encourage these manifestations. They show with what mighty force, at its first entrance into the world, Christianity took possession of the spirits which it touched. Each believer received, generally at his baptism, when the hands of the baptizer were laid on him, his special gift, which, if he remained faithful to it, he continued to exercise. It was the Holy Spirit, poured forth without stint, that entered into the spirits of men and distributed these gifts among them severally as He willed; and each member had to make use of his gift for the benefit of the whole body.

137. After the services just described were over, the members sat down together to a love-feast, which was wound up with the breaking of bread in the Lord's Supper; and then, after a fraternal kiss, they parted to their homes. It was a memorable scene, radiant with brotherly love and alive with outbreaking spiritual power. As the Christians wended their way homeward through the careless groups of the heathen city they were conscious of having experienced that which eye had not seen nor ear heard.

138. But truth demands that the dark side of the picture be shown as well as the bright one. There were abuses and irregularities in the church which it is painful to recall. They were due to two things—the antecedents of the members and the mixture in the church of Jewish and Gentile elements. If it be remembered how vast was the change which

most of the members had made in passing from the worship of the heathen temples to the pure and simple worship of Christianity, it will not excite surprise that their old life still clung to them or that they did not clearly distinguish which things needed to be changed and which might continue as they had been.

139. Yet it startles us to learn that some of them were living in gross sensuality, and that the more philosophical defended this on principle. One member, apparently a person of wealth and position, was openly living in a connection which would have been a scandal even among heathens, and though Paul had indignantly written to have him excommunicated, the church had failed to obey, affecting to misunderstand the order. Others had been allured back to take part in the feasts in the idol temples, notwithstanding their accompaniments of drunkenness and revelry. They excused themselves with the plea that they no longer ate the feast in honor of the gods, but only as an ordinary meal, and argued that they would have to go out of the world if they were not sometimes to associate with sinners.

140. It is evident that these abuses belonged to the Gentile section of the church. In the Jewish section, on the other hand, there were strange doubts and scruples about the same subjects. Some, for instance, revolted by the loose behavior of their Gentile brethren, had gone to the opposite extreme, denouncing marriage altogether and raising anxious questions as to whether widows might marry again, whether a Christian married to a heathen wife ought to put her away, and other points of the same nature. While some of the Gentile converts were participating in the idol feasts, some of the Jewish ones had scruples about buying in the market the meat which had been offered in sacrifice to idols, and looked with censure on their brethen who allowed themselves this freedom.

141. These difficulties belonged to the domestic life of the Christians; but in their public meetings also there were grave irregularities. The very gifts of the Spirit were perverted into instruments of sin; for those possessed of the more showy gifts, such as miracles and tongues, were too fond of displaying them, and turned them into grounds of boasting. This led to confusion and even uproar; for sometimes two or three of those who spoke with tongues would be pouring forth their unintelligible utterances at once, so that, as Paul said, if any stranger had entered their meeting he would have concluded that they were all mad. The prophets spoke at wearisome length, and too many pressed forward to take part in the services. Paul had sternly to rebuke these extravagances, insisting on the principle that the spirits of the prophets were subject to the prophets, and that therefore the spiritual impulse was no apology for disorder.

142. But there were still worse things inside the church. Even the sacredness of the Lord's Supper was profaned. It seems that the members were in the habit of taking with them to church the bread and wine which were needed for this sacrament. But the wealthy brought abundant and choice supplies, and instead of waiting for their poorer brethren and sharing their provisions with them, began to eat and drink so gluttonously that the table of the Lord actually resounded with drunkenness and riot.

143. One more dark touch must be added to this sad picture. In spite of the brotherly kiss with which their meetings closed, they had fallen into mutual rivalry and contention. No doubt this was due to the heterogeneous elements brought together in the church. But it had been allowed to go to great lengths. Brother went to law with brother in the heathen courts instead of seeking the arbitration of a Christian friend. The body of the members was split up into four theological factions. Some called themselves after Paul himself. These treated the scruples of the weaker brethren about meats and other things with scorn. Others took the name of Apollonians from Apollos, an eloquent teacher from Alexandria, who visited Corinth between Paul's second and third journeys. These were the philosophical party; they denied the doctrine of the resurrection because it was absurd to suppose that the scattered atoms of the dead body could ever be reunited again. The third party took the name of Peter, or Cephas, as in their Hebrew purism they preferred to call him. These were narrow-minded Jews, who objected to the liberality of Paul's views. The fourth party affected to be above all parties and called themselves simply Christians. Like many despisers of the sects since then who have used the name of Christian in the same way, these were the most bitterly sectarian of all and rejected Paul's authority with malicious scorn.

144. Such is the checkered picture of one of Paul's churches given in one of his own Epistles; and it shows several things with much impressiveness. It shows, for instance, how exceptional, even in that age, his own mind and character were, and what a blessing his gifts and graces of good sense, of large sympathy blended with conscientious firmness, of personal purity and honor, were to the infant church. It shows that it is not behind but in front that we have to look for the golden age of Christianity. It shows how perilous it is to assume that the prevalence of any ecclesiastical usage at that time must constitute a rule for all times. Everything of this kind was evidently at the experimental stage. Indeed, in the latest writings of Paul we find the picture of a very different state of things, in which the worship and discipline of the church were far more fixed and orderly. It is not for a pattern of the machinery of a church we ought to go back to this early time, but for a spectacle of fresh and transforming spiritual power. This is what will always attract to the

Apostolic Age the longing eyes of Christians; the power of the Spirit was energizing in every member, the tides of fresh emotion swelled in every breast, and all felt that the dayspring of a new revelation had visited them; life, love, light were diffusing themselves everywhere. Even the vices of the young church were the irregularities of abundant life, for the lack of which the lifeless order of many a subsequent generation has been a poor compensation.

CHAPTER IX His Great Constroversy

Paragraphs 145–162.

146–148. The Question at Issue.

149–153. The Settlement of it.

149, 150. By Peter; 151. By Paul; 152, 153. By the Council of Jerusalem.

154–156. Attempt to unsettle it.

157, 158. Paul crushes the Judaizers.

159–162. A subordinate Branch of the Question: the Relation of Christian Jews to the Law.

145. The version of the apostle's life supplied in his own letters is largely occupied with a controversy which cost him much pain and took up much of his time for many years, but of which Luke says little. At the date when Luke wrote it was a dead controversy, and it belonged to a different plane from that along which his story moves. But at the time when it was raging it tried Paul far more than tiresome journeys or angry seas. It was at its hottest about the close of his third journey, and the Epistles already mentioned as having been written then may be said to have been evoked by it. The Epistle to the Galatians especially was a thunderbolt hurled against his opponents in this controversy; and its burning sentences show how profoundly he was moved by the subject.

146. The question at issue was whether the Gentiles required to become Jews before they could be true Christians; or, in other words, whether they had to be circumcised in order to be saved.

147. It had pleased God in the primitive times to choose the Jewish race from among the nations and make it the repository of salvation; and, till the advent of Christ, those from other nations who wished to become partakers of the true religion had to seek entrance as proselytes within the sacred inclosure of Israel. Having thus destined this race to be the guardians of revelation, God had to separate them very completely from all other nations and from all other aims which might have distracted their attention from the sacred trust which had been committed to them. For this purpose he regulated their whole life with rules and arrangements intended to make them a peculiar people, different from all other races of the earth. Every detail of their life—their forms of worship, their social customs, their dress, their food—was prescribed for them; and all these prescriptions were embodied in that vast legal instrument which they called the law. This rigorous prescription of so many things which are

naturally left to free choice was a heavy yoke upon the chosen people; it was a severe discipline to the conscience, and such it was felt to be by the more earnest spirits of the nation. But others saw in it a badge of pride; it made them feel that they were the select of the earth and superior to all other people; and, instead of groaning under the yoke, as they would have done if their consciences had been very tender, they multiplied the distinctions of the Jew, swelling the volume of the prescriptions of the law with stereotyped customs of their own. To be a Jew appeared to them the mark of belonging to the aristocracy of the nations; to be admitted to the privileges of this position was in their eyes the greatest honor which could be conferred on one who did not belong to the commonwealth of Israel. Their thoughts were all pent within the circle of this national conceit. Even their hopes about the Messiah were colored with these prejudices; they expected Him to be the hero of their own nation, and the extension of His kingdom they conceived as a crowding of the other nations within the circle of their own through the gateway of circumcision. They expected that all the converts of the Messiah would undergo this national rite and adopt the life prescribed in the Jewish law and tradition; in short, their conception of Messiah's reign was a world of Jews.

148. Such undoubtedly was the tenor of popular sentiment in Palestine when Christ came; and multitudes of those who accepted Jesus as the Messiah and entered the Christian Church had this set of conceptions as their intellectual horizon. They had become Christians, but they had not ceased to be Jews; they still attended the temple worship; they prayed at the stated hours, they fasted on the stated days, they dressed in the style of the Jewish ritual; they would have thought themselves defiled by eating with uncircumcised Gentiles; and they had no thought but that, if Gentiles became Christians, they would be circumcised and adopt the styles and customs of the religious nation.

149. The question was settled by the direct intervention of God in the case of Cornelius, the centurion of Cæsarea. When the messengers of Cornelius were on their way to the Apostle Peter at Joppa, God showed that leader among the apostles, by the vision of the sheet full of clean and unclean beasts, that the Christian Church was to contain circumcised and uncircumcised alike. In obedience to this heavenly sign Peter accompanied the centurion's messengers to Cæsarea, and saw such evidences that the household of Cornelius had already, without circumcision, received the distinctively Christian endowments of faith and the Holy Ghost that he could not hesitate to baptize them as being Christians already. When he returned to Jerusalem his proceedings created wonder and indignation among the Christians of the strictly Jewish persuasion. But he defended himself by recounting the vision of the sheet and by an appeal to the clear

fact that these uncircumcised Gentiles were proved by their possession of faith and of the Holy Ghost to have been already Christians.

150. This incident ought to have settled the question once for all; but the pride of race and the prejudices of a lifetime are not easily subdued. Although the Christians of Jerusalem reconciled themselves to Peter's conduct in this single case, they neglected to extract from it the universal principle which it implied; and even Peter himself, as we shall subsequently see, did not fully comprehend what was involved in his own conduct.

151. Meanwhile, however, the question had been settled in a far stronger and more logical mind than Peter's. Paul at this time began his apostolic work at Antioch, and soon afterwards went forth with Barnabas upon his first great missionary expedition into the Gentile world; and, wherever they went, he admitted heathens into the Christian Church without circumcision. Paul in thus acting did not copy Peter. He had received his gospel directly from heaven. In the solitudes of Arabia, in the years immediately after his conversion, he had thought this subject out and come to far more radical conclusions about it than had yet entered the minds of any of the rest of the apostles. To him far more than to any of them the law had been a yoke of bondage; he saw that it was only a stern preparation for Christianity, not a part of it; indeed, there was in his mind a deep gulf of contrast between the misery and curse of the one state and the joy and freedom of the other. To his mind to impose the yoke of the law on the Gentiles would have been to destroy the very genius of Christianity; it would have been the imposition of conditions of salvation totally different from that which he knew to be the one condition of it in the gospel. These were the deep reasons which settled this question in this great mind. Besides, as a man who knew the world and whose heart was set on winning the Gentile nations to Christ, he felt far more strongly than did the Jews of Jerusalem, with their provincial horizon, how fatal such conditions as they meant to impose would be to the success of Christianity outside Judæa. The proud Romans, the high-minded Greeks, would never have consented to be circumcised and to cramp their life within the narrow limits of Jewish tradition; a religion hampered with such weights could never have become the universal religion.

152. But, when Paul and Barnabas came back from their first missionary tour to Antioch, they found that a still more decisive settlement of this question was required; for Christians of the strictly Jewish sort were coming down from Jerusalem to Antioch and telling the Gentile converts that unless they were circumcised they could not be saved. In this way they were filling them with alarm lest they might be

omitting something on which the welfare of their souls depended, and they were confusing their minds as to the simplicity of the gospel. To quiet these disturbed consciences it was resolved by the church at Antioch to appeal to the leading apostles at Jerusalem, and Paul and Barnabas were sent thither to procure the decision. This was the origin of what is called the Council of Jerusalem, at which this question was authoritatively settled. The decision of the apostles and elders was in harmony with Paul's practice: the Gentiles were not to be required to be circumcised; only they were enjoined to abstain from meat offered in sacrifice to idols, from fornication, and from blood. To these conditions Paul consented. He did not indeed see any harm in eating meat which had been used in idolatrous sacrifices, when it was exposed for sale in the market; but the feasts upon such meat in the idol temples, which were often followed by wild outbreaks of sensuality, alluded to in the prohibition of fornication, were temptations against which the converts from heathenism required to be warned. The prohibition of blood—that is, of eating meat killed without the blood being drained off—was a concession to extreme Jewish prejudice, which, as it involved no principle, he did not think it necessary to oppose.

153. So the agitating question appeared to be settled by an authority so august that none could question it. If Peter, John, and James, the pillars of the church of Jerusalem, as well as Paul and Barnabas, the heads of the Gentile mission, arrived at a unanimous decision, all consciences might be satisfied and all opposing mouths stopped.

154. It fills us with amazement to discover that even this settlement was not final. It would appear that, even at the time when it was come to, it was fiercely opposed by some who were present at the meeting where it was discussed; and although the authority of the apostles determined the official note which was sent to the distant churches, the Christian community at Jerusalem was agitated with storms of angry opposition to it. Nor did the opposition soon die down. On the contrary, it waxed stronger and stronger. It was fed from abundant sources. Fierce national pride and prejudice sustained it; probably it was nourished by self-interest, because the Jewish Christians would live on easier terms with the non-Christian Jews the less the difference between them was understood to be; religious conviction, rapidly warming into fanaticism, strengthened it; and very soon it was reinforced by all the rancor of hatred and the zeal of propagandism. For to such a height did this opposition rise that the party which was inflamed with it at length resolved to send out propagandists to visit the Gentile churches one by one, and, in contradiction to the official apostolic rescript, warn them that they were imperilling their souls by omitting circumcision, and could not enjoy the privileges of true Christianity unless they kept the Jewish law.

155. For years and years these emissaries of a narrow-minded fanaticism, which believed itself to be the only genuine Christianity, diffused themselves over all the churches founded by Paul throughout the Gentile world. Their work was not to found churches of their own; they had none of the original pioneer ability of their great rival. Their business was to steal into the Christian communities he had founded and win them to their own narrow views. They haunted Paul's foot-steps wherever he went, and for many years were a cause to him of unspeakable pain. They whispered to his converts that his version of the gospel was not the true one and that his authority was not to be trusted. Was he one of the twelve apostles? Had he kept company with Christ? They represented themselves as having brought the true form of Christianity from Jerusalem, the sacred headquarters; and they did not scruple to profess that they had been sent from the apostles there. They distorted the very noblest parts of Paul's conduct to their purpose. For instance, his refusal to accept money for his services they imputed to a sense of his own lack of authority: the real apostles always received pay. In the same way they misconstrued his abstinence from marriage. They were men not without ability for the work they had undertaken; they had smooth, insinuating tongues, they could assume an air of dignity, and they did not stick at trifles.

156. Unfortunately they were by no means without success. They alarmed the consciences of Paul's converts and poisoned their minds against him. The Galatian Church especially fell a prey to them; and the Corinthian Church allowed its mind to be turned against its founder. But, indeed, the defection was more or less pronounced everywhere. It seemed as if the whole structure which Paul had reared with years of labor was to be thrown to the ground. For this was what he believed to be happening. Though these men called themselves Christians, Paul utterly denied their Christianity. Their gospel was not another; if his converts believed it, he assured them they were fallen from grace; and in the most solemn terms he pronounced a curse on those who were thus destroying the temple of God which he had built.

157. He was not, however, the man to allow such seduction to go on among his converts without putting forth the most strenuous efforts to counteract it. He hurried when he could to see the churches which were being tampered with; he sent messengers to bring them back to their allegiance; above all, he wrote letters to those in peril—letters in which the extraordinary powers of his mind were exerted to the utmost. He argued the subject out with all the resources of logic and Scripture; he exposed the seducers with a keenness which cut like steel and overwhelmed them with sallies of sarcastic wit; he flung himself at his converts' feet and with all the passion and tenderness of his mighty heart

implored them to be true to Christ and to him. We possess the records of these anxieties in our New Testament; and it fills us with gratitude to God and a strange tenderness to Paul himself to think that out of his heartbreaking trial there has come such a precious heritage to us.

158. It is comforting to know that he was successful. Persevering as his enemies were, he was more than a match for them. Hatred is strong, but stronger still is love. In his later writings the traces of this opposition are slender or entirely absent. It had given way before the crushing force of his polemic, and its traces had been swept off the soil of the church. Had the event been otherwise, Christianity would have been a river lost in the sands of prejudice near its very source; it would have been at the present day a forgotten Jewish sect instead of the religion of the world.

159. Up to this point the course of this ancient controversy can be clearly traced. But there is another branch of it about whose true course it is far from easy to arrive at certainty. What was the relation of the Christian Jews to the law, according to the teaching and preaching of Paul? Was it their duty to abandon the practices they had been wont to regulate their lives by, and to abstain from circumcising their children or teaching them to keep the law? This would appear to be implied in Paul's principles. If Gentiles could enter the kingdom without keeping the law, it could not be necessary for Jews to keep it. If the law was a severe discipline intended to drive men to Christ, its obligations fell away when this purpose was fulfilled. The bondage of tutelage ceased as soon as the son entered on the actual possession of his inheritance.

160. It is certain, however, that the other apostles and the mass of the Christians of Jerusalem did not for many a day realize this. The apostles had agreed not to demand from the Gentile Christians circumcision and the keeping of the law. But they kept it themselves and expected all Jews to keep it. This involved a contradiction of ideas, and it led to unhappy practical consequences. If it had continued or been yielded to by Paul, it would have split up the church into two sections, one of which would have looked down upon the other. For it was part of the strict observance of the law to refuse to eat with the uncircumcised; and the Jews would have refused to sit at the same table with those whom they acknowledged to be their Christian brethren. This unseemly contradiction actually came to pass in a prominent instance. The apostle Peter, chancing on one occasion to be in the heathen city of Antioch, at first mingled freely in social intercourse with the Gentile Christians. But some of the stricter sort, coming thither from Jerusalem, so cowed him that he withdrew from the Gentile table and held aloof from his fellow-Christians. Even Barnabas was carried away by the same tyranny of

bigotry. Paul alone was true to the principles of gospel freedom. He withstood Peter to the face and exposed the inconsistency of his conduct.

161. Paul never, indeed, carried on a polemic against circumcision and the keeping of the law among born Jews. This was reported of him by his enemies; but it was a false report. When he arrived in Jerusalem at the close of his third missionary journey, the apostle James and the elders informed him of the damage which this representation was doing to his good name and advised him publicly to disprove it. The words in which they made this appeal to him are very remarkable. "Thou seest, brother," they said, "how many thousands of Jews there are who believe; and they are all zealous of the law; and they are informed of thee that thou teachest all the Jews who are among the Gentiles to forsake Moses, saying that they ought not to circumcise their children, neither to walk after the customs. Do therefore this that we say to thee: We have four men who have a vow on them. Take them and purify thyself with them and be at charges with them, that they may shave their heads; and all may know that those things whereof they were informed concerning thee are nothing, but thou thyself also walkest orderly and keepest the law." Paul complied with this appeal and went through the rite which James recommended. This clearly proves that he never regarded it as part of his work to dissuade born Jews from living as Jews. It may be thought that he ought to have done so—that his principles required a stern opposition to everything associated with the dispensation which had passed away. He understood them differently, however, and we find him advising those who were called into the kingdom of Christ being circumcised not to become uncircumcised, and those called in uncircumcision not to submit to circumcision; and the reason he gives is that circumcision is nothing and uncircumcision is nothing. The distinction was nothing more to him, in a religious point of view, than the distinction of sex or the distinction of slave and master. In short, it had no religious significance at all. If, however, a man preferred Jewish modes of life as a mark of his nationality, Paul had no quarrel with him; indeed, in some degree he preferred them himself. He stickled as little against mere forms as for them; only, if they stood between the soul and Christ or between a Christian and his brethren, then he was their uncompromising opponent. But he knew that liberty may be made an instrument of oppression as well as bondage, and therefore in regard to meats, for instance, he penned those noble recommendations of self-denial for the sake of weak and scrupulous consciences which are among the most touching testimonies to his utter unselfishness.

162. Indeed, we have here a man of such heroic size that it is no easy matter to define him. Along with the clearest vision of the lines of demarcation between the old and the new in the greatest crisis of human

history and an unfaltering championship of principle when real issues were involved, we see in him the most genial superiority to mere formal rules and the utmost consideration for the feelings of those who did not see as he saw. By one huge blow he had cut himself free from the bigotry of bondage; but he never fell into the bigotry of liberty, and had always far loftier aims in view than the mere logic of his own position.

CHAPTER X First and Second Imprisonments at Rome

Paragraphs 163–189.

163, 164.   Return to Jerusalem.

Prophecy of approaching Imprisonment.

165–168.   Arrest.

166.   Tumult in Temple; 167. Paul before the Sanhedrin; 168. Plot of Zealots.

169–172.   Imprisonment at Cæsarea.

170.   Providential Reason for this Confinement.

171.   Paul's later Gospel.

172.   His Ethics.

173–176.   Journey to Rome.

173.   Appeal to Cæsar.

174.   Voyage to Italy.

175.   Arrival in Rome.

176–182.   First Imprisonment at Rome.

176.   Trial delayed.

177–182.   Occupations of a Prison.

179.   His Guards converted; 180. Visits of Apostolic Helpers; 181. Messengers from his Churches; 182. His Writings.

183–188.   Last Scenes.

185.   Release from Prison; New Journeys.

186.   Second Imprisonment at Rome.

187, 188.   Trial and Death.

189.   Epilogue.

163. After completing his brief visit to Greece at the close of his third missionary journey, Paul returned to Jerusalem. He must by this time have been nearly sixty years of age; and for twenty years he had been engaged in almost superhuman labors. He had been travelling and preaching incessantly and carrying on his heart a crushing weight of cares. His body

had been worn with disease and mangled with punishments and abuse; and his hair must have been whitened and his face furrowed with the lines of age. As yet, however, there were no signs of his body breaking down, and his spirit was still as keen as ever in its enthusiasm for the service of Christ. His eye was specially directed to Rome, and before leaving Greece he sent word to the Romans that they might expect to see him soon. But, as he was hurrying towards Jerusalem along the shores of Greece and Asia, the signal sounded that his work was nearly done, and the shadow of approaching death fell across his path. In city after city the persons in the Christian communities who were endowed with the gift of prophecy foretold that bonds and imprisonment were awaiting him, and the nearer he came to the close of his journey these warnings became more loud and frequent. He felt their solemnity; his was a brave heart, but it was too humble and reverent not to be overawed with the thought of death and judgment. He had several companions with him, but he sought opportunities of being alone. He parted from his converts as a dying man, telling them that they would see his face no more. But when they entreated him to turn back and avoid the threatened danger, he gently pushed aside their loving arms, and said, "What mean ye to weep and to break my heart? for I am ready not to be bound only, but also to die at Jerusalem for the name of the Lord Jesus."

164. We do not know what business he had on hand which so peremptorily demanded his presence in Jerusalem. He had to deliver up to the apostles a collection on behalf of their poor saints which he had been exerting himself to gather in the Gentile churches; and it may have been of importance that he should discharge this service in person. Or he may have been solicitous to procure from the apostles a message for his Gentile churches, giving an authoritative contradiction to the insinuations of his enemies as to the unapostolic character of his gospel. At all events there was some imperative call of duty summoning him, and, in spite of the fear of death and the tears of friends, he went forward to his fate.

165. It was the feast of Pentecost when he arrived in the city of his fathers, and, as usual at such seasons, Jerusalem was crowded with hundreds of thousands of pilgrim Jews from all parts of the world. Among these there could not but be many who had seen him at his work of evangelization in the cities of the heathen and come into collision with him there. Their rage against him had been checked in foreign lands by the interposition of Gentile authority; but might they not, if they met with him in the Jewish capital, wreak on him their vengeance with the support of the whole population?

166. This was actually the danger into which he fell. Certain Jews from Ephesus, the principal scene of his labors during his third journey,

recognized him in the temple, and, crying out that here was the heretic who blasphemed the Jewish nation, law, and temple, brought about him in an instant a raging sea of fanaticism. It was a wonder he was not torn limb from limb on the spot; but superstition prevented his assailants from defiling with blood the court of the Jews, in which he was caught, and, before they got him hustled into the court of the Gentiles, where they would soon have despatched him, the Roman guard, whose sentries were pacing the castle ramparts which overlooked the temple courts, rushed down and took him under their protection; and when their captain learned that he was a Roman citizen, his safety was secured.

167. But the fanaticism of Jerusalem was now thoroughly aroused, and it raged against the protection which surrounded Paul like an angry sea. The Roman captain on the day after the apprehension took him down to the Sanhedrin in order to ascertain the charge against him; but the sight of the prisoner created such an uproar that he had to hurry him away lest he should be torn in pieces. Strange city and strange people! There was never a nation which produced sons more richly dowered with gifts to make her name immortal; there was never a city whose children clung to her with a more passionate affection; yet, like a mad mother, she tore the very goodliest of them in pieces and dashed them mangled from her breast. Jerusalem was now within a few years of her destruction; here was the last of her inspired and prophetic sons come to visit her for the last time, with boundless love to her in his heart; but she would have murdered him; and only the shields of the Gentiles saved him from her fury.

168. Forty zealots banded themselves together under a curse to snatch Paul even from the midst of the Roman swords; and the Roman captain was only able to foil their plot by sending him under a heavy guard down to Cæsarea. This was a Roman city on the Mediterranean coast; it was the residence of the Roman governor of Palestine and the headquarters of the Roman garrison; and in it the apostle was perfectly safe from Jewish violence.

169. Here he remained in prison for two years. The Jewish authorities attempted again and again either to procure his condemnation by the governor or to get him delivered up to themselves to be tried as an ecclesiastical offender; but they failed to convince the Roman that Paul had been guilty of any crime of which he could take cognizance or to hand over a Roman citizen to their tender mercies. The prisoner ought to have been released, but his enemies were so vehement in asserting that he was a criminal of the deepest dye that he was detained on the chance of new evidence turning up against him. Besides, his release was prevented by the expectation of the corrupt governor, Felix, that the life of the

leader of a religious sect might be purchased from him with a bribe. Felix was interested in his prisoner and even heard him gladly, as Herod had listened to the Baptist.

170. Paul was not kept in close confinement; he had at least the range of the barracks in which he was detained. There we can imagine him pacing the ramparts on the edge of the Mediterranean, and gazing wistfully across the blue waters in the direction of Macedonia, Achaia, and Ephesus, where his spiritual children were pining for him or perhaps encountering dangers in which they sorely needed his presence. It was a mysterious providence which thus arrested his energies and condemned the ardent worker to inactivity. Yet we can see now the reason for it. Paul was needing rest. After twenty years of incessant evangelization he required leisure to garner the harvest of experience. During all that time he had been preaching that view of the gospel which at the commencement of his Christian career he had thought out, under the influence of the revealing Spirit, in the solitudes of Arabia. But he had now reached a stage when, with leisure to think, he might penetrate into more recondite regions of the truth as it is in Jesus. And it was so important that he should have this leisure that, in order to secure it, God even permitted him to be shut up in prison.

171. During these two years he wrote nothing; it was a time of internal mental activity and silent progress. But when he began to write again the results of it were at once discernible. The Epistles written after this imprisonment have a mellower tone and set forth a profounder view of doctrine than his earlier writings. There is no contradiction, indeed, or inconsistency between his earlier and later views; in Ephesians and Colossians he builds on the broad foundations laid in Romans and Galatians. But the superstructure is loftier and more imposing. He dwells less on the work of Christ, and more on His person; less on the justification of the sinner, and more on the sanctification of the saint. In the gospel revealed to him in Arabia he had set Christ forth as dominating mundane history, and shown his first coming to be the point towards which the destinies of Jews and Gentiles had been tending. In the gospel revealed to him at Cæsarea the point of view is extramundane: Christ is represented as the reason for the creation of all things, and as the Lord of angels and of worlds, to whose second coming the vast procession of the universe is moving forward—of whom and through whom and to whom are all things. In the earlier Epistles the initial act of the Christian life—the justification of the soul—is explained with exhaustive elaboration; but in the later Epistles it is on the subsequent relations to Christ of the person who has been already justified that the apostle chiefly dwells. According to his teaching, the whole spectacle of the Christian life is due to a union between Christ and the soul; and for the description of this relationship

he has invented a vocabulary of phrases and illustrations: believers are in Christ, and Christ is in them: they have the same relation to him as the stones of a building to the foundation-stone, as the branches to the tree, as the members to the head, as a wife to a husband. This union is ideal, for the divine mind in eternity made the destiny of Christ and the believer one: it is legal, for their debts and merits are common property: it is vital, for the connection with Christ supplies the power of a holy and progressive life: it is moral, for in mind and heart, in character and conduct, Christians are constantly becoming more and more identical with Christ.

172. Another feature of these later Epistles is the balance between their theological and their moral teaching. This is visible even in the external structure of the greatest of them, for they are nearly equally divided into two parts, the first of which is occupied with doctrinal statements and the second with moral exhortations. The ethical teaching of Paul spreads itself over all parts of the Christian life; but it is not distinguished by a systematic arrangement of the various kinds of duties, although the domestic duties are pretty fully treated. Its chief characteristic lies in the motive which it brings to bear upon conduct. To Paul Christian morality was emphatically a morality of motives. The whole history of Christ, not in the details of his earthly life, but in the great features of his redemptive journey from heaven to earth and from earth back to heaven again, as seen from the extramundane standpoint of these Epistles, is a series of examples to be copied by Christians in their daily conduct. No duty is too small to illustrate one or other of the principles which inspired the divinest acts of Christ. The commonest acts of humility and beneficence are to be imitations of the condescension which brought him from the position of equality with God to the obedience of the cross; and the ruling motive of the love and kindness practised by Christians to one another is to be the recollection of their common connection with him.

173. After Paul's imprisonment had lasted for two years, Felix was succeeded in the governorship of Palestine by Festus. The Jews had never ceased to intrigue to get Paul into their hands, and they at once assailed the new ruler with further importunities. As Festus seemed to be wavering, Paul availed himself of his privilege of appeal as a Roman citizen and demanded to be sent to Rome and tried at the bar of the emperor. This could not be refused him; and a prisoner had to be sent to Rome at once after such an appeal was taken. Very soon therefore Paul was shipped off under the charge of Roman soldiers and in the company of many other prisoners on their way to the same destination.

174. The journal of the voyage has been preserved in the Acts of the Apostles and is acknowledged to be the most valuable document in

existence concerning the seamanship of ancient times. It is also a precious document of Paul's life; for it shows how his character shone out in a novel situation. A ship is a kind of miniature of the world. It is a floating island, in which there are the government and the governed. But the government is like that of states, liable to sudden social upheavals, in which the ablest man is thrown to the top. This was a voyage of extreme perils, which required the utmost presence of mind and power of winning the confidence and obedience of those on board. Before it was ended Paul was virtually both the captain of the ship and the general of the soldiers; and all on board owed him their lives.

175. At length the dangers of the deep were left behind; and Paul found himself approaching the capital of the Roman world by the Appian Road, the great highway by which Rome was entered by travellers from the East. The bustle and noise increased as he neared the city, and the signs of Roman grandeur and renown multiplied at every step. For many years he had been looking forward to seeing Rome, but he had always thought of entering it in a very different guise from that which now he wore. He had always thought of Rome as a successful general thinks of the central stronghold of the country he is subduing, who looks eagerly forward to the day when he will direct the charge against its gates. Paul was engaged in the conquest of the world for Christ, and Rome was the final stronghold he had hoped to carry in his Master's name. Years ago he had sent to it the famous challenge, "I am ready to preach the gospel to you that are at Rome also; for I am not ashamed of the gospel of Christ, for it is the power of God unto salvation to every one that believeth." But now, when he found himself actually at its gates and thought of the abject condition in which he was—an old, gray-haired, broken man, a chained prisoner just escaped from shipwreck, his heart sank within him and he felt dreadfully alone. At the right moment, however, a little incident took place which restored him to himself; at a small town forty miles out of Rome he was met by a little band of Christian brethren, who, hearing of his approach, had come out to welcome him; and ten miles farther on he came upon another group who had come out for the same purpose. Self-reliant as he was, he was exceedingly sensitive to human sympathy, and the sight of these brethren and their interest in him completely revived him. He thanked God and took courage; his old feelings came back in their wonted strength, and when, in the company of these friends, he reached that shoulder of the Alban Hills from which the first view of the city is obtained, his heart swelled with the anticipation of victory; for he knew he carried in his breast the force which would yet lead captive that proud city. It was not with the step of a prisoner, but with that of a conqueror, that he passed at length beneath the city gate. His road lay along that very Sacred Way by which many a

Roman general had passed in triumph to the Capitol, seated on a car of victory, followed by the prisoners and spoils of the enemy, and surrounded with the plaudits of rejoicing Rome. Paul looked little like such a hero. No car of victory carried him; he trod the causewayed road with wayworn foot. No medals or ornaments adorned his person; a chain of iron dangled from his wrist. No applauding crowds welcomed his approach; a few humble friends formed all his escort. Yet never did a more truly conquering footstep fall on the pavement of Rome or a heart more confident of victory pass beneath her gates.

176. Meanwhile, however, it was not to the Capitol his steps were bent, but to a prison; and he was destined to lie in prison long, for his trial did not come on for two years. The law's delays have been proverbial in all countries and at all eras; and the law of imperial Rome was not likely to be free from this reproach during the reign of Nero, a man of such frivolity that any engagement of pleasure or freak of caprice was sufficient to make him put off the most important call of business. The imprisonment, it is true, was of the mildest description. It may have been that the officer who brought him to Rome spoke a good word for the man who had saved his life during the voyage, or the officer to whom he was handed over, and who is known in profane history as a man of justice and humanity, may have inquired into his case and formed a favorable opinion of his character; but at all events Paul was permitted to hire a house of his own and live in it in perfect freedom, with the single exception that a soldier, who was responsible for his person, was his constant attendant.

177. This was far from the condition which such an active spirit would have coveted. He would have liked to be moving from synagogue to synagogue in the immense city, preaching in its streets and squares, and founding congregation after congregation among the masses of its population. Another man thus arrested in a career of ceaseless movement and immured within prison walls might have allowed his mind to stagnate in sloth and despair. But Paul behaved very differently. Availing himself of every possibility of the situation, he converted his one room into a centre of far-reaching activity and beneficence. On the few square feet of space allowed him he erected a fulcrum with which he moved the world, and established within the walls of Nero's capital a sovereignty more extensive than his own.

178. Even the most irksome circumstance of his lot was turned to good account. This was the soldier by whom he was watched. To a man of Paul's eager temperament and restlessness of mood this must often have been an intolerable annoyance; and, indeed, in the letters written during this imprisonment he is constantly referring to his chain, as if it

were never out of his mind. But he did not suffer this irritation to blind him to the opportunity of doing good presented by the situation. Of course his attendant was changed every few hours, as one soldier relieved another upon guard. In this way there might be six or eight with him every four-and-twenty hours. They belonged to the imperial guard, the flower of the Roman army. Paul could not sit for hours beside another man without speaking of the subject which lay nearest his heart. He spoke to these soldiers about their immortal souls and the faith of Christ. To men accustomed to the horrors of Roman warfare and the manners of Roman barracks nothing could be more striking than a life and character like his; and the result of these conversations was that many of them became changed men, and a revival spread through the barracks and penetrated into the imperial household itself. His room was sometimes crowded with these stern, bronzed faces, glad to see him at other times than those when duty required them to be there. He sympathized with them and entered into the spirit of their occupation; indeed, he was full of the spirit of the warrior himself. We have an imperishable relic of these visits in an outburst of inspired eloquence which he dictated at this period: "Put on the whole armor of God, that ye may be able to stand against the wiles of the devil; for we wrestle not against flesh and blood, but against principalities, against powers, against the rulers of the darkness of this world, against spiritual wickedness in high places. Wherefore take unto you the whole armor of God, that ye may be able to withstand in the evil day, and having done all, to stand. Stand therefore, having your loins girt about with truth, and having on the breastplate of righteousness, and your feet shod with the preparation of the gospel of peace; above all, taking the shield of faith, wherewith ye shall be able to quench all the fiery darts of the wicked. And take the helmet of salvation and the sword of the Spirit, which is the word of God." That picture was drawn from the life, from the armor of the soldiers in his room; and perhaps these ringing sentences were first poured into the ears of his warlike auditors before they were transferred to the Epistle in which they have been preserved.

179. But he had other visitors. All who took an interest in Christianity in Rome, both Jews and Gentiles, gathered to him. Perhaps there was not a day of the two years of his imprisonment but he had such visitors. The Roman Christians learned to go to that room as to an oracle or shrine. Many a Christian teacher got his sword sharpened there; and new energy began to diffuse itself through the Christian circles of the city. Many an anxious father brought his son, many a friend his friend, hoping that a word from the apostle's lips might waken the sleeping conscience. Many a wanderer, stumbling in there by chance, came out a new man. Such a one was Onesimus, a slave from Colossæ, who arrived in Rome as

a runaway, but was sent back to his Christian master, Philemon, no longer as a slave, but as a brother beloved.

180. Still more interesting visitors came. At all periods of his life he exercised a strong fascination over young men. They were attracted by the manly soul within him, in which they found sympathy with their aspirations and inspiration for the noblest work. These youthful friends, who were scattered over the world in the work of Christ, flocked to him at Rome. Timothy and Luke, Mark and Aristarchus, Tychicus and Epaphras, and many more came to drink afresh at the well of his ever-springing wisdom and earnestness. And he sent them forth again to carry messages to his churches or bring him news of their condition.

181. Of his spiritual children in the distance he never ceased to think. Daily he was wandering in imagination among the glens of Galatia and along the shores of Asia and Greece; every night he was praying for the Christians of Antioch and Ephesus, of Philippi and Thessalonica and Corinth. Nor were gratifying proofs wanting that they were remembering him. Now and then there would appear in his lodging a deputy from some distant church, bringing the greetings of his converts or, perhaps, a contribution to meet his temporal wants, or craving his decision on some point of doctrine or practice about which difficulty had arisen. These messengers were not sent empty away: they carried warm-hearted messages or golden words of counsel from their apostolic friend. Some of them carried far more. When Epaphroditus, a deputy from the church at Philippi, which had sent to their dear father in Christ an offering of love, was returning home, Paul sent with him, in acknowledgment of their kindness, the Epistle to the Philippians, the most beautiful of all his letters, in which he lays bare his very heart and every sentence glows with love more tender than a woman's. When the slave Onesimus was sent back to Colossæ, he received as the branch of peace to offer to his master the exquisite little Epistle to Philemon, a priceless monument of Christian courtesy. He carried too a letter addressed to the church of the town in which his master lived, the Epistle to the Colossians. The composition of these Epistles was by far the most important part of Paul's varied prison activity; and he crowned this labor with the writing of the Epistle to the Ephesians, which is perhaps the profoundest and sublimest book in the world. The church of Christ has derived many benefits from the imprisonment of the servants of God; the greatest book of uninspired religious genius, the "Pilgrim's Progress," was written in a jail; but never did there come to the church a greater mercy in the disguise of misfortune than when the arrest of Paul's bodily activities at Cæsarea and Rome supplied him with the leisure needed to reach the depths of truth sounded in the Epistle to the Ephesians.

182. It may have seemed a dark dispensation of providence to Paul himself that the course of life he had pursued so long was so completely changed; but God's thoughts are higher than man's thoughts and His ways than man's ways; and He gave Paul grace to overcome the temptations of his situation and do far more in his enforced inactivity for the welfare of the world and the permanence of his own influence than he could have done by twenty years of wandering missionary work. Sitting in his room, he gathered within the sounding cavity of his sympathetic heart the sighs and cries of thousands far away, and diffused courage and help in every direction from his own inexhaustible resources. He sank his mind deeper and deeper in solitary thought, till, smiting the rock in the dim depth to which he had descended, he caused streams to gush forth which are still gladdening the city of God.

183. The book of Acts suddenly breaks off with a brief summary of Paul's two years' imprisonment at Rome. Is this because there was no more to tell? When his trial came on did it issue in his condemnation and death? Or did he get out of prison and resume his old occupations? Where Luke's lucid narrative so suddenly deserts us tradition comes in proffering its doubtful aid. It tells us that he was acquitted on his trial and let out of prison; that he resumed his travels, visiting Spain among other places; but that before long he was arrested again and sent back to Rome, where he died a martyr's death at the cruel hands of Nero.

184. Happily, however, we are not altogether dependent on the precarious aid of tradition. We have writings of Paul's own undoubtedly subsequent to the two years of his first imprisonment. These are what are called the Pastoral Epistles—the Epistles to Timothy and Titus. In these we see that he regained his liberty and resumed his employment of revisiting his old churches and founding new ones. His footsteps cannot indeed be any longer traced with certainty. We find him back at Ephesus and Troas; we find him in Crete, an island at which he touched on his voyage to Rome and in which he may then have become interested; we find him exploring new territory in the northern parts of Greece. We see him once more, like the commander of an army who sends his aides-decamp all over the field of battle, sending out his young assistants to organize and watch over the churches.

185. But this was not to last long. An event had happened immediately after his release from prison which could not but influence his fate. This was the burning of Rome—an appalling disaster, the glare of which even at this distance makes the heart shudder. It was probably a mad freak of the malicious monster who then wore the imperial purple. But Nero saw fit to attribute it to the Christians, and instantly the most atrocious persecution broke out against them. Of course the fame of this

soon spread over the Roman world; and it was not likely that the foremost apostle of Christianity could long escape. Every Roman governor knew that he could not do the emperor a more pleasing service than by sending Paul to him in chains.

186. It was not long, accordingly, before Paul was lying once more in prison at Rome; and it was no mild imprisonment this time, but the worst known to the law. No troops of friends now filled his room, for the Christians of Rome had been massacred or scattered, and it was dangerous for any one to avow himself a Christian. We have a letter written from his dungeon, the last he ever wrote, the Second Epistle to Timothy, which affords us a glimpse of unspeakable pathos into the circumstances of the prisoner. He tells us that one part of his trial is already over. Not a friend stood by him as he faced the bloodthirsty tyrant who sat on the judgment-seat. But the Lord stood by him and enabled him to make the emperor and the spectators in the crowded basilica hear the sound of the gospel. The charge against him had broken down. But he had no hope of escape. Other stages of the trial had yet to come, and he knew that evidence to condemn him would either be discovered or manufactured. The letter betrays the miseries of his dungeon. He prays Timothy to bring him a cloak he had left at Troas to defend him from the damp of the cell and the cold of the winter. He asks for his books and parchments, that he may relieve the tedium of his solitary hours with the studies he had always loved. But, above all, he beseeches Timothy to come himself, for he was longing to feel the touch of a friendly hand and see the face of a friend yet once again before he died. Was the brave heart then conquered at last? Read the Epistle and see. How does it begin? "I also suffer these things; nevertheless I am not ashamed; for I know whom I have believed, and am persuaded that He is able to keep that which I have committed unto Him against that day." How does it end? "I am now ready to be offered, and the time of my departure is at hand. I have fought a good fight, I have finished my course, I have kept the faith. Henceforth there is laid up for me a crown of righteousness, which the Lord, the righteous Judge, shall give me at that day; and not to me only, but unto all them also that love his appearing." This is not the strain of the vanquished.

187. There can be little doubt that he appeared again at Nero's bar, and this time the charge did not break down. In all history there is not a more startling illustration of the irony of human life than this scene of Paul at the bar of Nero. On the judgment-seat, clad in the imperial purple, sat a man who in a bad world had attained the eminence of being the very worst and meanest being in it—a man stained with every crime, the murderer of his own mother, of his wives, and of his best benefactors; a man whose whole being was so steeped in every namable and

unnamable vice that body and soul of him were, as some one said at the time, nothing but a compound of mud and blood; and in the prisoner's dock stood the best man the world possessed, his hair whitened with labors for the good of men and the glory of God. Such was the occupant of the seat of justice, and such the man who stood in the place of the criminal.

188. The trial ended, Paul was condemned and delivered over to the executioner. He was led out of the city with a crowd of the lowest rabble at his heels. The fatal spot was reached: he knelt beside the block; the headsman's axe gleamed in the sun and fell; and the head of the apostle of the world rolled down in the dust.

189. So sin did its uttermost and its worst. Yet how poor and empty was its triumph! The blow of the axe only smote off the lock of the prison and let the spirit go forth to its home and to its crown. The city falsely called eternal dismissed him with execration from her gates; but ten thousand times ten thousand welcomed him in the same hour at the gates of the city which is really eternal. Even on earth Paul could not die. He lives among us to-day with a life a hundred-fold more influential than that which throbbed in his brain while the earthly hull which made him visible still lingered on the earth. Wherever the feet of them who publish the glad tidings go forth beautiful upon the mountains he walks by their side as an inspirer and a guide; in ten thousand churches every Sabbath and on a thousand thousand hearths every day his eloquent lips still teach that gospel of which he was never ashamed; and wherever there are human souls searching for the white flower of holiness or climbing the difficult heights of self-denial, there he whose life was so pure, whose devotion to Christ was so entire, and whose pursuit of a single purpose was so unceasing, is welcomed as the best of friends.

Hints to Teachers and questions to Bible Students

Teacher's Apparatus.—The English theology of this century has no juster cause for pride than the books it has produced on the Life of Paul. Perhaps there is no other subject in which it has so outdistanced all rivals. Conybeare and Howson's "Life and Epistles of St. Paul" will probably always keep the foremost place; in many respects it is nearly perfect; and a teacher who has mastered it will be sufficiently equipped for his work and require no other help. The works of Lewin and Farrar are written on the same lines; the former is rich in maps of countries and plans of towns; and the strong point of the latter is the analysis of Paul's writings—the exposition of the mind of Paul. The German books are not nearly as valuable as these three. Hausrath's "The Apostle Paul" is a brilliant performance, but it is as weak in handling the deeper things as it is strong in coloring up the external and picturesque features of the subject. Baur's work is an amazingly clever *tour de force*, but it is not so much a well-proportioned picture of the apostle as a prolonged paradox thrown down as a challenge to the learned. The French essay by Sabatier is highly spoken of, but I have not seen it. Adolphe Monod's "St. Paul," a series of five discourses, is an inquiry into the secret of the apostle's life, written with deep sympathy and glowing eloquence. But the best help is to be found in the original sources themselves—the cameo-like pictures of Luke and the self-revelations of Paul's Epistles. The latter especially, read in the fresh translation of Conybeare, will show the apostle to anyone who has eyes to see. Johnstone's wall-map of Paul's journeys is indispensable in the class-room.

CHAPTER XI Who Authored the Book of Hebrews: A Defense for Pauline Authorship

Edward D. Andrews

Introduction

Who is the author of the Book of Hebrews? Why does it really matter, if the book is canonical, authoritative and inspired? The book was not signed, and so there have been many suggestions over the centuries. This article will provide evidence that the author of the book of Hebrews is, in fact, the Apostle Paul. To be quite frank at the outset, there is no absolute determinative evidence for any suggested author, even Paul. However, we do not live in an absolute world. God is absolute and the Word of God in the original is absolute. It seems that most researchers that address this seem to offer just a few suggestions to live with the belief that it is best to say that we do not know. Having gotten that out of the way, I view biblical evidence like a criminal court views the level needed for a decision. Let us take a moment to consider just that.

Warrants Further Investigation

Reasonable (30%): This is a low-level burden of proof in that it is enough to accept something as fairly likely, being so unless proven otherwise by a deeper look, which may bring in more evidence.

Probable (40%): This is also a low-level burden of proof in that it is enough to accept something as likely being so unless proven otherwise by a deeper look, which may bring in more evidence.

Conviction for Claim

The Preponderance of Evidence (51%): This is a higher level burden of proof that makes something to be more likely to be true than not true.

Clear and Convincing Evidence (85%): This is an even higher level of burden of proof that something is substantially more likely than not.

Beyond Reasonable Doubt (99%): This is the highest level of burden of proof that something is true, having absolutely no doubt. It must be understood that having absolutely no doubt is not the same as 100% absolute evidence of certainty. If one has doubts that affect their belief of certainty, it is not beyond reasonable doubt. This too must be qualified, because it is reasonable to have doubts on certain aspects of the whole that does not have all the answers as of yet, but it does not affect the level of certainty as a whole.

Suggested Authors

There have been many suggested authors since the first century. James, Philip, and Jude have been offered as suggested authors of the book of Hebrews. Below is a short summary of evidence that is presented for some of the more common suggestions.

Luke as the Author: The Greek of the book of Hebrews is literary Koine Greek, like what is found in the Gospel of Luke and the book of Acts. Luke had an extensive association with Timothy, who is mentioned twice in Hebrews. There are the similarities with the doctrines of Paul. Luke was also a traveling companion of Paul.

Barnabas as the Author: He was a traveling companion of Paul and a companion of Timothy. As was mentioned above, he was a Levite of the island of Cyprus (Ac 4:36) and was a Hellenist, he was a Greek-speaking Jew.

Silas as the Author of Hebrews: He was a traveling companion of Paul and a companion of Timothy. There are many personal characteristics that contribute to his name being offered. He was a Jew from Jerusalem, and well respected, and viewed as a prophet. (Acts 15:32) He played a major role in the circumcision issue in Antioch. (Acts 15:23)

Apollos as the Author: The literary Koine Greek fits the training that he had received, he is from Alexandria, and the birthplace of the Septuagint (280-150 B.C.E.), and the Old Testament quotes from the book of Hebrews reflects his emphasis and the Septuagint. He was an eloquent speaker, with matches the eloquence of the book of Hebrews.

Priscilla and Aquila as the Authors: This view is supported by Adolf Harnack, who suggested Priscilla, because of her close ministry and working relationship with Paul. However, it really lacks in internal and external evidence. The fact that she is a woman would be reason enough to leave the letter anonymous.

Clement of Rome as the Author: (d. about 100 C.E.) There are a few similarities between the Book of Hebrews and the apocryphal book 1 Clement. (Heb. 11:7 and 1 Clem 9; Heb. 11:31 and 1 Clem 12; Heb. 1:3-13 and 1 Clem 36) In addition, there is a similarity in the way the two books cite Scripture. (Heb. 2:6; 4:4 and 1 Clem 15; 21) Then, there are the similarities of: connecting multiple Scripture quotations together, similarity in flow of argument, and the movement from example to application.

Up until the 1800's, the most recognized suggested author is the Apostle Paul. In 1930, there was a discovery of the Chester Beatty P46 (papyrus No. 46), which had been copied (150 C.E.), about 100 years after the death of the Apostle Paul. (Comfort and Barret 2001, pp. 203-06) P46 contains Hebrews among nine of Paul's letters, coming after Romans. The early church unanimously viewed Paul as the author. Pantaenus, who ran the Catechetical School in Alexandria around 180 C.E., accepted Paul as the author. This holds true of both his successors: Clement of Alexandria (150-215 C.E.) and Origen (184-254 C.E.). It should be mentioned that the Western church doubted that Paul was the author. It was Jerome and Augustine who accepted the authorship of Paul, which contributed to the West eventually accepting it as well. Thus, Hebrews is listed among "fourteen letters of Paul the apostle" in "*The Canon of Athanasius*," of the fourth-century C.E.

Excursus on Origen

Origen is the most noted early scholar of Alexandria, Egypt. In relation to the authorship of Hebrews, many commentaries quote him out of context and do not even reflect the whole of his comment if their quote was accurate. For example, Dr. George H. Guthrie in his NIV Application Commentary on Hebrews writes, "With Origen we confess our ignorance: 'Who wrote the epistle, God only knows the truth.'" (G. H. Guthrie 1998, p. 27) Let us say for the sake of argument that Origen was referring to the author of Hebrews. What Guthrie leaves out is that just prior to that statement, Origen writes, "If then, any church considers this epistle as coming from Paul, let it be commended for this, for neither did those ancient men deliver it as such without cause." (Cruse 1998, 6.25.13-14, p. 216) In addition, Origen quoted from the book of Hebrews over 200 times as being Paul's epistle. It is a bit disingenuous to quote the small phrase of Origen, and not include the fact that Origen "accepted Pauline authorship," and "consistently quoted Hebrews as Paul's and commended those Churches that held to the Pauline authorship." (Lea 1999, p. 496) Worse still, Origen was quoted out of context, as the quote, "Who wrote the epistle, God only knows the truth," was not meant for the author of Hebrews, it was an uncertainty about the scribe that took down the letter to the Hebrews as Paul spoke.

The Grouping of Certain Books

First, it must be understood that the synoptic Gospels were published orally for many years before the written text came to market. With many of the writers of the Christian Greek Scriptures, you have the author himself penning the book (rough draft), making needed corrections, and then producing the 'authorized' text. From this authorized text, other copies were made. For those authors who dictated their writings, the scribe would take it down initially in shorthand and then create a rough draft to be corrected by the author and himself. From this, the scribe would produce the authorized text for the author to sign in his own hand. After the individual books had been in circulation for a few decades, the community of Christians throughout the Roman Empire started to form collections, such as combined books of the Gospels, and compilations of the Apostle Paul's letters. These groupings were accomplished by 125 C.E., with the total collection of the 27 books of the Christian Greek Scriptures coming together by 325 C.E. There is no doubt that throughout this process of publishing, copying, collecting, and canonizing of the Christian Greek Scriptures, those involved recognized these writings as being authoritative, no less than the graphē [Scriptures] of the Hebrew Old Testament books. (Andrews 2012, p. 65)

In other words, toward the close of the first century, Christians were gathering certain New Testament books together, and dispensing them as a collection. The first to be collected were the four Gospels and then the Gospels and Acts. Running neck-and-neck with these collections were the letters of the Apostle Paul. These groupings were available by the early part of the second century, and we have P46, which dates to 150 C.E., and just so happens to be a collection of Paul's letters, and included the books of Hebrews in the prominent position, right after Romans.

Doctrinal and Stylistic Similarities Between Paul and Hebrews

1. The book of Hebrews begins with Jesus Christ's work in creation, as does the book of Colossians. (Heb. 1:2; Col 1:16)
2. Jesus took on the form of his brothers, to be like them in every respect, as he suffered in his ransom sacrifice. (Heb. 2:14-17; Phil 2:5-8)
3. Christ mediates and new and better covenant. (Heb. 8:6; 2 Cor. 3:4-11)

4. The gifts that were given by way of the Holy Spirit. (Heb. 2:4; 1 Cor. 12:11)

5. The warning example of unbelief to the Hebrews from the Israelite history. (Heb. 3:7-11; 4:6-11; 1 Cor. 10:1-11)

6. The similarity of a request that the readers pray for Paul and his work. (Heb. 13:18;Rom 15:30)

7. "Now may the God of peace," is exact. (Heb. 13:20; 1 Thess. 5:23)

8. "Our brother Timothy" is similar to four of Paul's other letters. (Heb. 13:23; 2 Cor. 1:1, Col 1:1, I Thess. 3:2; Phm. 1)

9. Paul's letters to the Philippians, the Colossians, and Philemon, were written from Rome, as Paul was imprisoned, and Timothy was at his side. This circumstance fits the circumstances of the closing of Hebrews. (Heb. 13:23-24; Php 1:1; 2:19; Col 1:1, 2; Phm 1)[3]

10. Paul's trademark ending "be with all of you," is found in Hebrews and a number of Paul's letters, whether it be 'grace' or 'peace' or 'love' or 'holy Spirit,' or 'the Lord' or Jesus Christ' "be with all of you." (Heb. 13:25; Rom. 15:33; 1 Cor. 16:24; 2 Cor. 13:14; 2 Thess. 3:16, 18; Tit 3:15)

11. When we look at the textual evidence, the evidence points to ending in the manuscripts of the autographs were much shorter. For example, Philemon would have ended with "grace be with you," rather than the longer ending, "grace of our Lord Jesus Christ be with your spirit. Amen."

Differences Between Paul and Hebrews

1. The book of Hebrews is anonymous, whereas no other writing of Paul is anonymous. Sometimes we are quick to dismiss exceptions to the rule, this lack of clear proof of identity of the writer would clearly not rule out Paul. If there is a reasonable reason for the omission of the name, and other evidence supports Paul, let us leave it at that. Other New Testament books do not name the author, who is then identified by internal evidence and external support. Some have logically suggested that Paul intentionally omitted his name, as the letter was to go to the Hebrew

---

[3] It should be noted that this is Paul's first imprisonment (59 to 61 C.E.), and Timothy, a very close traveling companion of Paul for some 15 years is mentioned twice. Timothy could have served as served as Paul's amanuensis, the person to write from Paul's dictation of what would become the book of Hebrews.

Christians in Judea, and his name was greatly hated by the Jews there, and the Hebrew Christians were under stress from them as it was. (Acts 21:28)

2. Hebrews 2:3: "how shall we escape if we neglect such a great salvation? It was declared at first by the Lord, and it was attested to us by those who heard." This verse has cause most to suggest that if Paul were the author of Hebrews, it would conflict with his words at Galatians 1:1, 11-12, where he states that he received the Gospel through Jesus Christ. However, Hebrews 2:3 seems to suggest that the author is a second generation Christian, having been taught the Gospel by others who had heard it. However, the context seems to suggest otherwise. It seems that Paul is merely stating here that he did not receive the Gospel during Jesus' three and half year ministry here on earth, like the others.

3. It is a fact that the Greek in most of Paul's letters is more of a conversational Koine; Hebrews is more of a literary Koine. This could be a simple case of different settings and audiences requiring different levels of writing. There is likely no scholar that would ever suggest that Paul could not write in the literary Koine. (1 Cor. 13)

4. Jesus is the great high priest of the book of Hebrews, which is not to be found in Paul's other writings. This logical fallacy is known as an argument from silence, an assumption drawn-out based on the lack of evidence, as opposed the presence of evidence. Again, different setting, require different subject matter.

Canonicity of the Book of Hebrews

What is the Bible canon, and how did this term come about? What are some of the aspects that are used to determine a book's canonicity?

The English word "canon" goes back to the Greek word kanon and then to the Hebrew qaneh. Its basic meaning is "reed," our English word "cane" being derived from it. Since a reed was sometimes used as a measuring rod, the word kanon came to mean a standard or rule. It was also used to refer to a list or index and when so applied to the Bible denotes the list of books which are received as Holy Scripture. Thus if one speaks of "canonical" writings, one is speaking of those books which are regarded as having divine authority and which comprise our Bible. (Lightfoot 1963, 1988, 2003, p. 152)

Before reading the rest of this paragraph, ponder and consider this question: how many books of the New Testament were written by

Archippus, Claudia, Damaris, Linus, Persis, Pudens, and Sopater? None right? Why? All of those mentioned were traveling companions of the Apostle Paul. However, Paul had over 100 traveling companions. These were some of the most unfamiliar, because they received little press in the New Testament, and were unknown to most of the New Testament world at that time. Using a modern day example, if I were to ask, 'who knows Pastor Rodney Uhlig?' While he too is a person that would have been willing and qualified to travel with someone like the Apostle Paul, you do not know him, as he is mostly known to his local community and congregation. However, what if I were to ask, 'who is Reverend Billy Graham,' would you know him? Most of the world would know who he is. There are a lot of aspects that signal a book of the Bible as canonical. However, we are going to focus our attention on one criterion. "Every New Testament book was written by an apostle or prophet. Thus each book has either apostolic authorship or apostolic teaching."[4]

All of the writers of the Greek New Testament somehow or other were closely affiliated with the Jerusalem Council (Acts 15:1–35), which was made up of apostles personally selected by Jesus, Jesus' half-brother and elders. Matthew, John, and Peter were of the original twelve apostles. The apostle Paul, while he was an apostle, though not of the twelve, he was specifically selected by Jesus after Jesus had ascended to heaven. James, Jude (half-brother of Jesus) and Mark were at the outpouring of Holy Spirit at Pentecost. (Acts 1:14) Peter clearly reckons the letters of Paul in with "the other Scriptures." (2 Pet. 3:15, 16) Both Mark and Luke were friends and traveling companions of the Apostle Paul, as well as Peter. (Acts 12:25; 1 Pet. 5:13; Col. 4:14; 2 Tim. 4:11) In fact, the Gospel of Mark is recognized as being from both Peter and Mark: Peter's account, Mark penning it. "That relationship notwithstanding, Mark had his own God-given ministry (Acts 12:25; 2 Tim. 4:11)." (Geisler and Nix 1996, p. 212-13) Each of these writers had received Holy Spirit, at either Pentecost on the road to Damascus (Acts 9:17, 18), or by the laying of hands by the apostles. (Acts 8:14-17) All of these writers were well-known in the first century Christian congregation.

Within the Old Testament, we see that the books were written by persons that were known to all of Israel: such as Moses, Joshua, David, Isaiah, Jeremiah, Ezra and Nehemiah. "In the New Testament as well as the Old, the determining factor in whether a book was canonical was its propheticity." (Geisler and Nix 1996, p. 212) If we readDeuteronomy 13:1-8, where Moses sets out the criteria of a prophet, we see that, he was a man of signs and wonders, as well as a proclaimer of God's Word.

---

[4] Norman L. Geisler and William E. Nix, A General Introduction to the Bible, Rev. and expanded. (Chicago: Moody Press, 1996), 212.

Whether the people of God were the Israelites or the first century Christian congregation, they accepted the proclamations from men who possessed supernatural gifts as the inspired Word of God

More so, in the New Testament era, the apostle filled the office of prophet (a proclaimer of the gospel) as well. At Acts 1:21-22, Peter informs us as to the qualifications to be an apostle, it must be "one of the men who have accompanied us during all the time that the Lord Jesus went in and out among us, beginning from the baptism of John until the day when he was taken up from us, one of these men must become with us a witness to his resurrection." Of course, this criterion was to fill the position of one of the twelve apostles. The Apostle Paul was not one of the twelve, but he was handpicked specifically by Jesus himself. This apostle has penned 13 books, half of the New Testament books. If you accept that he penned Hebrews, as this writer does, then he has penned over half. At 2 Corinthians, Paul tells us that "the signs of a true apostle were performed among you with utmost patience, with signs and wonders and mighty works." If a person was not appointed, had not seen Christ, or had not evidenced his office with signs or miracles, his claims would have been unacceptable. "Every New Testament book was written by an apostle or prophet." (Geisler and Nix 1996, p. 212)

In Conclusion

Is there absolute certainty that the Apostle Paul wrote the book of Hebrews? No. We cannot place absolute certainty on it, and it is unfair to take this one book and suggest that this is the criterion that we need. Based on the evidence above, is it fairly likely that Paul wrote the book of Hebrews? Yes, so we can say that it is reasonably so. Can we say that it is fairly likely that Luke, Clement of Rome, Apollos, or another wrote the book of Hebrews? Yes, it is reasonable. What about the level of being probable, is it likely for either Paul or any of the other recommendations? Yes, it is probable. Can we say that it is more likely to be true than not true that Paul or any of the other recommendations wrote the book of Hebrews? Yes for Paul, but a few of the other recommended writers would fall off at this point, such as Clement of Rome, Luke, Silas and Priscilla and Aquila.

Is the evidence clear and convincing that Paul wrote the book of Hebrews, being substantially more likely than not? Yes. What about the others who are still in the running at this level of certainty? There are those that would argue that Barnabas and Apollos are serious candidates, and would be retained at this level of certainty. I would not. I personally believe that when weighed, the evidence points to the Apostle Paul as being beyond reasonable doubt. Is it absolute evidence of certainty? No. However, some issues that can be raised are not really issues at all, when they are looked at more deeply. Regardless, it is acceptable to have concerns on certain aspects of the whole, yet this does not affect the certainty of the whole. Therefore, for this writer, it is beyond reasonable doubt that the Apostle Paul did pen the book of Hebrews. Am I at odds with most of scholarship today? Yes. However, the majority of anything is not right merely because they are the majority.

Bibliography for This Chapter

Barclay, William. The Letter to the Hebrews (New Daily Study Bible). Louisville, KY: Westminster John Knox Press, 2002.

Bercot, David W. A Dictionary of Early Christian Beliefs. Peabody: Hendrickson, 1998.

Bruce, F. F. The New International Commentary on the New Testament: The Epistle to the Hebrews (Revised). Grand Rapids, MI: William B. Eermans Publishing Company, 1990.

Carson, D. A, and Douglas J Moo. An Introduction to the New Testament. Grand Rapids, MI: Zondervan, 2005.

Comfort, Philip, and David Barret. The Text of the Earliest New Testament Greek Manuscripts. Wheaton: Tyndale House Publishers, 2001.

Cruse, C. F. Eusebius' Eccliatical History. Peabody, MA: Hendrickson, 1998.

Ellingworth, Paul. The Epistle to the Hebrews: A Commentary on the Greek Text. Grand Rapids, MI: W.B. Eerdmans, 1993.

Geisler, Norman L, and William E Nix. A General Introduction to the Bible. Chicago: Moody Press, 1996.

Guthrie, Donald. Introduction to the New Testament (Revised and Expanded). Downers Grove, IL: InterVarsity Press, 1990.

Guthrie, George H. The NIV Application Commentary: Hebrews. Grand Rapids, MI: Zondervan, 1998.

Kistemaker, Simon J, and William Hendriksen. New Testament Commentary: vol. 15, Exposition of Hebrews. Grand Rapids: Baker Book House, 1953-2001.

Lea, Thomas D. Holman New Testament Commentary: Hebrews, James. Nashville, TN: Broadman & Holman Publishers, 1999.

Lightfoot, Neil R. How We Got the Bible. Grand Rapids, MI: Baker Books, 1963, 1988, 2003.

Outlaw, W. Stanley. The Book of Hebrews . Nashville, TN: Randall House, 2005.

Pink, Arthur Walkington. An Exposition of Hebrews. Swengel, PA: Bible Truth Depot, 1954.

Wright, N. T. Hebrews for Everyone. London: Westminster John Knox Press, 2003.

APPENDIX A The Conversion of Saul

Edward D. Andrews

Historical Setting

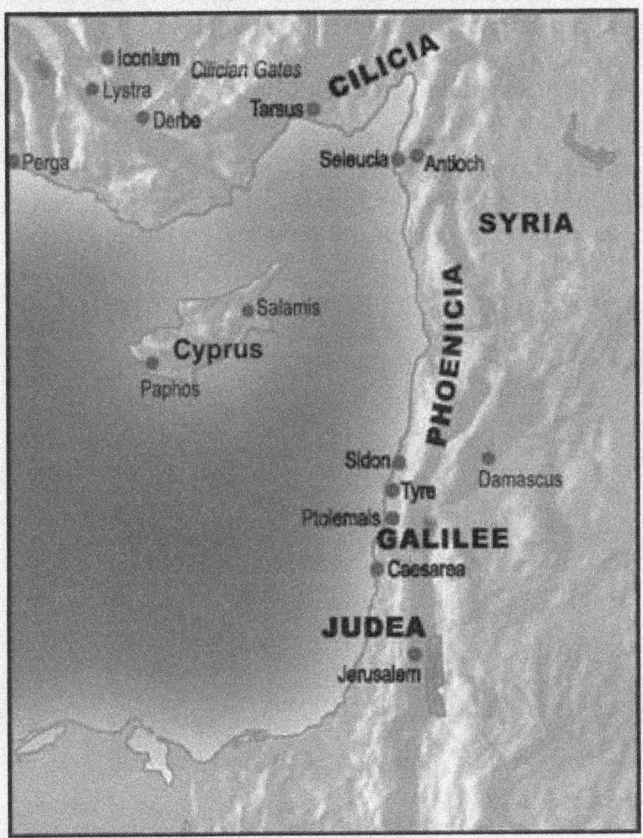

Saul's Persecution and Conversion (8:1–9:30). A great persecution entered Jerusalem that very day, causing a dispersion of everyone except the apostles. Philip, one of the seven travels to Samaria, where many accept the Good News. Peter and John are sent to Samaria, lying "their hands on them and they received the Holy Spirit." (8:17-18) shortly thereafter, an angel sends Philip "south to the road that goes down from Jerusalem to Gaza." (8:26) There, Philip finds a court official of Ethiopia, a eunuch, riding in a chariot, and reading from the book of Isaiah. Philip is sent to witness to him, offering him the meaning of what he was reading, and then baptizes him.

In the meantime, Saul, "still breathing threats and murder against the disciples of the Lord ... asked him for letters to the synagogues at Damascus, so that if he found any belonging to the Way, men or women, he might bring them bound to Jerusalem." Suddenly, light flashes from the heavens, blinding Saul, he falls to the ground. He hears a voice from heaven say, "Saul, Saul, why are you persecuting me?" To which Saul responds, "Who are you, Lord?" And he said, "I am Jesus, whom you are persecuting. But rise and enter the city, and you will be told what you are to do." (9:4-6) In one moment, the one who was persecuting the Christians, would then spend the rest of his Christian missionary life, being the persecuted.

A Period of Peace (9:31). The Christian congregation "now throughout all Judea and Galilee and Samaria had peace and was being built up. And walking in the fear of the Lord and in the comfort of the Holy Spirit, it multiplied."

Based on Acts 9:1-19

Acts 9:1-2 Updated American Standard Version (UASV)

9 But Saul,[5] still breathing threats and murder against the disciples of the Lord, went to the high priest **2** and asked him for letters to the synagogues at Damascus, so that if he found any belonging to the Way, men or women, he might bring them bound to Jerusalem.

Travelers heading for Damascus were still breathing threats, seeking to wreak even more havoc on the fledgling Christian community. Their

---

[5] I.e. the apostle Paul prior to his conversion. Saul is his Hebrew name and Paul is his Roman name.

objective was to pull the Christian disciples of Jesus from their homes, damaging their dignity publicly as they bound them, and then take them by force back to Jerusalem to face the vengeance of the Sanhedrin.

A Pharisee named Saul, who had already given his approval as others stoned the first Christian martyr, Stephen, led this large of an unruly crowd of radical Jews. (Acts 7:57–8:1) Saul was not satisfied with the terror being inflicted up the Jewish Christians within Jerusalem. Saul was zealous to no end, seething with rage, seeking to persecute this sect, known as "the Way."[6] The phrase "'breathing out threats and murder' is an idiomatic expression for 'making threats to murder' (see L&N 33.293)."[7] Luke helps his readers of the book of Acts to understand the ferocity of Saul, as he sought to go after "men or women." (Ac 8:3; 9:2; 22:4)

Acts 9:3-5 Updated American Standard Version (UASV)

3 Now as he was traveling and nearing Damascus, suddenly a light from heaven flashed around him. **4** And falling to the ground he heard a voice saying to him, "Saul, Saul, why are you persecuting me?" **5** And he said, "Who are you, Lord?" And he said, "I am Jesus, whom you are persecuting.

Unexpectedly, an intense light from heaven overwhelms Saul. Those who were traveling with him had seen the light, but were so stunned by the event, it left them without words. Saul was unable to see, but he heard a voice[8] saying, "Saul, Saul, why are you persecuting me?" Shock, but still able to respond, Saul asks, "Who are you, Lord?" The words that came next had to be very much unexpected, and wrenching to his heart, "I am Jesus, whom you are persecuting."

What we notice about Jesus words should comfort every Christian. Jesus **did not** ask Saul, "Saul, Saul, why are you persecuting my disciples?"

---

[6] Was not Rome over this region of their Empire? Where did Saul's authority come from, empowering him to travel to a foreign city? The Sanhedrin had moral authority (in essence, legal authority) over every Jew, regardless of where they resided. This power carried with it the high priest's authority to extradite criminals. Therefore, the elders of the Damascus synagogues would honor letters from the high priest.

[7] Biblical Studies Press, *The NET Bible First Edition Notes* (Biblical Studies Press, 2006), Ac 9:1.

[8] **Acts 22:9** (LEB) **9** (Now those who were with me saw the light **but did not hear the voice** of the one who was speaking to me.) (ESV) **9** Now those who were with me saw the light but **did not understand the voice** of the one who was speaking to me.

When a light from heaven blinded Saul, did those with him hear the voice that Saul heard?

Rather, he asked, "why are you persecuting me?" Yes, for Jesus, his disciple's pain is his pain. (Matt. 25:34-40, 45)

Acts 9:6-9 Updated American Standard Version (UASV)

6 But get up and enter into the city, and it will be told to you what you must do." **7** The men who were traveling with him stood speechless, hearing the voice[9] but seeing no one. **8** Saul rose from the ground, and although his eyes were opened, he saw nothing. And leading him by the hand, they brought him into Damascus. **9** And for three days he was without sight, and neither ate nor drank.

When a light from heaven blinded Saul, did those with him hear the voice that Saul heard? Acts 9:7 says, "The men who were traveling with him stood speechless, hearing the voice." Yet, a restatement of the same account at Acts 22:9, Paul (Saul) says, **(LEB)** **9** "(Now those who were with me saw the light **but did not hear the voice** of the one who was speaking to me.)" (ESV) **9** "Now those who were with me saw the light but **did not understand the voice** of the one who was speaking to me." Do we have a discrepancy here? No. The Greek word for "voice" (*phone*) at Acts 9:7 in in the genitive case (*phones*), which has the sense of hearing the sound of the voice, but not being able to understand it. At Acts 22:9, *phone* is in the accusative case (*phonen*), which means that the men did not hear the voice with comprehension or understanding. In other words, they heard the voice, but did not understand the words. Therefore, this is not a discrepancy. See Box below.

Another so-called "contradiction" of which a great deal is made is that which seems to exist between two different accounts of the conversion of Saul of Tarsus. We are told in Acts 9:7 that those who journeyed with Saul to Damascus *heard the voice* that spoke to Saul, but saw no man. On the other hand Paul, in relating to the Jews in Jerusalem the story of his conversion, says, "They that were with me beheld indeed the light, but they *heard not the voice* of him that spoke to me" (Acts 22:9, RV). Now these two statements seem to flatly contradict one another. Luke, in recounting the conversion, says that the men that journeyed with Paul heard the voice; but Paul himself in recounting his conversion says that they did not hear the voice. Could there possibly be a flatter contradiction than this?

However, this apparent contradiction disappears when we look at the Greek of the two passages. The Greek word translated "heard" governs two cases, the genitive and the accusative. When the voice of a

---

[9] Or *sound* (See footnote on Acts 22:9)

person or thing, which is heard, is spoken of, it is followed by the genitive. When the message that is heard is spoken of it is followed by the accusative. In Acts 9:7, the genitive is used. They did hear the voice, the sound. In Acts 22:9 the words translated "the voice" are in the accusative. They did not hear the message of the One that spoke. The word rendered "voice" also has two meanings: first, "a sound, a tone," and second, "a voice," that is, "a sound of uttered words" (Thayer's *Greek-English Lexicon of the New Testament*). The voice as a mere sound they heard; they did not hear the voice as the sound of uttered words; they did not hear the message.

Therefore, another seeming difficulty entirely disappears when we look exactly at what the Bible in the original says. Instead of having an objection to the Bible we have another illustration of its absolute accuracy, not only down to a word but down to a single letter that ends a word and by which a case in indicated.

Ananias Sent to Saul

Acts 9:10-12 Updated American Standard Version (UASV)

10 Now there was a disciple at Damascus named Ananias; and the Lord said to him in a vision, "Ananias." And he said, "Here I am, Lord." **11** And the Lord said to him, "Get up and go to the street called Straight, and inquire at the house of Judas for a man from Tarsus named Saul, for he is praying, **12** and he has seen in a vision a man named Ananias come in and lay his hands on him so that he might regain his sight."

It was nice of Luke to give his readers, a little chronological and geographical note to move the historical account. A Jewish Christian, converted by Jewish Christians, named Ananias from Damascus, received an unexpected and amazing assignment. "The Lord said to him, "Rise and go to the street called Straight, and at the house of Judas look for a man of Tarsus named Saul, for behold, he is praying." (9:11)

"Straight Street" is actually one of the main roads going through Damascus (the *cardo maximus*), the main east-west route through the city." (Arnold 2002, 293) It was about a mile long. Looking at the sketch, we can picture what the street may have looked like about 34 C.E., when Ananias received his assignment. It may have taken him quite some time, as he went along searching for the house of Judas.

We should note, "The dialog throughout this part of the chapter indicates that conversations with both Saul and Ananias are coming directly from Jesus, not from the Father. That becomes particularly clear in verses 14–16." (Gangel 1998, 141)

Jesus is telling Ananias that Saul/Paul "has seen in a vision a man named Ananias come in and **lay his hands on him**." In the Old Testament, we see Jehovah instructed Moses to commission Joshua as his replacement, by laying hands on him. (Num. 27:23) Jesus laid his hands on people before he healed them, "Now when the sun was setting, all those who had any who were sick with various diseases brought them to him, and he lay his hands on every one of them and healed them." (Lu 4:40) Here we have Ananias being instructed to lay his hands on Saul, to heal him, as Saul/Paul was about to be commissioned an apostle to the nations and kings and the children of Israel, having a greater impact toward the growth of Christianity than all the apostles combined.

Acts 9:13-16 Updated American Standard Version (UASV)

[13] But Ananias answered, "Lord, I have heard from many about this man, how much evil he has done to your holy ones at Jerusalem; [14] and here he has authority from the chief priests to bind all who call on your name." [15] But the Lord said to him, "Go, for he is a chosen instrument of mine, to bear my name before the Gentiles and kings and the sons of Israel. [16] For I will show him how much he must suffer for the sake of my name."

We are told numerous times throughout the New Testament that the world will hate Christians and Christianity. However, we need not prejudge the individuals who make up the world alienated from God. Verses 13-16 are an evident demonstration that circumstances can change a person's heart and mind. Clearly, Saul of Tarsus was a vehement enemy of Christianity, going from an opposer and persecutor, to one who walked with God and became the most faithful and effective evangelist of the first-century.

Ananias says, "**I have heard from many about this man**." There was probably no Jew in the whole of Palestine, who was not aware of Saul's violent persecution of the Christians, all the time thirsting for more opportunities. Therefore, one can certainly appreciate Ananias' pause about visiting Saul. Ananias had no knowledge that Jesus had appeared to Saul on the road to Damascus. We notice that Jesus did not admonition Ananias for his reluctance to take on this assignment. Another thing we might note is Ananias not being surprised at Jesus speaking with him, as he engages the conversation, as if he were talking with some friend in the congregation. It would not be too much of a stretch to suspect that Ananias actually saw Jesus in this vision, while they carried on this brief exchange.

Ananias speaks of "how much evil [Saul/Paul] has done to **your saints** [holy ones] at Jerusalem." (9:13) "This is the first time that this expression is used to refer to Christians." (Arnold 2002, 294) The Bible refers to holy ones, or saints. God is spoken of as "the Holy One [Greek, hagion]." (1 Pet. 1:15-16; see Leviticus 11:45.) Jesus Christ is described as "the Holy One [hagios] of God" when on earth and as "holy [one] [hagios]" in heaven. (Mark 1:24; Rev. 3:7) The angels too are "holy." (Acts 10:22) The same Greek term is applied to numerous ones on earth.—*The New Greek to English Interlinear New Testament*

This writer does not prefer the term "saints." Dr. Don Wilkins, the head of the New American Bible committee writes to me in an email, "I do not see a problem with using 'holy ones.' My camp doesn't like "saints" that much either (even though it's in the NAS). In addition, I don't see 'saints' listed as an option for hagios in BDAG. About the only time I use the term is when I'm formally designating one of the apostles, and even then I don't really like it; it's just a matter of convenience." The three dictionaries below help us better appreciate this,

SAINTS

ENCARTA DICTIONARY

1. **somebody honored by church after death:** a member of a religion who after death is formally designated as having led a life of exceptional holiness

2. **somebody in heaven:** somebody who goes to heaven after death

3. **virtuous person:** a particularly good or holy person, or one who is exceptionally kind and patient in dealing with difficult people or situations

VINE'S EXPOSITORY DICTIONARY

In the plural, as used of believers, it designates all such and is not applied merely to persons of exceptional holiness, or to those who, having died, were characterized by exceptional acts of "saintliness."[10]

MOUNCE's EXPOSITORY DICTIONARY

233x. *hagios* is an adjective that means "holy," but it is used at least 45x as a substantive to designate "saints." Esp. in Paul's letters those who name Jesus as their Lord are called *hagioi* ("saints"; lit., "holy ones").[11]

In all likelihood, the humble Christian servants who are given the term "saint," would not like it, based on the way it is thought of today.

Verse 15 is the most important verse of this chapter, because Paul's witness to Agrippa fulfilled the prophecy that he would carry Jesus' name before kings, but it also identifies the intended purpose of taking the Good News to the nations, not just to the sons of Israel. (Rom. 1:1, 5; 9:24; Gal. 1:15–16; Eph. 3:7–13) Ananias was made aware of God's will and purposes before the older men of Israel down in Jerusalem. Paul was Jesus' **chosen instrument to carry his name**.

Jesus also informed Ananias that the greatest persecutor of the Christian Way was about to '**suffer for the sake of Jesus' name**.' He will experience the hatred of the Jews, the pagans, and the Roman government throughout the course of his ministry. However, Saul/Paul is quite pleased at the privilege of suffering for the name of Christ. (2 Cor. 11:23–33)

Acts 9:17-19 Updated American Standard Version (UASV)

17 So Ananias departed and entered the house, and after laying his hands on him said, "Brother Saul, the Lord Jesus, who appeared to you on the road by which you were coming, has sent me so that you may regain your sight and be filled with the Holy Spirit." **18** And immediately something like scales fell from his eyes and he regained his sight and got up and was baptized; **19** and taking food, he was strengthened.

Saul Proclaims Christ in Synagogues

Now for several days he was with the disciples who were at Damascus.

---

[10] W. E. Vine, Merrill F. Unger, and William White Jr., *Vine's Complete Expository Dictionary of Old and New Testament Words* (Nashville, TN: T. Nelson, 1996), 544.

[11] William D. Mounce, *Mounce's Complete Expository Dictionary of Old & New Testament Words* (Grand Rapids, MI: Zondervan, 2006), 609.

The general rule of the Holy Spirit being passed on was that it took place through the apostles lying on their hands. However, this was the exception to the rule, as it appears that Jesus approved Ananias to transfer the gifts of the Spirit, to Jesus' chosen instrument, Saul.[12] Ananias' laying his hands on Paul had a threefold purpose, (1) demonstrating that Saul/Paul was now being accepted as a fellow believer, this was no ruse, (2) to restore his sight, and (3) to transmit the Holy Spirit. As Ananias carried out his commission, as he spoke to Saul, this scale like substance fell from his eyes. Saul rose up, as he could now see once more, and was immediately baptized by Ananias. Thereafter, he was given some food to eat, as he had not eaten for some three days. As to Saul's baptism, New Testament scholar Clinton E. Arnold writes,

> In later church tradition, there is a one- to three-year delay for baptism, which follows a long period of instruction. The New Testament pattern appears to be that the rite is performed in a short time after a person professes faith in Christ. It is also important here to observe that Paul experiences the work of the Spirit in his life prior to his baptism. (Arnold 2002, 295)

The account at Acts 9:19b-25 says that Paul 'for some days he was with the disciples at Damascus, and **immediately** he proclaimed Jesus in the synagogues.' Luke goes on to inform us of Paul's preaching activity, until he was obligated to leave Damascus, because "the Jews plotted to kill him." However, in his letter to the Galatians, Paul tells his readers that after his conversion, "I did not immediately consult with anyone; nor did I go up to Jerusalem to those who were apostles before me, but I went away into Arabia, and returned again to Damascus." (Gal 1:15-17) One can only infer where the trip to Arabia fits within these events.

It may be that Paul went to Arabia immediately after his conversion. If this were the case, Luke's use of the term **immediately**, would mean after Paul "returned again to Damascus," he immediately spent some time with the disciples, and began proclaiming Jesus in the synagogues. However, in Paul's letter to the Galatians, he is making the point that he "did not immediately" go to "Jerusalem." In other words, Arabia was the **only place outside of Damascus** to which Paul traveled. Thus, his going to Arabia need not necessarily have to come right after his conversion. It may simply be that Paul spent a few days in Damascus, renouncing his former crusade against the Christians, and expressing his newfound faith in Christ, in the synagogues. He then went on his trip to

---

[12] Donald Guthrie, *New Testament Theology* (Downers Grove: Inter-Varsity, 1981), pp. 541–42.

Arabia (why we do not know), "and returned again to Damascus," to continue his preaching work in the synagogues.

Apologist and Old Testament Bible Scholar Dr. Gleason L. Archer

Did Paul's companions hear the Voice on the Damascus Road?

An apparent contradiction arises between the first account of Paul's conversion on the Damascus Road (Acts 9:7) and the second account (Acts 22:9) in regard to Paul's companions. Did they hear the Voice from heaven or did they not? Acts 9:7 states: "But the men who were journeying with Paul were standing speechless, hearing the Voice (*akouontes men tēs phōnēs*), but beholding no one." In Acts 22:9, on the other hand, we are told, "And those who were with me beheld the light, but they did not hear the Voice [*tēn de phōnēn ouk ēkousan*] of the one who was talking to me."

In the original Greek, however, there is no real contradiction between these two statements. Greek makes a distinction between hearing a sound as a noise (in which case the verb "to hear" takes the genitive case) and hearing a voice as a thought-conveying message (in which case it takes the accusative). Therefore, as we put the two statements together, we find that Paul's companions heard the Voice as a sound (somewhat like the crowd who heard the sound of the Father talking to the Son in John 12:28, but perceived it only as thunder); but they did not (like Paul) hear the message that it articulated. Paul alone heard it intelligibly (Acts 9:4 says Paul *ēkousen phōnēn*—accusative case); though he, of course, perceived it also as a startling sound at first (Acts 22:7: "I fell to the ground and heard a voice [*ēkousen phōnēn*] saying to me," NASB). However, in neither account is it stated that his companions ever heard that Voice in the accusative case.

There is an instructive parallel here between the inability to hear the voice as an articulated message and their inability to see the glory of the risen Lord as anything but a blaze of light. Acts 22:9 says that they saw the light, but Acts 9:7 makes it clear that they did not see the Person who displayed Himself in that light. There is a clear analogy between these differing levels of perception in each case.

(For the technical case-distinction in Greek, cf. W. W. Goodwin and C. B. Gulick, *Greek Grammar* [Boston: Ginn & Co., 1930], #1103: "The partitive genitive is used with verbs signifying to taste, to smell, to hear, to perceive, etc."—with the example from Aristophanes' *Pax: phōnēs akouein moi dokō*—'Methinks I hear a voice." See also #1104: "Verbs of hearing, learning, etc. may take an accusative of the thing heard etc., and

> a genitive of the person heard from." This comes very close to the distinction made above, that the accusative indicates the voice as a communicated message or thought, rather than as simply a sound vibrating against the eardrum.)[13]

---

[13] Gleason L. Archer, *New International Encyclopedia of Bible Difficulties*, Zondervan's Understand the Bible Reference Series (Grand Rapids, MI: Zondervan Publishing House, 1982), 382–383.

APPENDIX B Gamaliel Taught Saul of Tarsus

The International Standard Bible Encyclopedia, Revised

Rabbi Gamaliel I, son of Simon and grandson (according to the Talmud) of Rabbi Hillel (founder of the more liberal of the two main schools of the Pharisees, Shammai being the other). Although an alternate tradition makes Gamaliel the son of Hillel, the Talmud is surely to be preferred on this point. A member of the Sanhedrin and a teacher of the law (Acts 5:34), he was known in rabbinical writings as Gamaliel the Elder to distinguish him from his grandson, Gamaliel II. He was the first of seven successive leaders of the school of Hillel to be honored with the title *Rabban* ("Our Rabbi/Master").

Illustration from the *Pollak-Pratto Haggadah* (Spain, ca a.d. 1300) showing Gamaliel instructing two pupils (Jewish Theological Seminary Library).

While believing the law of God to be divinely inspired, Gamaliel tended to emphasize its human elements. He recommended that sabbath observance be less rigorous and burdensome, regulated current custom with respect to divorce in order to protect women, and urged kindness toward Gentiles. Scholarly, urbane, a man of great intellect, he studied Greek literature avidly. What we know of his tolerance and cautious spirit is entirely in keeping with the account of his appeal in the Sanhedrin to spare the lives of Peter and his companions (Acts 5:33-39).

TB *Shabbath* 30b mentions a student of Gamaliel who displayed "impudence in matters of learning," a young man identified by some as the apostle Paul. Paul himself says, "Under Gamaliel, I was thoroughly trained in the law of our fathers and was just as zealous for God as any of you are today" (Acts 22:3, NIV). Several indications from elsewhere in the NT tend to corroborate Paul's claim as recorded by Luke.

(1) Although Paul usually quotes from the LXX when referring to OT passages, he sometimes clearly makes use of the Hebrew text (Job 41:3 in Rom. 11:35; Job 5:12f in 1 Cor. 3:19; Ex. 16:18 in 2 Cor. 8:15; Nu. 16:5 in 2 Tim. 2:19).

---

ca *circa*, about

TB Babylonian Talmud

LXX Septuagint

(2) In Gal. 1:14 Paul mentions a period of advanced and specialized study of the very kind that one might expect under a teacher of Gamaliel's stature, and he does so in language strongly reminiscent of Acts 22:3: "I was advancing in Judaism beyond many Jews of my own age and was extremely zealous for the traditions of my fathers" (NIV).

(3) In Phil. 3:6f Paul asserts that before his conversion to faith in Christ he was faultless as far as legalistic righteousness is concerned. In accordance with the Judaism of his day, Paul had earlier believed in the possibility of salvation through works, but after exercising faith in Christ he came to realize that only through Him could the righteous requirements of the law be fully met in redeemed sinners like himself (Rom. 8:3f.).

(4) Paul made use of five of the seven hermeneutical principles usually associated with Gamaliel's grandfather Hillel. This is understandable in the light of the fact that Gamaliel consistently and faithfully perpetuated the teachings and methodology of his grandfather. For example, Paul uses the hermeneutical principle of arguing from the lesser to the greater in 1 Cor. 9:9-12, which begins as follows: "Do not muzzle an ox while it is treading out the grain." After thus quoting Dt. 25:4, the apostle makes application—in typical Halakic fashion—by stating that if God is concerned about oxen He is all the more concerned that His faithful human servants receive the support they deserve and need.

(5) In 1 Cor. 14:21 Paul quotes Isa. 28:11f as a citation from "the law"—a statement entirely fitting for a student of Gamaliel.

Luke's characteristic restraint in his references to Gamaliel in Acts may be contrasted with two later passages that also mention him. According to Clement *Recognitions* i.65, the apostle Peter states that Gamaliel was "our brother in the faith," and Photius (*Bibliothecae codices* 171 [PG, p. 199]) asserts that he was baptized by Peter and Paul. But both of these traditions are now universally rejected as spurious.

Gamaliel's reputation as one of the greatest teachers in the annals of Judaism, however, remains untarnished and is perhaps best exemplified in Mish *Sotah* ix.15: "Since Rabban Gamaliel the Elder died there has been no more reverence for the law, and purity and abstinence [$p^e r\hat{i}\check{s}\hat{u}t$, cf. "Pharisee"] died out at the same time." [14]

PG J. P. Migne, ed., *Patrologia Graeca* (162 vols., 1857–1866)

Mish Mishnah (*See* TALMUD 1)

[14] Youngblood R. F., "Gamaliel," ed. Geoffrey W Bromiley, *The International Standard Bible Encyclopedia, Revised* (Wm. B. Eerdmans, 1979–1988), 393–394.

Bibliography.—J. Jeremias, "Paulus als Hillelit," in E. E. Ellis and M. Wilcox, eds., *Neotestamentica et Semitica* (1969), pp. 88–94; E. F. Harrison, "Acts 22:3—A Test Case for Luke's Reliability," in R. N. Longenecker and M. C. Tenney, eds., *New Dimensions in NT Study* (1974), pp. 251–260.

Baker Encyclopedia of the Bible

Jewish scholar. This man lived in the 1st century a.d. and died 18 years before the destruction of Jerusalem in A.D. 70 by Titus, the Roman general.

Gamaliel is mentioned in Acts 22:3 as the rabbi with whom the apostle Paul studied as a youth in Jerusalem.

When Peter and the other apostles were brought before the enraged and threatening council in Jerusalem, Gamaliel, who was highly respected by the council, offered cautionary advice that probably saved the apostles' lives in that situation (Acts 5:27–40).

During that period in Israel a number of rabbinical schools evolved. Two of the most influential were the rival Pharisaic schools of Hillel and Shammai. Both of those teachers had vast influence on Jewish thinking. Hillel's school emphasized tradition even above the Law. Shammai's school preserved the teaching of the Law over the authority of tradition. Hillel's school was the most influential, and its decisions have been held by a great number of later rabbis.

Traditionally Gamaliel is considered to be the grandson of Hillel, and was thoroughly schooled in the philosophy and theology of his grandfather's teaching. Gamaliel was a member of the Sanhedrin, the high council of Jews in Jerusalem, and served as president of the Sanhedrin during the reigns of the Roman emperors Tiberius, Caligula, and Claudius. Unlike other Jewish teachers, he had no antipathy toward Greek learning.

The learning of Gamaliel was so eminent and his influence so great that he is one of only seven Jewish scholars who have been honored by the title "Rabban." He was called the "Beauty of the Law." The Talmud even says that "since Rabban Gamaliel died, the glory of the Law has ceased."[15]

---

[15] Walter A. Elwell and Barry J. Beitzel, *Baker Encyclopedia of the Bible* (Grand Rapids, MI: Baker Book House, 1988), 838.

APPENDIX C Citizenship, the rights and privileges of

The International Standard Bible Encyclopedia, Revised

Citizenship [Gk. *politeía*] (Acts 22:28); AV FREEDOM. The "citizens of Shechem" in Jgs. 9 are citizens by virtue of their being landowners. The NT words come from Gk. *pólis*, "city," and indicate variously the inhabitants of a country (Lk. 15:15), the subjects of a feudal lord (19:14), legal rights of citizenship (Acts), and figuratively, "members of God's household" (Eph. 2:19). In He. 8:11 *polítēs* means "fellow-citizen" (AV, NEB; RSV "fellow"). A few MSS have *plēsíon*, "neighbor." In the Apocrypha cf. 2 Macc. 4:50; 5:6; 9:19.

Roman citizenship is of special interest to the Bible student because of the apostle Paul's relation to it. It was one of his qualifications as the apostle to the Gentiles. Luke shows him in Acts as a Roman citizen, who, though a Jew and a Christian, receives for the most part justice and courtesy from the Roman officials, and more than once successfully claims the privileges of his citizenship.

Paul himself declared that he was a citizen of Tarsus (Acts 21:39). He was not only born in that city but had a citizen's rights in it (*See* Paul the Apostle VII.A; Tarsus). But this citizenship in Tarsus did not of itself confer upon Paul the higher dignity of Roman citizenship. Had it done so, Claudius Lysias would not have ordered him to be scourged, as he did, after having learned that he was a citizen of Tarsus (Acts 21:39; cf. 22:25). So, over and above this Tarsian citizenship was the Roman one, which availed for him not in one city only, but throughout the Roman world, and secured for him everywhere certain great immunities and rights. Precisely what all of these were we are not certain; but we know that, by the Valerian and Porcian laws, exemption from shameful punishments, such as scourging with rods or whips, and especially crucifixion, was secured to every Roman citizen; also the right of appeal to the emperor, with certain limitations. This sanctity of person had become almost a part of their religion, so that any violation was esteemed a sacrilege. Cicero's oration against Verres indicates the almost fanatical extreme to which this feeling had been carried. Yet Paul was thrice beaten with rods, and five times received from the Jews forty lashes save one (2 Cor. 11:24f). Perhaps it was as at Philippi before he made known his citizenship (Acts

---

MSS manuscript(s)

16:22f), or the Jews had the right to whip those who came before their own tribunals. Roman citizenship included also the right of appeal to the emperor in all cases, after sentence had been passed, and no needless impediment must be interposed against a trial. Furthermore, the citizen had the right to be sent to Rome for trial before the emperor himself, when charged with capital offenses (Acts 16:37; 22:25–29; 25:11).

How then had Paul, a Jew, acquired this valued dignity? He himself tells us. In contrast to the *parvenu* citizenship of the chief captain, who seems to have thought that Paul also must have purchased it, though apparently too poor, Paul quietly says, "But I was born (a citizen)" (Acts 22:28). Thus either Paul's father or some other ancestor had acquired the right and had transmitted it to the son.

What more natural than that Paul should sometimes use this civic privilege to illustrate spiritual truths? He does so a number of times. Before the Sanhedrin he says, in the words of our English versions, "I have lived before God in all good conscience" (Acts 23:1). But this translation does not fully bring out the sense. Paul uses a noticeable word, *politeúōi*, "to live as a citizen." He adds, "to God" (*tṓ theṓ*). That is to say, he had lived conscientiously as God's citizen, as a member of God's commonwealth. The day before, by appealing to his Roman citizenship, he had saved himself from ignominious whipping, and now what more natural than that he should declare that he had been true to his citizenship in a higher state? What was this higher commonwealth in which he has enjoyed the rights and performed the duties of a citizen? What but the theocracy of his fathers, the ancient Church, of which the Sanhedrin was still the ostensible representative, but which was really continued in the kingdom of Christ without the national restrictions of the older one? Thus Paul does not mean to say simply, "I have lived conscientiously before God," but "I have lived as a citizen to God, of the body of which He is the immediate Sovereign." He had lived theocratically as a faithful member of the Jewish church, from which his enemies claimed he was an apostate. Thus Paul's conception was a kind of blending of two ideas or feelings, one of which came from the old theocracy, and the other from his Roman citizenship.

Later, writing from Rome itself to the Philippians, who were proud of their own citizenship as members of a *colonia*, a reproduction on a small scale of the parent commonwealth, where he had once successfully maintained his own Roman rights, Paul forcibly brings out the idea that Christians are citizens of a heavenly commonwealth, urging them to live worthy of such honor (Phil. 1:27, RV mg).

---

mg margin

A similar thought is brought out when he says, "But our commonwealth [*politeúma*] is in heaven" (Phil. 3:20; cf. NEB, "for we are citizens of heaven"). The state to which we belong is heaven. Though absent in body from the heavenly commonwealth, as was Paul from Rome when he asserted his rights, believers still enjoy its civic privileges and protections; sojourners upon earth, citizens of heaven. The OT conception, as in Isa. 60–62, would easily lend itself to this idea, which appears in He. 11:10, 16; 12:22–24; 13:14; Gal. 4:26, and possibly in Rev. 21.[16]

Baker Encyclopedia of the Bible

Citizenship.

In NT usage (1) designation of belonging to the city or city-state where one was born and reared, and (2) status of sharing in the privileges and responsibilities of the Roman empire. Thus the apostle Paul claimed to be a citizen of both Tarsus (Acts 21:39) and Rome (Acts 22:28).

The right of Roman citizenship most commonly was acquired by birth, as was true of Paul (Acts 22:28). The status of a child whose parents were married was determined by the status of the father at the time of conception. The status of a child born out of wedlock was determined by that of the mother at the child's birth. Slaves automatically became citizens when freed by their masters. Although known as "freedmen," they were often denied the rights of regular freeborn citizens. Greedy magistrates frequently sold the right of citizenship for a high price. The tribune Claudius Lysias received his citizenship in that manner (Acts 22:28). Citizen rights could also be granted by treaty or imperial declaration. Following the Social War (about 90–85 b.c.), citizenship was granted to all the inhabitants of Italy. Julius Caesar extended the right to colonies in Gaul (France) and provinces in Asia Minor. According to the census of the emperor Augustus (Lk 2:1), there were approximately 4,233,000 Roman citizens at the time of Christ's birth. By the time of Paul's ministry the number had reached 6,000,000.

Roman citizens were often required to give proof of their citizenship. That was usually accomplished by reference to the census archives, where the name of every citizen was recorded. In addition, freeborn citizens possessed a small wooden birth certificate containing information about their status at birth. Military documents and taxation tables also carried

---

[16] G. H. Trever, "Citizenship," ed. Geoffrey W. Bromiley, *The International Standard Bible Encyclopedia, Revised* (Wm. B. Eerdmans, 1979–1988), 704–705.

NT New Testament

the names of registered citizens. Further, every Roman citizen had three names, whereas noncitizens generally had only one.

The rights of Roman citizenship were extensive, including the right to vote; to hold office; to serve in the military; to purchase, possess, sell, and bequeath property; to enter into a legal contract; to have a fair trial; and to appeal to Caesar. Thus Paul, upon mention of his Roman citizenship, received an apology from magistrates at Philippi for having been imprisoned without a trial (Acts 16:39). He also avoided a scourging in Jerusalem (Acts 22:24–29) and was able to request a trial before Caesar (Acts 25:10–12; cf. 26:32).

Since the privileges and responsibilities of citizenship originated in Rome, that city came to be a symbol of power, success, and national purpose for people throughout the empire. In that light, Paul reminded the Christians at Philippi, a Roman colony, of their identity as citizens of heaven and their responsibility to live accordingly (Phil 3:20). Paul evidently wanted the Philippian Christians to recognize that their new relationship to God conveyed upon them certain rights and duties, as did their Roman citizenship.[17]

---

cf. compare

[17] Walter A. Elwell and Barry J. Beitzel, *Baker Encyclopedia of the Bible* (Grand Rapids, MI: Baker Book House, 1988), 468.

APPENDIX D Areopagus, A Unique Athenian Rock

The International Standard Bible Encyclopedia, Revised

Areopagus ar-ē-op'ə-gəs [GK. *Areios Pagos*] (Acts 17:19, 22); AV MARS' HILL (v 22); NEB "Court of Areopagus." A hill NW of the Acropolis in ATHENS.

There are two traditions as to how the hill got its name. According to one, it was named for Ares the god of War, who was put on trial there for the slaying of Halirrhotios the son of Poseidon; hence the AV designation in Acts 17:22 (Ares has been identified with the Roman god Mars). The other tradition understands the name Areopagus to mean the "hill of the Arai." The Arai ("curses"), more popularly known as the Furies, were goddesses whose task was avenging murder. If this tradition is true the name was very fitting, for the Areopagus was the place where cases of homicide were tried. Moreover, at the foot of this hill there is a cave wherein the shrine of these goddesses was located. The goddesses are also known by the names Semnai and Erinyes. Pausanias of Sparta tells of a tradition that the first trial on the Areopagus was that of Orestes, whom the goddesses cursed and pursued relentlessly for the murder of his own mother, Clytemnestra.

A staircase hewn out of the rock leads to the summit of this hill (which is about 370 ft [113 m] high), where traces of benches are visible forming three sides of a square, also cut out of the stone. At one time, two white stones were also there, upon which the defendant and his accuser stood. They were named "The Stone of Shamelessness" and "The Stone of Pride," respectively.

The name of the hill was given later to the council whose meetings were held upon it. The council of the Areopagus retained this name even when its meetings were transferred from the hill to the Royal Stoa, which should, perhaps, be identified with the stoa of Zeus Eleutheros in the agora. It is suggested that the council met at times on the Acropolis as well. The council of the Areopagus was similar to a council of elders, and was subject to the king of Athens. It was very influential in the formation of the aristocracy. Aristotle (*Pol.* viii.2) describes the scope of its power as including the appointment to all offices, the work of administration, and the right to punish all cases. Through the reforms of Solon (594 b.c.) the

---

ft foot, feet

authority of the Areopagus was greatly limited, though the council did maintain jurisdiction in cases of conspiracy against the state. During the time of Pericles its functions were mainly those of a criminal court. Further transfers of its functions to the Boule, the Ecclesia, and the Popular Court of Law detracted from the prestige of the court, though it retained jurisdiction in cases of homicide. Under Demosthenes it recaptured some of its power and was able to annul the election of certain officers. In times of Roman domination the council of the Areopagus concerned itself with cases of forgery, maintaining correct standards of measure, supervision of buildings, and matters of religion and education. The Areopagus was the court where Socrates met his accusers.

The apostle Paul was brought to the Areopagus by certain Epicureans and Stoics who wished to hear more of his teaching about Jesus and the Resurrection. Since the name Areopagus may be applied to the hill or to the council, there is an ambiguity which has given rise to debate as to whether Paul spoke publicly on the hill or was examined for his religious teaching before the council. Ramsay (SPT) rejected the view that they took Paul to the summit of the Areopagus in an effort to find a more suitable place for him to address the crowd. He considers that pride would have prevented the Athenians from asking Paul, a despised person, to address them in such an honored locality. Furthermore, he asserts that the language of the text will not allow it, for one cannot stand "in the midst of the hill." It is likely that Paul was examined by the council on account of the religious tenets he was proclaiming. The control the council exercised over public instruction is illustrated by Plutarch's statement with respect to Cratippus the peripatetic, that Cicero "got the court of Areopagus, by public decree, to request his stay at Athens, for the instruction of their youth, and the honor of their city" (Plutarch *Cicero* 24.5). Although it is recognized that the council met in various places, its common practice to convene on the hill from which it took its name makes plausible the position of Wright and certain others who consider that Paul stood before the council on the hill of the Areopagus.[18]

Bibliography.—SPT; WBA; F. F. Bruce, *Book of the Acts* (NIC, 1954); W. A. McDonald, BA, 4 (1941), 1–10; O. Broneer, BA, 21 (1958), 2–28.

SPT W. Ramsay, *St. Paul the Traveller and Roman Citizen* (1920)

[18] D. H. Madvig, "Areopagus," ed. Geoffrey W. Bromiley, *The International Standard Bible Encyclopedia, Revised* (Wm. B. Eerdmans, 1979–1988), 287–288.

SPT W. Ramsay, *St. Paul the Traveller and Roman Citizen* (1920)

WBA G. E. Wright, *Biblical Archaeology* (rev. ed. 1962)

BA *The Biblical Archaeologist*

Baker Encyclopedia of the Bible

Areopagus.

Hill northwest of the Acropolis in Athens overlooking the marketplace (Acts 17:19). "Areopagus" also refers to the Athenian council or court that met there. The irregular limestone outcropping was also known as Mars Hill, Mars being the Roman equivalent of the Greek god Ares. Paul was taken to the Areopagus after he had been reasoning with Jews and God-fearing Gentiles in the Athenian synagogue and marketplace (*agora*) for several days (Acts 17:16–21). Some Epicurean and Stoic philosophers involved in those discussions brought Paul before the council, but evidently not for an official arraignment. Trials were held at the Areopagus; there, some five centuries earlier, Socrates had faced those who accused him of deprecating the Greek gods. By Paul's day the council of the Areopagus was responsible for various political, educational, philosophical, and religious matters as well as for legal proceedings. The general tone of Paul's address does not suggest judicial proceedings. He spoke as an intelligent Christian believer who was able to meet the intellectual Athenians on their own ground (Acts 17:22–31). Some remained skeptical, but his address was convincing to a few who "joined him and believed" (Acts 17:32–34).[19]

BA *The Biblical Archaeologist*

[19] Walter A. Elwell and Barry J. Beitzel, *Baker Encyclopedia of the Bible* (Grand Rapids, MI: Baker Book House, 1988), 167–168.

APPENDIX E The Unknown God

The International Standard Bible Encyclopedia, Revised

Unknown God [Gk. *ágnōstos theós*] (Acts 17:23). In the opening sentences of his address on the Areopagus Paul referred to an altar inscribed "to an unknown god" that was among the many objects of worship of the Athenians. Paul identified this "unknown god" as the God he proclaimed (Acts 17:23).

The AV has translated the inscription with the definite article, "to the unknown god" (similarly Phillips). In Greek the article may be omitted with nouns designating persons (BDF § 254), but the neuter article and pronoun in 17:23b and the neuter to *theión* in v 29 favor the translation "to an unknown god" (as in ASV, RSV, NEB, JB, NIV).

The existence of altars to "unknown gods" (plural) in the early Christian centuries is attested. Pausanias (2nd cent a.d.) referred to those at Olympia and near Phalerum (v 14.8; i.l.4). Philostratus (3rd cent. a.d.) quoted Apollonius (late 1st cent. a.d.) as referring to such altars in Athens (*Life of Apollonius of Tyana* 4.3). In the ruins of the temple of Demeter at Pergamum (modern Bergama) in Asia Minor was found a partially broken inscription. The preserved portion of the first line, with a plausible restoration, reads *theois agnōstois*.

The absence of the singular "unknown god" in classical literature and inscriptions hardly justifies the suggestion that the NT author changed the plural to the singular (as E. Norden [*Agnostos Theos* (1913)] and others have suggested); the lack of evidence allows nothing more than an argument from silence. R. E. Wycherley (JTS, 19 [1968], 620f) made the novel suggestion that the square pillars—similar to the Herms—excavated in the Athenian agora may represent attempts to placate various unknown deities offended by the disturbance of Mycenaean burials in Athens.

The inclusive character of Greek religion makes such altars to unknown gods plausible (see the summary of evidence in E. des Places, Bibl, 40 [1959], 795–97). Paul capitalized on this feature and effectively

---

BDF F. Blass and A. Debrunner, *A Greek Grammar of the New Testament*, tr. and rev. R. W. Funk (1961)

JTS *Journal of Theological Studies*

Bibl *Biblica*

used such an altar as a point of contact and an occasion to proclaim the "knowable God" of his religion. The double meaning ("unknown" and "unknowable") of the verbal adjective *ágnōstos* may figure in the further development of Paul's speech (cf. vv 23–31). In any case, Paul made clear that God is "knowable" from His revelation in creation and providence (v 27) and hardly deserves the designation "unknown" or "unknowable."[20]

---

[20] B. Vanelderen, "Unknown God," ed. Geoffrey W. Bromiley, *The International Standard Bible Encyclopedia, Revised* (Wm. B. Eerdmans, 1979–1988), 947.

APPENDIX F Athens, the "City of Many Gods"

Baker Encyclopedia of the Bible

Athens.

Capital of modern Greece and for centuries chief city of the province of Attica. Athens' famous landmark is the Acropolis, a steep flat rock that rises about 200 feet above the plain around it and which still holds several masterpieces of architecture. Walls dating from 1100 B.C. indicate an advanced community by that time.

The Acropolis in Athens.

Athens began its rise to glory in the 6th century B.C., first under the leadership of Solon (d. 559 B.C.), who established democratic forms of government, and later under Pericles (d. 429 B.C.), when the magnificent buildings of the Acropolis took form. In this golden age, Athens became the center of philosophy, art, architecture, and drama.

By the time Paul brought the Christian message to Athens (Acts 17:15–34) the city had only a portion of its former glory and prestige. Roman emperors continued to extend patronage by providing for new buildings and the restoration of the Agora (marketplace). Athens continued to be the home of the most prominent university in the Greek world. Both Epicurean and Stoic philosophy had worthy representatives in the city.

The Christian message was first brought to Athens by the apostle Paul on his second missionary journey about a.d. 50. His only reference to Athens is in 1 Thessalonians 3:1, where he indicated that he and Timothy arrived in the city together, but that shortly thereafter he sent Timothy back to Thessalonica while he remained alone in Athens.

Luke has provided a more complete account of Paul's ministry there (Acts 17:16–34). His arrival in a city marked by many statues to the gods, which surpassed anything he had seen in other cities, provoked in him strong feelings against such rampant idolatry. Reared in the strict monotheism of Judaism, Paul apparently viewed Athens as the epitome of sin, and the cultural majesty of the city could not undo this impression.

As did almost all cities of that day, Athens had its community of Jews, and Paul began to speak, according to his custom, with his own kinsmen. Before long he was also in the marketplace, speaking about Jesus to anyone who would listen, including some of the philosophers, who spoke condescendingly of him as peddling "scrap-ideas." Paul's preaching of Jesus and the resurrection sounded as though he was proclaiming a new deity, which earned him a summons before the Areopagus, a civic body responsible for the religious and moral life of Athens. As such it had to approve any new deity. The name Areopagus came from a small hill just off the Acropolis where the body formerly sat for deliberations. By Paul's time its meetings were commonly held in a portico at one end of the marketplace.

Most of Luke's account consists of Paul's message to the Areopagus, in which he referred to the many gods, even to an "unknown god." Paul declared that he was making known to them the God who was not known. He closed his address with a call to repentance and judgment. His reference to the resurrection brought division, but some individuals wanted to hear more.

Luke says only that a few followed Paul, including Dionysius, a member of the Areopagite council, and a woman named Damaris. Athens seems to be one of the few places where Paul did not succeed in establishing a church, and thus it did not figure prominently in early Christian history.

Today Athens is one of the cities that best illuminates the setting of apostolic ministry. Many of the monuments surviving today were seen by Paul. Acts 17:23 implies that he examined thoroughly the sculpture and architecture of the city.

The Acropolis was the site of palaces of the Mycenaean kings of Athens. The city was sacred to the goddess Athena, and several temples were built in her honor, including the Erechtheum (with its porch of maidens), the small temple of Athena Nike (Victory), and the temple of Athena Parthenos (the Virgin), known as the Parthenon. A huge statue of Athena Promachos stood beside the temple, and sunlight flashing on the statue's spear was said by Pausanias to be visible to ships off Cape Sounion.

Excavations by the American School of Classical Studies since 1931 in the Athenian Agora have illuminated the city's life and its architectural pre- and early Christian history. Pottery fragments scratched with the names of political leaders were found in a ballot jar where they had been cast.

Important buildings in the Agora are the Temple of Hephaestus, the Stoa (portico) of Attalus, and the Odeum (small theater) of Agrippa. The Panathenaic Way, which led through the Agora and up to the Acropolis, was used for festival processions and ceremonial occasions. The Horologion (Tower of the Winds) in the Agora still stands. It contained sundials and a water clock.

Excavations at the Ceramicus near the Agora yielded fine grave stelae and artifacts, some of which are now at the National Archaeological Museum in Athens. At the foot of the Acropolis stands the Odeum of Herod Atticus, built in the 2nd century A.D. A 535-foot stoa nearby was presented to Athens by King Eumenes II of Pergamum (197–159 b.c.). The theater of Dionysus, dating from the 5th century B.C. and later replaced in stone by Lycurgus, held more than 15,000 spectators. Add to these splendid monuments the remains of the once-massive temple of Olympian Zeus, 104 columns over 90 feet high, and it is possible to imagine what a glorious city Athens was in her prime. The temple to Zeus, begun by Pesistratus, was roofless in the time of Paul and was not completed until the reign of the emperor Hadrian, lavish benefactor of the city.

Though smaller and less influential than its rivals Corinth and Ephesus, Athens was honored as a cultural and religious center until the time of Julian the Apostate (A.D. 361–63), who studied philosophy there. He tried unsuccessfully to revive the city's pagan spirit.[21]

---

[21] Walter A. Elwell and Barry J. Beitzel, *Baker Encyclopedia of the Bible* (Grand Rapids, MI: Baker Book House, 1988), 230-231.

APPENDIX G Gallio, the Proconsul of Achaia

Baker Encyclopedia of the Bible

Gallio.

M. Annaeus Seneca's son, and brother of the philosopher Seneca, who lived from 3 B.C.–A.D. 65. Born in Cordoba, Spain, Gallio came to Rome during Tiberius' reign. His given name was Marcus Annaeus Novatus, but he assumed the name Gallio after his adoption by the rhetorician Lucius Junius Gallio. The wealthy Lucius trained him for his career in administration and government.

Gallio served as Roman proconsul of Achaia sometime between A.D. 51 and 53. During the apostle Paul's first visit to Corinth the Jews brought the apostle before the proconsul, accusing him of having persuaded people to practice religion in an unlawful manner (Acts 18:12–17). Gallio abruptly dismissed the charge since it dealt with Jewish and not Roman law. His action reflected the characteristic behavior of Roman governors toward religious disputes.

Forced to leave Achaia because of illness, Gallio returned to Rome as consul suffectus under Nero. His involvement in a conspiracy against Nero resulted in temporary pardon but eventual obligatory suicide.

Gallio Inscription.

Dated Greek inscription found in Delphi, Greece mentioning Gallio as proconsul, and establishing the time of Paul's initial visit to Corinth (cf. Acts 18:12–17).[22]

---

cf. compare

[22] Walter A. Elwell and Barry J. Beitzel, *Baker Encyclopedia of the Bible* (Grand Rapids, MI: Baker Book House, 1988), 838.

APPENDIX H Vow, Paul's Observance of Law as to Vows

Baker Encyclopedia of the Bible

Vow.

Serious promise or pledge. The making of vows to God is a religious practice which is frequently mentioned in Scripture. Most references to vows are found in the OT, especially in the psalms, but there are a few in the NT as well.

Unlike tithing, sacrifices and offerings, Sabbath-keeping, and circumcision, vow making was not something commanded by the Mosaic law. There are rules regulating the carrying out of vows which have been taken (even to the possible cancellation of a woman's careless vow by a discerning father or husband—Nm 30:5, 8), but the making of them seems to be more a traditional and personal matter.

For example, Psalm 50:14 says, "Offer to God a sacrifice of thanksgiving; and pay your vows to the Most High." The command is to "pay," that is, to keep or fulfill a pledge that has already been made. No order is given to make such promises in the first place. The practice is accepted and regulated, but not demanded.

The purpose of a vow is either to win a desired favor from the Lord, to express gratitude to him for some deliverance or benefit, or else simply to prove absolute devotion to him by way of certain abstinences and non-conformities.

The NT information about vows sets the stage for reviewing the background information concerning what was by then a long-established custom. The term "vow" occurs just twice in the NT, both times in association with the apostle Paul (Acts 18:18; 21:23, 24). But the same principle is involved in the case of the word "Corban" (Mk 7:11–13; cf. Mt 15:5, 6). The Lord in these two passages severely rebukes those who have made a vow that served as a clever escape from meeting obligations to care for aged parents. A monetary figure was involved in such a "gift" or "offering." But Jesus declares that God does not want a gift which is designed to deprive someone.

In the case of Paul, he may have entered into his vows for the very purpose of forestalling objections which either antagonistic Jews or Jewish

---

cf. compare

Christian believers had to his removing the yoke of Mosaic regulations from the shoulders of Gentile believers. At least he did not despise this practice of OT piety. This is especially true of the second of the two passages cited above. Paul was in Jerusalem under the keen surveillance of Jewish authorities. He made it a point to join with four other Jewish believers in the payment of vows in the temple. This action, however, was misconstrued by his enemies, who charged that he was bringing Gentiles into the holy temple.

Although vows seemed to be an important expression of spiritual commitment in OT times, there is little information and no real stress on vows in the NT. Spirituality is elevated to a higher plane for the Spirit-filled NT believer. Demonstration of devotion to the Lord is not an occasional thing. The all-pervasive reason for and measure of dedication to God in Christ is well summed up in 1 Corinthians 6:20: "You were bought with a price. So glorify God in your body."

The opening verses of Psalm 132 afford an excellent example of the expression of unselfish devotion on the part of David. He calls upon God to remember his strong determination to build a permanent home for the ark of the covenant, his determination to do something that expresses love for his great Redeemer. David exclaims, "I will not enter my house or get into my bed; I will not give sleep to my eyes or slumber to my eyelids, until I find a place for the Lord, a dwelling place for the Mighty One of Jacob" (Ps 132:3-5).

Dedication of self and separation to the Lord is the primary feature of the Nazirite vow. Samson, Samuel, and John the Baptist are the most familiar examples of this type of vow. Numbers 6:1-8 prescribes the conditions of this commitment, and verses 13-21 tell how release may be obtained by fulfillment and certain sacrifices. Women as well as men might take this vow of separation which could be of limited duration. The Rechabite clan pledged themselves to an ascetic and nomadic life. They constitute a compelling illustration of loyalty to the God of Israel (Jer 35).

Frequently, however, vows were taken as a type of bargain with God. At Bethel Jacob promised God worship and the tithe if he would protect him and supply his needs. Jephthah vowed to sacrifice whatever first met him on his return home victorious over the Ammonites (Jgs 11:30, 31). Hannah offered to return her son to God (1 Sm 1:11, 27, 28). In the psalms, payment of vows is often associated with thanksgiving for deliverance from danger or affliction (e.g., 22:24, 25; 56:12, 13).

---

e.g. for example

Most important is that once a vow is made, the obligation is serious. To refrain from making any vow is no sin (Dt 23:22), but once declared, the vow must be kept (Dt 23:21-23; see also Nm 30:2; Eccl 5:4-6).[23]

Paul's Observance of Law as to Vows. The apostle Paul made a vow, whether a Nazirite vow or not is uncertain; also, whether he had made the vow before becoming a Christian is not stated. He may have concluded the period of his vow at Cenchreae, near Corinth, when he had his hair clipped (Ac 18:18) or, as some believe, when he went to the temple in Jerusalem with four other men who were completing their vows. However, this latter action was taken by Paul on the advice of the Christian governing body to demonstrate that Paul was walking orderly and not teaching disobedience to the Law, as rumored in the ears of some of the Jewish Christians. It was common practice for a person to pay for others the expenses involved in the ceremonial cleansing at the expiration of the period of a vow, as Paul here did.—Ac 21:20-24.

As to why the apostle Paul and his associates in the Christian governing body approved the carrying out of certain features of the Law, even though the Law had been moved out of the way by the sacrifice of Jesus Christ, the following things may be considered: The Law was given by Jehovah God to his people Israel. Accordingly, the apostle Paul said, "The Law is spiritual," and of its regulations he said, "The Law is holy, and the commandment is holy and righteous and good." (Ro 7:12, 14) Consequently, the temple and the services carried on there were not despised by Christians, or looked down upon as wrong. They were not idolatrous. Furthermore, many of the practices had become ingrained as custom among those who were Jews. Moreover, since the Law was not merely religious but was also the law of the land, some things, such as the restrictions on work on the Sabbaths, had to be followed by all those living in the land.

However, in considering this matter, the main point is that the *Christians did not look to these things for salvation.* The apostle explained that certain things, such as the eating of meat or vegetables, the observing of certain days as above others, even the eating of meat that had been offered to idols before being put up for regular sale in the marketplaces, were matters of conscience. He wrote: "One man judges one day as above another; another man judges one day as all others; let each man be fully convinced in his own mind. He who observes the day observes it to Jehovah. Also, he who eats, eats to Jehovah, for he gives thanks to God; and he who does not eat does not eat to Jehovah, and yet gives thanks to

---

[23] Walter A. Elwell and Barry J. Beitzel, *Baker Encyclopedia of the Bible* (Grand Rapids, MI: Baker Book House, 1988), 2127-2128.

God." Then he summed up his argument by stating the principle: "For the kingdom of God does not mean eating and drinking, but means righteousness and peace and joy with holy spirit," and he concluded: "Happy is the man that does not put himself on judgment by what he approves. But if he has doubts, he is already condemned if he eats, because he does not eat out of faith. Indeed, everything that is not out of faith is sin."—Ro 14:5, 6, 17, 22, 23; 1Co 10:25-30.

An enlightening comment is made on this point by Bible scholar Albert Barnes, in his *Notes, Explanatory and Practical, on the Acts of the Apostles* (1858). Making reference to Acts 21:20—which reads: "After hearing this [an account of God's blessing on Paul's ministry to the nations] they began to glorify God, and they said to him: 'You behold, brother, how many thousands of believers there are among the Jews; and they are all zealous for the Law'"—Barnes remarks: "The reference here is, to the law respecting circumcision, sacrifices, distinctions of meats and days, festivals, &c. It may seem remarkable that they should still continue to observe those rites, since it was the manifest design of Christianity to abolish them. But we are to remember, (1.) That those rites had been appointed by God, and that they were trained to their observance. (2.) That the apostles conformed to them while they remained in Jerusalem, and did not deem it best to set themselves violently against them. [Ac 3:1; Lu 24:53] (3.) That the question about their observance had never been agitated at Jerusalem. It was only among the Gentile converts that the question had risen, and there it *must* arise, for if they were to be observed, they must have been *imposed* upon them by authority. (4.) The decision of the council (ch. xv.) related only to the *Gentile* converts. [Ac 15:23] ... (5.) It was to be presumed, that as the Christian religion became better understood—that as its large, free, and [universal] nature became more and more developed, the peculiar institutions of Moses would be laid aside of course, without agitation, and without tumult. Had the question been agitated [publicly] at Jerusalem, it would have excited tenfold opposition to Christianity, and would have rent the Christian church into factions, and greatly retarded the advance of the Christian doctrine. We are to remember also, (6.) That, in the arrangement of Divine Providence, the time was drawing near which was to destroy the temple, the city, and the nation; which was to put an end to sacrifices, and *effectually* to close for ever the observance of the Mosaic rites. As this destruction was so near, and as it would be so effectual an *argument* against the observance of the Mosaic rites, the Great Head of the church did not suffer the question of their obligation to be needlessly agitated among the disciples at Jerusalem."[24]

---

[24] it-2 pp. 1163-1164 Vow

APPENDIX I Thorn In the Flesh

The International Standard Bible Encyclopedia, Revised

Thorn in the Flesh [Gk. *skólops tḗ sarkí*] (2 Cor. 12:7); NEB "sharp physical pain." Paul's vague reference to a thorn in his flesh has stirred an enormous amount of discussion. The actual term "thorn" (*skólops*) means "splinter," "thorn," "sharpened stake," or even "cross." It can indicate something tiny or huge, physical or mental; the context does not identify exactly what it is. God permitted Satan to afflict Paul as he did Job (Job 2:6). Paul understood the reason for his suffering to lie in the visions and revelations that he had received (v 7): these had the potential of making him drunk with elation and therefore proud and boastful. The Lord used Satan's affliction to discipline Paul (cf. He. 12:10) and to demonstrate cogently that His power did not require human effort to be effective (v 9). The affliction seemed to hamper Paul's work, and he prayed for its removal three times (v 8). But it was to be permanent, as Paul soon learned, and productive of many blessings (vv 9f, 12; 13:3).

The thorn, called "a messenger of Satan," could possibly refer to Paul's opponents, who are mentioned so frequently in the context (e.g., 2 Cor. 11:13). But the phrase itself does not require a personal reference: the thorn may equally well be a mental or physical liability. Exactly the same figure of speech occurs in Nu. 33:55; here the reference of the thorns is explicit—the inhabitants of Canaan as potential enemies of Israel. Possibly 2 Corinthians itself offers a clue in its references to Paul's great sufferings in Asia (1:8f) or even his afflictions in Macedonia (7:5). Nevertheless, the allusion is stubbornly vague.

There has, however, been no dearth of efforts to pinpoint it. Tertullian thought that the "thorn" was an earache or headache (*On Modesty* 13). Chrysostom was sure that it referred to Paul's enemies (*Hom 26 in 1 Cor.*). Augustine saw in it a general description of Paul's physical sufferings. Influenced by a bad translation in the Vulgate (*stimulus carnis*), many Catholic interpreters detected an allusion to sexual lusts. Among the solutions proposed by modern scholars are an eye affliction (cf. Gal. 6:11), epilepsy (cf. Acts 22:17), hysteria, malaria, and speech impediment. P. H. Menoud believed that Paul referred to the continual anguish caused by Israel's unbelief.

Hom Homily

This remarkable confusion has resulted from attempts to supply information that Paul did not provide. Possibly Paul's readers knew his reference. Some interpreters (e.g., Hughes) have refused to guess, and so should we all. The word "thorn" is a general term in Scripture for sorrow and suffering, and nothing in it can indicate whether the suffering was physical or spiritual. Many of the suggested interpretations are clearly possible, but none can be proved or disproved.[25]

---

[25] C. H. Pinnock, "Thorn in the Flesh," ed. Geoffrey W. Bromiley, *The International Standard Bible Encyclopedia, Revised* (Wm. B. Eerdmans, 1979–1988), 843.

APPENDIX J Governor Felix Fails to Pass Judgment

Baker Encyclopedia of the Bible

Felix, Antonius.

Roman procurator (governor) of Judea (A.D. 52–60) succeeding Cumanus, appointed by Claudius and succeeded by Festus Porcius. Felix's brother, Pallas, a prominent, more influential Roman, interceded on his behalf after he was recalled from his procuratorship by Nero. During his oppressive rule, Felix utilized the aid of robbers to have Jonathan, the high priest, murdered. His tyranny has been cited as the cause for the Jewish War that broke out 6 years after he was recalled. Felix had 3 wives: one unknown, another the granddaughter of Mark Antony and Cleopatra, and another the Jewess sister of Agrippa II, whose name was Drusilla. At the age of 16, Drusilla left her husband, King Azizus of Emesa, to marry Felix. She later bore him a son, Agrippa.

Felix was serving as governor when the apostle Paul was brought before him in Caesarea to answer charges against him after the riot in Jerusalem (Acts 23:24–24:27). After a 5-day delay, Tertullus, spokesman for the Jews, and others arrived to state their charges. Felix put off a decision until he could hear from Lysias, the tribune. In the meantime, Paul was placed in limited custody. Felix hoped to obtain bribe money for his release. As a result, Paul was detained for 2 years, during which time he and Felix often conversed. The apostle's message of "justice, self-control, and future judgment" alarmed Felix greatly (24:25). Record of his life after being recalled by Nero is not available.[26]

---

[26] Walter A. Elwell and Barry J. Beitzel, *Baker Encyclopedia of the Bible* (Grand Rapids, MI: Baker Book House, 1988), 788–789.

APPENDIX K Shipwreck, Paul and His Traveling Companions

McClintock and Strong Biblical Cyclopedia

Shipwreck, a term that occurs but twice in the New Test. in the verbal form ναυαγέω, once literally (2Co 11:25) and once metaphorically (1Ti 1:19). We learn from the former of these passages that Paul had already three times experienced this mishap prior to his more notable instance on the way to Rome. The interest that centers around this latter event, and the light it sheds upon many points of Biblical history, geography, and archaeology, are so great as to justify a special treatment of the topic in addition to the remarks given under previous heads. It is a singular coincidence that another Jew, a contemporary of Paul, should have suffered a similar mishap on the same route, viz. Josephus (*Life*, § 3); but the account left is so brief as to afford but little illustration: of the case. Luke's narratives of the shipwreck of the apostle, on the contrary, is so full and graphic that we are enabled to trace the causes, progress, and culmination of the catastrophe in great detail; and his nice but artless discriminations show not only his truthfulness, but his careful habits of observation. His language, although of course not professional, is yet highly appreciative of the technical particulars to which he was an eye witness. We here present a brief outline of the results of the accurate and most interesting investigations of. Mr. Smith, of Jordanhill, in his work — *On the Voyage and Shipwreck of. St. Paul* (3d ed. Lond. 1866). A winter's residence in Malta afforded this learned writer ample opportunities for personal examination of the localities of the shipwreck. Having been a yacht sailor of more than thirty years' standing, and with much practical experience in planning, building, and altering vessels, he was able to bring a kind of knowledge to the interpretation of the passage which no commentator had possessed.

Paul's company embarked in a ship of Adramyttium, a seaport of Mysia on the eastern shore of the Aegean, opposite Lesbos. On the second day they touched at Sidon, sixty-seven geographical miles from Caesarea. Loosing from thence, they were forced, by contrary winds, to run under the lee of Cyprus. A ship's course from Sidon to Myra is W.N.W., leaving Cyprus on the right. The contrary wind must have been from the west, which prevails in this part of the Mediterranean in the summer. Under these circumstances, they left Cyprus on the left hand, doing as the most accomplished seamen of the present day would do under similar circumstances. Favored, as they probably were, by, the land breeze and currents, they arrived, without any unusual incident, at Myra in Lycia, then a flourishing city, now a desolate waste and about three miles from the sea. The company were there transferred to a corn ship from Alexandria bound for Italy. From the dimensions of one of these ships given by Lucian, they appear to have been quite as large as the largest class of merchant ships of modern times. Myra lies due north from Alexandria, and its bay is well fitted to shelter a wind bound ship. Their progress after leaving Myra was extremely slow, for it was many days before they came over against Cnidus, at the entrance to the Aegean Sea. As the distance between Myra and Cnidus is not more than 130 geographical miles, the delay was probably caused by unfavorable winds, which may be inferred from the words "with difficulty." The course of a ship on her voyage from Cnidus to Italy is by the north side of Crete, through the archipelago, W. by S. But this would be impossible with a northwest wind. With that wind the ship would work up to Cnidus, because she had the advantage of a weather shore and a westerly current; but there the advantage would cease. The only alternative would be to wait at Cnidaus for a fair wind, or else to run- under the lee of Crete in the direction. of Salmonie, which is the eastern end of Crete. As the south side of this island is a weather shore, they would be able, with northwest winds, to work up as far as Cape Matala. Here, however, the land bends suddenly to the north, and their only resource would be to make for a harbor. Fair Havens is the harbor nearest to Cape Matala. This was probably no more than an open roadstead, or, rather, two roadsteads contiguous to each other. The site of the city Lasaea is but recently known. It was now after the autumnal equinox, and sailing was dangerous. It was a question whether they should winter here or sail to port Phoenice, on the same side of Crete, about forty miles west. Paul strongly urged the officers to remain, but his advice was overruled. Pheenice, the harbor which they expected to reach, looks; (Luke says) "towards the southwest and northwest," or, as Mr. Smith translates the preposition, *in the same direction as*, i.e. the point *towards* which, the wind Libs blows; so that the harbor would open, not to the southwest, but to the north east. It seems to have been the one now called Lutro, which looks towards the east. The. south wind, which now blew, is a fair wind for a ship going from Fair Havens to Lutro. The island of Clauda is exactly opposite to Lutro, the Claudos of Ptolemy, and the Gozzo of the modern charts.

Sailing from Fair Havens close the land, they might hope, with a south wind, to reach Phoenice, in a few hours. But soon the weather changed; the ship, was caught in a typhoon which blew with such violence that they could not face it, but were forced, in the first instance, to scud before it. It follows from this that the wind must have blown off the land, else they would have been stranded on the Cretan coast. This sudden change from a south wind to a violent northerly wind is a common occurrence in these seas. The Greek term *typhonic* means that the wind was accompanied by the agitation and whirling motion of the clouds caused by the meeting of the opposite currents of air. By this single word are expressed the violence and direction of the gale. The wind Euroclydon (according to the most ancient versions, Euroaquilo= east northeast) forced them to run under the lee of Clauda. Here they availed themselves of the smooth water to prepare the ship to resist the fury of the storm. Their first care was to secure the boat by hoisting it on board. Luke tells us that they had much difficulty in doing this, probably because it was filled with water. The next care was to undergird the ship. Only one naval officer with whom Mr. Smith had met had ever seen it put in practice. Mr. Henry Hartley, who piloted the Russian fleet in 1815 from England to the Baltic, mentions that one of the ships, the "Jupiter," was wrapped round the middle by three or four turns of a stream cable. Sir George Back, on his return from his perilous arctic voyage in 1837, was forced, on account of the shattered condition of his ship, to undergird her.

We are next told that, fearing they should be driven towards the Syrtis, they lowered the gear (not "strake sail," which would be equivalent to saying that, being apprehensive of a certain danger, they deprived themselves of the only possible means of avoiding it). A ship preparing for a storm sends down upon deck the "top hamper," or gear connected with the fair weather sails, such as the *suppara*, or topsails. When the ship was thus borne along, she was not only undergirded and made snug, but had storm sails set and was on the starboard tack, i.e. with her right side to the wind, which was the only course by which she could avoid falling into the Syrtis (q.v.). On the next day, they threw overboard the ship's tackling. From the expression "with our own hands," Mr. Smith supposes the main yard is meant, an immense spar, probably as long as the ship, and which might require, the united efforts of passengers and men. The storm continued with unabated fury for eleven days more. "All hope was taken away, probably not so much from the fury of the gale as from the state of the ship, their exertions to keep her from foundering being unavailing. At length, on the fourteenth night, the seamen suspected (to use the graphic sea phrase of Luke) "the land was nearing them," probably from the noise of the breakers. No ship can enter St. Paul's Bay in Malta from the east without passing within a quarter of a mile of the point of Koura; but before reaching it the land is too low and too far from the track of a ship driven from the eastward to be seen on a dark night. When she does come within this distance, it is impossible to avoid observing the breakers, which are so violent as to form its distinctive character. On Aug. 10, 1810, the British frigate "Lively" went to pieces on these very breakers at the point of. Koura. Mr. Smith here goes into calculations in order to show that a ship starting late, in the evening from Clauda would, by midnight, on the 14th, be less than three miles from the entrance of St. Paul's Bay. A coincidence so close as this is, to a certain extent, accidental; but it is an accident: which could not have happened had there been any inaccuracy on the part of the author of the narrative with, regard to the. numerous incidents upon which the calculations are founded. or had, the ship been wrecked anywhere but at Malta. The number of conditions required in order to make any locality agree with the narrative are so numerous as to render it impossible to suppose that the agreement in the present case can be the effect of chance. The first circumstance is that the shipmen suspected the approach of land evidently without, seeing it. The quartermaster of the "Lively" states, in his evidence at the court martial, that at the distance of a quarter of a mile the land could not be seen, but that he saw the surf on the shore. Another point is, this: the shipmen when they sounded found twenty fathoms, and then fifteen fathoms. Every ship, indeed, in approaching the land must, pass over twenty fathoms and fifteen fathoms; but here must not only the twenty fathom depth be close to the spot where they had the indications of land, but it must bear east by south from the fifteen-fathom depth, and at such a distance as would allow of preparation for anchoring with four anchors from the stern, which must have required some time. Now, about half an hour farther the depth was fifteen fathoms. Fearing lest they should fall upon rocks, they cast four anchors out of the stern. This implies that there were rocks to leeward on which they were in danger of falling; but the fifteen-fathom depth is, as nearly as possible, a quarter of a mile from the shore; which is here girt with mural precipices, and on which the sea must have been breaking violently. Their only chance of safety was to anchor; but to do this in a gale on a lee shore not only requires time, but very tenacious holding ground. Is there such ground here? In the *English*

Sailing Directions it is said (to repeat an important fact given under a previous article), "The harbor of St. Paul is open to easterly and northeast winds. It is, notwithstanding, safe for small ships, the ground generally being very good; and while the cables hold there is no danger, *as the anchors will never start.*" But why anchor from the stern? "The anchor is cast from the prow," it being much easier to arrest a ship's way by the bow than the stern. Ships constructed like, those of the ancients, were, of necessity, amply provided with anchors and cables, It seems, too, from the figure of the ship in the picture of Theseus, deserting Ariadne, that they could anchor by the stern, as they had hawse holes aft, (a hawser is seen towing astern, it passes through the rudder port, and within board it is seen coiled round an upright beam or capstan in front of the break of the poop deck). The advantages, of being anchored in, this manner are that by cutting away the anchors, loosing the bands of the rudders, and hoisting the artemon (the foresail, not the mainsail), all of which could be done simultaneously, the ship was immediately under command, and could be directed with precision to any part of the shore which offered a prospect of safety. But if anchored in the usual mode, she might have taken "the wrong cast" or drifted on the rocks. The number of anchors let go show that nothing was neglected. The shipmen, after taking a meal, lightened the ship, not only by pumping, but by throwing the wheat into the sea. When day broke, they knew not the land, but it had certain peculiarities: the shore was rocky, it being, in fact, skirted with precipices. They then discovered a creek with a *sandy beach* (the Greek word, in a restricted sense, means this, in contradistinction to a rocky coast). Into this creek they were minded to thrust the ship. They now cut their cables and left the anchors in the sea; and, loosing the lashings of the rudder and hoisting the foresail, they made for the creek. On the west side of the bay there are two creeks. One of them, Mestara Valley, has a shore. The other, though its sandy beach has been worn away by the action of the sea, was probably the scene: of the wreck. for here "two seas meet." At the entrance of the bay, where the ship anchored, it could not have been suspected that at the bottom of it there was a communication with the sea outside. But such is the case. Salmone island, which separates the bay from the sea outside, is formed by a long, rocky ridge separated from the mainland by a channel of not more than a hundred yards in breadth. Near this channel they ran the ship ashore; the fore part stuck fast, but the stern was dashed in pieces. A ship impelled by a gale into a creek such as that in St. Paul's Bay would strike a bottom of mud graduating into a tenacious clay, into which the fore part would fix itself and be held fast, while the stern would be exposed to the force of the waves.

The correspondence in the direction and distance is no less striking. A modern merchant ship can sail within six points. Taking the mean between these, we cannot be so much as a point wrong if we assume that an ancient ship would, under favorable circumstances, make good her course about seven points from the wind. But there is another element which must be taken into account when we calculate the course of a ship in a storm — it is the lee way, which in a modern ship, in a gale such as described in Acts 27, is about six points. Now, if we apply these elements to Luke's account of Paul's voyage, the result will be found to be very striking. The facts mentioned in the narrative are

(1.) The point of departure — Clauda.

(2.) The direction of the wind in the received text, Euroclydon, but since the discovery of the Codex Sinaiticus the reading of the Vulg.,

Euroaquilo, east northeast (that is, a wind between *eurrus*, east, and *aquilo*), must be considered established.

(3.) The ship's course seven points from the wind, which, with six points of leeway added, must have been thirteen points to the west of east northeast, or west by north, which is as nearly as possible the bearing of Malta.

(4.) Distance; this is inferred from the ship's rate of sailing and the time consumed.

In the voyage in question we know within very narrow limits the time consumed: it was "about midnight on the fourteenth night" (Ac 27:27), and therefore thirteen days complete and a fraction. With regard to the rate at which a ship would drive under the circumstances described by Luke, Mr. Smith, in the work already alluded to, taking the mean from the determinations of skilful and scientific seamen, assumed that it would be about thirty-six and one twelfth miles in the twenty-four hours, and the distance ascertained from the nautical observations of admiral Smyth' is four hundred and seventy-seven miles to the nearness of a mile. Now a ship laid to, in a gale from east northeast, according to these calculations, founded on the incidental notices of the narrative, would — about midnight, "when the fourteenth night was come" of their being driven *through*(διαφερομένων), not up and down, Adria — have been exactly at Malta, and within two or three miles of St. Paul's Bay. Such were the results arrived at by Mr. Smith, and given in the first edition of his treatise on the *Voyage and Shipwreck of St. Paul.* Since then Dr. Howson in his researches discovered that admiral sir Charles Penrose had made a similar calculation, agreeing with the above to about four hours in time and six miles in distance but, as such results can only be approximations, a nearer agreement could not have been anticipated from the most accurately kept dead reckoning.

We here note an incidental fact with regard to Salmone, the east point of the island of Crete. In the account of Paul's voyage to Rome this promontory is mentioned in such a way (Ac 27:7) as to afford a curious illustration both of the navigation of the ancients and of the minute accuracy of Luke's narrative. We gather from other circumstances of the voyage that the wind was blowing from the northwest (ἐναντίους, ver. 4; βραδυπλοοῦντες, ver. 7). We are then told that the ship, on making Cnidus, could not, by reason of the wind, hold on her course, which was past the south point of Greece, west by south. She did, however, just fetch Cape Salmone, which bears southwest by south from Cnidus. Now we may take it for granted that she could have made good a course of less than seven points from the wind; and, starting from this assumption, ye are at once brought to the conclusion that the wind must have been between north northwest and west northwest. Thus what Paley would have called an "undesigned coincidence" is elicited by a cross examination of the narrative. This ingenious argument is due to Mr. Smith, of Jordainhmil.(*Voyage and Shipwreck of St. Paul*, p. 73, 74, 2d ed.), and from him was quoted by Conybeare and Howson (*Life and Epistles St. Paul* 393, 2d d.). To these books we must refer for filler details. We may just add that the ship had had the advantages of a weather shore, smooth water, a favoring current, before, reaching Cnidus, a that by running down to Cape Salmone the sailors obtained similar advantages under the lee of Crete, as far as Fair Havens, near Lasaea.

APPENDIX L Timothy, A Genuine Child in the Faith

Baker Encyclopedia of the Bible

Timothy, Timotheus (Person).

Paul's convert and companion, whose name means "one who honors God." His name is often spelled Timotheus in the KJV.

Timothy first appears in Acts 16:1–3 as Paul's disciple whose mother "was a believer; but his father was a Greek" (v 1). He was a third-generation Christian after his mother Eunice and grandmother Lois (2 Tm 1:5). The apostle Paul, undoubtedly Timothy's spiritual father, refers to him as "my true child in the faith" (1 Tm 1:2); he perhaps converted Timothy on his first or second missionary journey. The son of a Greek (or gentile) father, Timothy was yet uncircumcised; however, when Paul decided to take Timothy with him on the second journey, he had him circumcised, so as not to hinder their missionary endeavors among the Jews.

Timothy, who was "well spoken of by the brethren at Lystra and Iconium" (Acts 16:2), became Paul's companion and assistant on his second missionary journey at Lystra.

He traveled with Paul into Europe following the Macedonian vision. When Paul decided to go to Athens, he left Silas and Timothy at Beroea to better establish the church there (Acts 17:14). Timothy and Silas eventually joined Paul in Corinth (18:5). He next appears with Paul in Ephesus on his third journey (19:22), from where Paul sends Erastus and him into Macedonia ahead of himself. In the last mention of Timothy in Acts 20:4, he was included in the list of goodwill ambassadors who were to accompany Paul to Jerusalem with the offering for the Christian Jews.

Timothy is often mentioned in the Pauline letters. His name is included in the introductory salutations of 2 Corinthians, Philippians, Colossians, 1 and 2 Thessalonians, and Philemon. Timothy's presence with Paul when he wrote these letters confirms the accuracy of the references to him in Acts. He was in Corinth on the second journey when Paul wrote 1 and 2 Thessalonians, at Ephesus on the third journey when Paul wrote 2 Corinthians, and in Rome during Paul's first Roman imprisonment, when he wrote Philippians, Colossians, and Philemon. He is mentioned in the

---

v verse (*pl.* vv)

introductions of 1 and 2 Timothy as the recipient of those two pastoral letters.

In the closing salutations of Romans 16:21, Timothy is listed along with others who send their good wishes to the believers in Rome. In 1 Corinthians 4:17 and 16:10, Paul speaks words of praise for Timothy as he sends him with a message to Corinth (see also Phil 2:19–23; 1 Thes 3:2–6). In 2 Corinthians 1:19 Timothy is named along with Paul and Silas as men who were telling about Jesus Christ.

In Hebrews 13:23 the author (Pauline authorship uncertain) tells his readers that Timothy has been released from prison, and hopes to come with Timothy to visit the readers of that letter.

Paul put Timothy in charge of the church at Ephesus and wrote him two pastoral letters addressed with his name to help him perform that responsible task.[27]

---

[27] Walter A. Elwell and Barry J. Beitzel, *Baker Encyclopedia of the Bible* (Grand Rapids, MI: Baker Book House, 1988), 2069–2070.

APPENDIX M Titus, A Fellow Worker

Baker Encyclopedia of the Bible

Titus (Person).

One of Paul's converts—"my true child in a common faith" (Ti 1:4)—who became an intimate and trusted associate of the apostle in his mission of planting Christianity throughout the Mediterranean world (2 Cor 8:23; 2 Tm 4:10; Ti 1:5). Mentioned frequently in Paul's letters (eight times in 2 Cor, twice in Gal, once each in Ti and 2 Tm), his name occurs nowhere in Acts, a puzzling silence some have sought to explain with the fascinating, but uncertain, suggestion that he was a brother of Luke, the author of Acts.

Unlike Timothy, who was half Jewish, Titus was born of gentile parents. Nothing is recorded of the circumstances surrounding his conversion and initial encounter with Paul. He is first introduced as a companion of Paul and Barnabas on a visit to Jerusalem (Gal 2:3). The occasion appears to have been the Jerusalem Council, about a.d. 50, which Paul and Barnabas attended as official delegates from the church at Antioch not long after the apostle's first missionary journey (Acts 15).

With the hotly contested issue of compulsory circumcision of gentile converts to Christianity before the Council, Paul decided to make a test case of Titus. The Council decided in Paul's favor against the Judaizing party, and Titus was accepted by the other apostles and leaders of the Jerusalem church without submitting to the rite of circumcision. Thus Titus became a key figure in the liberation of the infant church from the Judaizing party.

Very likely Titus accompanied Paul from that time on, but he does not appear again until Paul's crisis with the church at Corinth during his third missionary journey. According to 2 Corinthians, while Paul was conducting an extended ministry in Ephesus, he received word that the Corinthian church had turned hostile toward him and renounced his apostolic authority. Other attempts at reconciliation, including a personal visit, having failed, he sent Titus to Corinth to try to repair the breach. When Titus rejoined Paul somewhere in Macedonia, where the apostle had traveled from Ephesus to meet him, he bore the good news that the attitude of the Corinthians had changed and their former love and friendship were now restored (2 Cor 7:6, 7). In view of this development Paul sent Titus back to Corinth bearing 2 Corinthians and with instructions to complete the collection of the relief offering for the Jewish Christians of Judea which he had previously begun, but not finished (8:6, 16). In this venture also Titus was apparently successful (Rom 15:26).

On the assumption that Paul was released after his first Roman imprisonment, recorded in the final chapters of Acts, it appears that Titus accompanied him on a mission to the island of Crete. On departing from Crete, Paul left Titus behind as his apostolic deputy to consolidate the new Christian movement there (Ti 1:5). The assignment was difficult, for the Cretans were unruly and the struggling church was already invaded by false teachers (vv 10–16). His handling of the Corinthian problem some years before, however, demonstrated that Titus possessed the spiritual earnestness, skillful diplomacy, and loving concern required to meet the present challenge, and Paul was confident that this new commission was therefore safe in his hands.

Paul's letter to Titus, one of his three pastoral letters, was written somewhat later to encourage Titus in his Cretan ministry. The letter closes with the apostle's request that Titus join him at Nicopolis, a town on the west coast of Greece, where he planned to spend the winter (Ti 3:12). Most likely it was from Nicopolis, or else later from Rome where the apostle was imprisoned again and eventually martyred, that Paul sent Titus on the mission to Dalmatia, a Roman province in what is now Yugoslavia, on which he had embarked when Paul wrote 2 Timothy, the last of his letters (2 Tm 4:10). If later tradition is correct, Titus returned to Crete, where he served as bishop until advanced age.[28]

---

vv verse (pl. vv)

[28] Walter A. Elwell and Barry J. Beitzel, *Baker Encyclopedia of the Bible* (Grand Rapids, MI: Baker Book House, 1988), 2072–2073.

APPENDIX N Why Has God Permitted Suffering and Evil?

Edward D. Andrews

"God has morally sufficient reasons for permitting the evil and suffering in the world."—William Lane Craig

That *morally sufficient reason* lies below.

"The significant issue that drove me to Agnosticism [Bible Scholar Dr. Bart D. Ehrman is now an Agnostic] has to do not with the Bible, but with the pain and suffering in the world." He writes, "I eventually found it impossible to explain the evil so rampant among us—whether in terms of genocides (which continue), unspeakable human cruelty, war, disease, hurricanes, tsunamis, mudslides, the starvation of millions of innocent children, you name it—if there was a good and loving God who was actively involved in this world." *Misquoting Jesus* (p. 248)

As you will see below, Ehrman's issue is simply a matter of starting with the wrong assumption. **Point One**: He starts with 'if God is a God of love, who has the power to fix anything, how can there have been such horrific pain and suffering in imperfection over the last 6,000 years?' **Point Two**: He also likely begins with the premise that 'God is responsible for everything that happens.' If one starts with the wrong assumption, there is no doubt that he will reach the wrong conclusion(s). **Point One** is dealt with below, but let it be said that Ehrman is looking through the binoculars from the opposite end, the big side through the small. When we do that, we get a narrow, focused outlook. God looks through the binoculars the correct way, and can see the big picture. Ehrman can only see but a fraction and a moment of time, 70 – 80 years, while God has seen everything that has happened over these past 6,000 plus years in the greatest of detail, and can see what the outcome would be if he had handled things in a variety of ways.

Point Two is certainly one reason suffering and evil is often misunderstood. God is responsible for everything, but not always directly. If he started the human race, and we end up with what we now have, in essence, he is responsible. Just as parents, who have a child are similarly responsible for the child committing murder 21 years into his life, because they procreated and gave birth to the child. The mother and father are indirectly responsible. King David commits adultery with Bathsheba and has her husband Uriah killed to cover things up, and impregnates Bathsheba, but the adulterine child, who remains nameless, died. Is God responsible for the death of that child? We can answer yes and no to that question. He is responsible in two ways: **(1)** He created humankind, so there would have been no affair, murder, adulterine child if he had not. **(2)** He did not step in and save the child, when he had the power to do so. However, he is not directly responsible, because he did not make King David and Bathsheba commit the acts that led to the child being born, nor did he bring an illness on the adulterine child, he just did not move in to protect the child, in a time that had a high rate of infant deaths.

The reason people think that God does not care about us is the words of some religious leaders, which have made them, feel this way. When tragedy strikes, what do some pastors and Bible scholars often say? When 9/11 took place, with thousands dying in the twin towers of New York, many ministers said: "It was God's will. God must have had some good reason for doing this." When religious leaders make such comments or similar ones, they are actually blaming God for the bad things that happened. Yet, the disciple James wrote, "Let no one say when he is tempted, 'I am being tempted by God,' for God cannot be tempted with evil, and he himself tempts no one." (James 1:13) God never directly causes what is bad. Indeed, "far be it from God that he should do wickedness, and from the Almighty that he should do wrong." Job 34:10.

The history of humans has been inundated with pain and suffering on an unprecedented scale, much of which they have brought on themselves. The problem/question that has plagued many persons is, 'why if there is a loving God, would he allow it to start with, and worse still, why allow it to go on for over 6,000 years?' Some apologist scholars have struggled to answer this question, because they are over analyzing, as opposed to just looking for the answer in God's Word. Therefore, if we are to answer this question, we must go back to Adam and Eve at the time of the first sin. Many have read this account, but I will list the texts as a refresher.

Genesis 2:17 Updated American Standard Version (UASV)

17 but from the tree of the knowledge of good and evil you shall not eat,[29] for in the day that you eat from it you shall surely die."[30]

Genesis 3:1-5 Updated American Standard Version (UASV)

1 Now the serpent was more crafty than any beast of the field which Jehovah God had made. And he said to the woman, "Did God actually say, 'You[31] shall not eat of any tree in the garden'?" **2** And the woman said to the serpent, "From the fruit of the trees of the garden we may eat, **3** but from the tree that is in the midst of the garden, God said, 'You shall not eat from it, nor shall you touch it, lest you die'." **4** And the serpent said to the woman, "<u>You shall not surely die</u>. **5** For God knows that when you eat of it your eyes will be opened, and you will be like God, knowing good and evil." knowing good and evil.

Later Bible texts establish Satan the Devil as the one using a serpent as his mouthpiece like a ventriloquist would a dummy. Anyway, take note that Satan contradicts the clear statement that God made to Adam at Genesis 2:17, "you will not surely die." Backing up a little, we see Satan asking an inferential question, "Did God actually say, 'You shall not eat of any tree in the garden'?" First, he is overstating what he knows to be true, not "any tree," just one tree. Second, Satan is inferring, 'I can't believe that God would say . . . how dare he say such.' Notice too that Eve has been told so thoroughly about the tree that she even goes beyond what Adam told her, not just that you 'do not eat from it,' no, 'you do not even touch it!' Then, Satan out and out lied and slandered God as a liar, saying that 'they would not die.' To make matters much worse, he infers that God is withholding good from them, and by rebelling they would be better off, being like God, 'knowing good and bad.' This latter point is not knowledge of; it is the self-sovereignty of choosing good and bad for

---

[29] Lit *eat from it*

[30] Lit *dying you* [singular] *shall die*. Heb *moth tamuth*; the first reference to death in the Scriptures

[31] In Hebrew *you* is plural in verses 1–5

oneself and act of rebellion for created creatures. What was symbolized by the tree is well expressed in a footnote on Genesis 2:17, in The Jerusalem Bible (1966):

> This knowledge is a privilege which God reserves to himself and which man, by sinning, is to lay hands on, 3:5, 22. Hence it does not mean omniscience, which fallen man does not possess; nor is it moral discrimination, for unfallen man already had it and God could not refuse it to a rational being. It is the power of deciding for himself what is good and what is evil and of acting accordingly, a claim to complete moral independence by which man refuses to recognize his status as a created being. The first sin was an attack on God's sovereignty, a sin of pride.

The Issues at Hand

(1) Satan called God a liar and said he was not to be trusted, as to the life or death issue.

(2) Satan's challenge, therefore, took into question the right and legitimacy of God's rightful place as the Universal Sovereign.

(3) Satan also suggested that people would remain obedient to God only as long as their submitting to God was to their benefit.

(4) Satan all but said that humankind was able to walk on his own, there being no need for dependence on God.

(5) Satan argued that man could be like God, choosing for himself what is right and wrong.

(6) Satan claimed that God's way of ruling was not in the best interests of humans, and they could do better without God.

Job 1:6-11 Updated American Standard Version (UASV)

6 Now there was a day when the sons of God came to present themselves before Jehovah, and Satan also came among them. **7** Jehovah said to Satan, "From where do you come?" Then Satan answered Jehovah and said, "From roaming about on the earth and walking around on it." **8** Jehovah said to Satan, "Have you considered my servant Job? For there is no one like him on the earth, a blameless and upright man, fearing God and turning away from evil." **9** Then Satan answered Jehovah, "<u>Does Job fear God for nothing?</u> **10** Have you not made a hedge about him and his house and all that he has, on every side? You have blessed the work of his hands, and his possessions have increased in the land. **¹¹** But <u>put forth your hand now and touch all that he has; he will surely curse you to your face</u>."

Job 2:4-5 Updated American Standard Version (UASV)

⁴ Satan answered Jehovah and said, "Skin for skin! Yes, all that <u>a man</u> has he will give for his life. **⁵** However, put forth your hand now, and touch his bone and his flesh; he will curse you to your face."

This general reference to "a man," as opposed to explicitly naming Job, is suggesting that all men [and women] will only obey God when things are good, but when the slightest difficulty arises, he will not obey. If you were put to the test, would you prove your love for your heavenly Father and show that you preferred His rule to that of any other?

God Settles the Issues

There is one thing that Satan did not challenge, namely, the power of God. Satan did not suggest that God was unable to destroy him as an opposer. However, he did challenge God's way of ruling, not His right to rule. Therefore, a moral issue must be settled.

An illustration of how God chose to deal with the issue can be demonstrated in human terms. A neighbor down the street slandered a man, who had a son and daughter. The slanderer said that he was not a good father, i.e., he withheld good from his children and was so overbearing, to the point of being abusive. The slanderer stated that the children would be better off without their father. He further argued that the children had no real love for their father and only obeyed him because of the food and shelter. How should the father deal with these false, i.e., slanderous accusations? If he were to go down the road and pummel the slanderer, it would only validate the lies, making the neighbors believe the accuser is telling the truth.

The answer lies within his family as they can serve as his witnesses. (Pro 27:11; Isa 43:10) If the children stay obedient and grow to be successful adults, turning out to be loving, caring, honest people with spotless character, it proves the accusations false. If the children accept the lies and rebel and grow up to be despicable people, it just further validates that they would have been better off by staying with the father. This is how God chose to deal with the issues. The issues that were raised must be settled beyond all reasonable doubt.

If God had destroyed the rebellious three: Satan, Adam, and Eve; he would not have resolved the issues of

(1) Whether man could walk on his own,

(2) if he would be better off without his Creator,

(3) if God's rulership were not best, and

(4) if God were hiding good from man.

(5) In addition, there was an audience of untold billions of angelic spirit creatures looking on.

If God destroyed without settling things, these spirit persons would be following God out of dreadful fear, not love, fear of displeasing God. Moreover, say He did kill them, and start over, and ten thousand years down the road (with billions of humans now on earth), the issues were raised again, He would have to destroy billions of people again, and again, and again all throughout time, until these issues were laid to rest.

What God has done is, allow time to pass, and the issues to be resolved. Man thought he was better off without God, and could walk on his own. In addition, man has attempted every kind of rulership imaginable, and one must ask, 'have they proven themselves better than rulership under the sovereignty of their Creator?' (Proverbs 1:30-33; Isaiah 59:4, 8) Sadly, the issues must be taken up to the brink of destroying man. (Rev 11:18) otherwise, the argument would be that if given enough time, they could have turned things around. If man goes up to the point of destroying himself and Armageddon comes at the last minute, it will have set a case law, solved the issue, and the Bible can serve as the example forever. If the issues of God's sovereignty or the loyalty of His created creatures, angelic or human, is ever questioned again, we would have the Holy Bible that will serve as a law established based on previous verdicts of not guilty, please see below.

What Have the Results Been?

(1) God does not cause evil and suffering. Romans 9:14.

(2) The fact that God has allowed evil, pain and suffering has shown that independence from God has not brought about a better world. Jeremiah 8:5, 6, 9.

(3) God's permission of evil, pain and suffering has also proved that Satan has not been able to turn all humans away from God. Exodus 9:16; 1 Samuel 12:22; Hebrews 12:1.

(4) The fact that God has permitted evil, pain and suffering to continue has provided proof that only God, the Creator, has the capability and the right to rule over humankind for their eternal blessing and happiness. Ecclesiastes 8:9.

(5) Satan has been the god of this world since the sin in Eden (over 6,000 years), and how has that worked out for man, and what has been the result of man's course of independence from God and his rule? Matthew 4:8-9; John 16:11; 2 Corinthians 4:3-4; 1 John 5:19; Psalm 127:1.

Satan's impact on the earth's activities has carried with it conflict, evil and death, and his rulership has been by means of deception, power and his own self-interest. He has demonstrated himself an unfit ruler of everything. Therefore, God is now completely vindicated in putting an end to this corrupted rebel along with all who have shared in his evil deeds.—Romans 16:20.

God has tolerated evil, sickness, pain, suffering and death until our day in order to resolve all the issues raised by Satan. We are self-centered in thinking that this has only pained us. Imagine that you are holding a rope on a sinking ship that 20 other men, women and children are clinging to, when your child loses her grip and falls into the ocean. You can either hold the rope, saving 20 people, or you can let go and attempt to rescue your daughter. God has been watching the suffering of billions from the day of Adam and Eve's sin. Moreover, it has been His great love for us, which causes Him to cling to the rope of issues, saving us from a future of repeated issues. Nevertheless, he will not allow this evil to remain forever. He has set a fixed time when He will end this wicked system of Satan's rule.

Daniel 11:27 Updated American Standard Version (UASV)

²⁷ As for both kings, their heart will be inclined to do what is evil, and they will speak lies to each other at the same table; but it will not succeed, for the end is still to come at the appointed time.

Unlike what many people of the world may think (the world that lies in the hands of Satan), being obedient to God is not difficult. We simply must set our pride aside and accept that the wisdom of God is so far greater than our own, and accept that He has worked for the good of obedient humankind, as He loves each one of us.

Matthew 7:21 Updated American Standard Version (UASV)

²¹ "Not everyone who says to me, 'Lord, Lord,' will enter the kingdom of heaven, but the one who does the will of my Father who is in heaven.

1 John 2:15-17 Updated American Standard Version (UASV)

¹⁵ Do not love the world or the things in the world. If anyone loves the world, the love of the Father is not in him. ¹⁶ For all that is in the world, the lust of the flesh and the lust of the eyes and the boastful pride

of life, is not from the Father, but is from the world. **¹⁷** The world is passing away, and its lusts; but the one who does the will of God remains forever.

As Christians, there is a love we must not have. We must 'not love the world or anything in it.' Instead, we need to keep from becoming infected by the corruption of unrighteous human society that is alienated from God and must not breathe in its mental disposition or be moved by its sinful dominant attitude. (Ephesians 2:1, 2; James 1:27) If we were to have the views of those in the world that are in opposition to God, "the love of the Father" would not be in us. (James 4:4)

An Overview

Was Satan Punished?

Yes.

COMMON QUESTION: Why did God not destroy the Satan, Adam, and Eve right away?

I would follow up with what would have happened if God had chosen that path. Hundreds of billions of angels with free will were watching, and they knew of the issues raised. What would their love of God have been like if God did not address the issues raised? Was Satan right? Was God lying? Would free will creatures, spirit and humans, be better off? Will God just destroy us over anything? First, the spirit creatures would have followed God out of dreadful fear, rather than fear of displeasing the one they loved so much up to that point, like a child to a parent. Second, what happens if the issue is raised a hundred thousand years after a restart and there are 30 billion perfect humans on the planet? Would God simply destroy everyone again and start over. Do we think it wise that he does this reboot every time or was it not better that he settled the issue once and for all?

POINT: Satan raised Issues of sovereignty in the Garden of Eden.

POINT: Can humans walk on their own; do they really need their Creator? Are they better off without God?

POINT: Was God lying and withholding?

When a teenager becomes a rebel in our house, we have a choice: (1) severe punishment or (2) teach them an object lesson.

HUMANS AND ANGELS are a created product no different than a car coming off of an assembly line, i.e., (1) they owe their existence to their creator and (2) they were created to function based on the design of the creator. If we take a ford escort and treat it like a heavy duty four-wheel drive truck and go off roading (not what the car was designed to do), what will happen?

God wisely chose to teach both angels and humans an object lesson. Neither was designed to walk on their own. Both angel and human were given relative freedom (under the sovereignty of God), not absolute freedom. They were not designed to choose what is right and what is wrong on their own. They were given God's moral standards by way of an internal conscience. How can we tell a rebel that we do not have absolute freedom, we are better off under the umbrella of our creator's sovereignty, we cannot walk on our own? They will just reject it as a rebel teenager would.

OBJECT LESSON: We let them learn from their choice, no matter how painful it is, and hard love means that we do not step in until the lesson is fully learned. Humankind was essentially told, "Oh, you think you can walk on your own, well go ahead, we will see how that works out." After six-thousand-years, God could actually use a common saying among young people today: "How is that absolute freedom working out for you?"

When will the lesson fully be learned? Humankind will walk right up to the very edge of the cliff of killing themselves, actually falling over, when God will step in and stop the object lesson. To stop it any time before, will cause doubts. If it had been stopped a century ago, the argument would have been; God simply stepped in before we got to the scientific age because he knew we were going to find true peace and security, along with something to give us eternal life. However, if humanity has actually fallen over the edge of the cliff and the destruction of us is definite, and God steps in, there is no argument that can be raised, the object lesson is learned.

Why Was Satan Not Kicked Out of Heaven Right Away?

Satan stayed in his realm, just as humans stayed in theirs. God changed nothing right away because he would have been accused of adjusting the pieces on the chessboard to get the desired outcome, i.e., cheating. When will Satan be kicked out of heaven? Satan and the Demons lost access to the person of God long age, and they lost some of their powers, such as being able to materialize in human form, like they did when they took human women for themselves at the flood, producing the Nephilim.

Satan would be thrown to the earth very shortly before the end of his age of rulership, when "he knows that his time is short." (Rev 12:9-12) This, then, means that Satan will be thrown from heaven likely sometime before the Great Tribulation and Christ's return. Revelation 12:12 says, "'Therefore, rejoice, O heavens and you who dwell in them! But woe to you, O earth and sea, for the devil has come down to you in great wrath because he knows that his time is short!'"

Notice that it is at a time, when "Satan knows that his time is short!" What comes next for Satan? He will be abyssed, thrown into a super-maximum-security prison for a thousand years (for lack of a better way to explain it) while Jesus fixes all that Satan done. After the thousand years, he will be let loose for a little while, and he will tempt perfect humans, and sadly some will fall away. In the end, Satan and those humans will be destroyed, and Jesus will hand the kingdom back over to the father.

APPENDIX O Why is Life So Unfair?

Edward D. Andrews

On December 14, 2012, 20-year-old Adam Lanza fatally shot twenty children and six adult staff members in a mass murder at Sandy Hook Elementary School, in the village of Sandy Hook in Newtown, Connecticut. Before driving to the school, Lanza shot and killed his mother Nancy at their Newtown home. As first responders arrived, he committed suicide by shooting himself in the head.[32]

Parents, who sent their children to school that morning, never expected that by the end of the day, Adam Lanza would have murdered them. Worse still, there were signs that, if paid attention to, things may not have turned out the way they did. These parents are certainly, what comes to mind when we think of life being unfair.

Unfairness the World Over

The world is full of these type of accounts the world over. We have social depravities everywhere we look. In the United States, there are hundreds of thousands living in homeless shelters, under bridges, eating at soup kitchens, and many have young children with them as well. On the

---

[32] http://en.wikipedia.org/wiki/Sandy_Hook_Elementary_School_shooting

other hand, the United States throws away more food than any other country. Sadly, the hungry in the United States, while truly unfair, rates very low when one considers the inhumane conditions of other countries. In some countries, like Mexico, you have a millionaire living in a mansion, with a poor person living in a shack next door, and a person living in a car, living next door to him. Almost two billion people live in such hopeless poverty and inhuman conditions that those in the Western part of the world could never relate.

Poverty is defined as a state of want; lacking means; inadequacy. Poverty "brings hunger, disease, high infant mortality, homelessness, and even war." Poverty "falls on the more vulnerable groups in society, such as women, the elderly, minority groups, and children." About 1 billion people around the world live on less than $1 a day.[33]

God's View of Fairness

Leviticus 19:15 Updated American Standard Version (UASV)

[15] 'You shall do no injustice in judgment; you shall not be partial to the poor nor defer to the great, but in righteousness shall you judge your neighbor.

The New American Commentary (Leviticus) says, "Even though those who are disadvantaged are to be treated properly, no special favors are to be given to the poor in judicial settings (19:15; see Exod 23:3). All proceedings are to be characterized by justice, just as God is just (Job 36:3; Pss 85:10; 89:14; 97:2; 119:42; Isa 42:6; 45:18, 19; Jer 11:20; Hos 2:19)."[34] The irony is, one of the charges Satan made against God was that he is unfair. In addition, he said God was not rightly exercising his sovereignty. Then, he believed that God was going to hear his case fairly and deal with his rebellion in a fair and just way. In other words, he believed God would allow him to live if Satan could prove the charges he had raised. Thus, Satan's charge of God being unfair was self-defeating in that he depended on him to be fair in hearing the issues. God is just and impartial.

Deuteronomy 32:4 Updated American Standard Version (UASV)

[4] "The Rock, his work is perfect,
for all his ways are just.

---

[33] ttp://prezi.com/8duqy_es2rmu/inadequate-living-conditions-around-the-world/

[34] (Rooker, Leviticus: The New American Commentary 2001, p. 258)

A God of faithfulness and without injustice,
 righteous and upright is he

"This word [**rock**], representing the stability and permanence of God, was placed at the beginning of the verse for emphasis and was followed by a series of phrases which elaborated the attributes of God as the rock of Israel. It is one of the principal themes in this song (see vv. 15, 18, 30, 31), emphasizing the unchanging nature of God in contrast to the fickle nature of the people."[35] All of God's actions are perfect in that he expresses his attributes of justice, wisdom, love, and power in perfect balance.

Acts 10:34-35 Updated American Standard Version (UASV)

[34] So Peter opened his mouth and said: "Truly I understand that God shows no partiality, [35] but in every nation anyone who fears[36] him and works righteousness[37] is acceptable to him.

Kenneth O. Gangel writes, "Cornelius and his family already were worshipers of God and thus had some prior preparation for the gospel. Peter could have assumed such knowledge on their part and not have to start by first introducing the basic monotheistic message of faith in God as he did when preaching to pagan Gentiles. Peter's sermon at Cornelius's basically followed the pattern of his prior sermons to the Jews but with several significant differences. One is found at the very outset, where he stressed that God shows no favoritism, accepts people from every nation and that Jesus is "Lord of all." This emphasis on the universal gospel is particularly suited to a message to Gentiles. Peter's vision had led him to this basic insight that God does not discriminate between persons, that there are no divisions between "clean" and "unclean" people from the divine perspective. The Greek word used for favoritism (v. 34) is constructed on a Hebrew idiom meaning *to lift a face*.[38] Peter saw that God does not discriminate on the basis of race or ethnic background, looking up to some and down on others. But God does discriminate

---

[35] MacArthur, John (2005-05-09). *The MacArthur Bible Commentary* (Kindle Locations 9334-9337). Thomas Nelson. Kindle Edition.

[36] This is a reverential fear of displeasing God because of one's great love for him. It is not a dreadful fear.

[37] I.e., *does what is right*

[38] For God's judgment on the basis of one's conduct, see also Gen 4:7; Rom 2:6; Rev 20:12f. For God's impartiality cf. Eph 6:9; Col 3:25, Jas 2:1, 9; 1 Pet 1:17; Rev 22:12. The idiom "lifting a face" pictures God as an oriental monarch lifting the face of a petitioner. To lift the petitioner's face is to receive him or her with favor (cf. Esth 4:11; 5:2, where the custom is different but the import is the same).

between those whose behavior is acceptable and those whose attitude is not acceptable. Those who reverence God and practice what is right are acceptable to him (v. 35; cf. Luke 8:21)." (Polhill 2001, p. 261)

From Where Does Unfairness Stem?

Genesis 2:17 Updated American Standard Version (UASV)

¹⁷ "but from the tree of the knowledge of good and evil you shall not eat, for in the day that you eat from it you shall surely die."

"The tree of the knowledge of good and evil," resulted in man's failure to respect God's decree and his sovereignty, which brought man's fall.

Genesis 3:4-5 Updated American Standard Version (UASV)

⁴ And the serpent **[Satan the Devil]** said to the woman, "You shall not surely die. ⁵ For God knows that when you eat of it your eyes will be opened, and you will be like God, knowing good and evil." knowing good and evil.

⁶ So when the woman saw that the tree was good for food, and that it was a delight to the eyes, and that the tree was to be desirable to make one wise, and she took of its fruit and ate, then she also gave some to her husband when with her, and he ate.

Satan the Devil, a very powerful angelic spirit person rebelled against God, seeking glory and power for himself. He use the serpent hanging from the tree, like a ventriloquist uses a dummy to project his voice to deceive Eve and inevitably cause Adam to rebel.

Genesis 3:24 Updated American Standard Version (UASV)

²⁴ So he drove the man out, and at the east of the garden of Eden he placed the cherubim and a flaming sword that turned every way to guard the way to the tree of life.

The New American Commentary (Genesis) says, "Such imagery effectively depicts the excommunication of the man and woman from the presence of God. Later Israel was all too aware that an audience with God was the exclusive privilege of Aaron's lineage and only at the invitation of God once a year. Our parents squandered what men and women have longed to regain ever since. However, not all is lost since God initiates for Israel a new way into his presence but at the costly price of innocent blood. In spite of man's inability to obtain life through the garden's tree, the tabernacle revealed at Sinai enabled Israel to live with God, though imperfectly. The means and extent of access to God's presence was altered because of sin, but divine mercy overtook the wayward man and woman. For their future generations provision was afforded through Israel. This all, however, only foreshadowed the perfect and final passage into the presence of God by the very body of Jesus Christ, whose blood cleanses us so that we might know life through his death (Heb. 9:6–14)." (Mathews 2001, p. 258)

John 8:44 Updated American Standard Version (UASV)

⁴⁴ You are of your father the devil, and your will is to do your father's desires. That one was a manslayer from the beginning, and does not stand in the truth, because there is no truth in him. When he lies, he speaks out of his own character, for he is a liar and the father of lies.

John MacArthur writes, "Jesus' words refer to the fall when Satan tempted Adam and Eve and successfully killed their spiritual life (Gen. 2:17; 3:17–24; Rom. 5:12; Heb. 2:14)."[39]

Revelation 12:9 Updated American Standard Version (UASV)

⁹ And the great dragon was thrown down, the serpent of old who is called the devil and Satan, who deceives the whole inhabited earth; he was thrown down to the earth, and his angels were thrown down with him.

The MacArthur Bible Commentary says, "Satan and his demons were cast out of heaven at the time of their original rebellion, but still have access to it (cf. Job 1:6; 2:1). That access will then be denied, and they will be forever barred from heaven. Devil and Satan. Cf. 20:2. Devil comes from a Greek verb meaning "to slander" or "to falsely accuse." He is a malignant liar (John 8:44; 1 John 3:8). His accusations against believers (v. 10) are unsuccessful because of Christ our Advocate (1 John 2:1). Satan, meaning "adversary," or "enemy," appears especially in Job and the Gospels. deceives the whole world. As he has throughout human history, Satan will deceive people during the Tribulation (cf. 13:14; 20:3; John 8:44). After his temporary release from the bottomless pit at the end of the Millennium, he will briefly resume his deceitful ways (20:8, 10)."[40]

---

[39] MacArthur, John (2005-05-09). *The MacArthur Bible Commentary* (Kindle Locations 47425-47426). Thomas Nelson. Kindle Edition.

[40] MacArthur, John (2005-05-09). The MacArthur Bible Commentary (Kindle Locations 67207-67213). Thomas Nelson. Kindle Edition.

Unfairness in the Last Days

Revelation 12:12 Updated American Standard Version (UASV)

¹² Therefore, rejoice, O heavens and you who dwell in them! Woe to you, O earth and sea, for the devil has come down to you in great wrath, because he knows he has a short time."

The Holman New Testament Commentary (Revelation) says, "Satan's overthrow means that his accusations can never again ascend to the throne of God. This is great news for all the holy angels. It is cause for **you who dwell in** the heavens to **rejoice**. What brings heavenly joy causes **woe to the earth and the sea**. More terrors await them from the sea beast and from the land beast that the dragon will call up. The dragon is **filled with fury**, for he has never before been so utterly defeated. He recognizes this as a sign: **his time is short** to damage God and his people, so he must act quickly with renewed energy. (Easley 1998, p. 213)

Daniel 12:4 Updated American Standard Version (UASV)

⁴ But as for you, O Daniel, conceal these words and seal up the book until the time of the end; many will go to and fro,⁴¹ and knowledge will increase."

The angel "Gabriel, therefore, was instructing Daniel to preserve "the words of the scroll," not merely this final vision146 but the whole book147 for those who will live at "the time of the end" when the message will be needed. This future generation will undergo the horrors of the tribulation ("time of distress") and will need the precious promises contained in the Book of Daniel–that God will be victorious over the kingdoms of this world and that the suffering will last for only a brief time–to sustain them." (Miller 1994, p. 321)

Difficult Times In the Last Days

2 Timothy 3:1-5 Updated American Standard Version (UASV)

3 But realize this, that in the last days difficult times will come. ² For men will be lovers of themselves, lovers of money, boastful, arrogant, revilers, disobedient to parents, ungrateful, unholy, ³ unloving, irreconcilable, malicious gossips, without self-control, brutal, not loving good, ⁴ treacherous, reckless, conceited, lovers of pleasure rather than lovers of God, ⁵ having the appearance of godliness, but denying its power; avoid such men as these.

---

⁴¹ I.e. examine the book thoroughly

The MacArthur Bible Commentary says, "**3:1 the last days.** This phrase refers to this age, the time since the first coming of the Lord Jesus. See note on 1 Timothy 4:1. perilous times. Perilous is used to describe the savage nature of two demon-possessed men (Matt. 8:28). The word for times had to do with epochs, rather than clock or calendar time. Such savage, dangerous eras or epochs will increase in frequency and severity as the return of Christ approaches (v. 13). The church age is fraught with these dangerous movements accumulating strength as the end nears. Cf. Matthew 7:15; 24:11, 12, 24; 2 Peter 2:1, 2. **3:2–4** This list of attributes characterizing the leaders of the dangerous seasons is a description of unbelievers similar to the Lord's in Mark 7:21, 22. **3:5 having a form of godliness but denying its power.** Form refers to the outward shape or appearance. Like the unbelieving scribes and Pharisees, false teachers and their followers are concerned with mere external appearances (cf. Matt. 23:25; Titus 1:16). Their outward form of Christianity and virtue makes these individuals all the more dangerous."[42]

Unfairness Removed

Romans 16:20 Updated American Standard Version (UASV)

²⁰ The God of peace will soon crush Satan under your feet. The grace of our Lord Jesus Christ be with you.

Do Not Love the World

1 John 2:15-17 Updated American Standard Version (UASV)

¹⁵ Do not love the world or the things in the world. If anyone loves the world, the love of the Father is not in him. ¹⁶ For all that is in the world, the lust of the flesh and the lust of the eyes and the boastful pride of life, is not from the Father, but is from the world. ¹⁷ The world is passing away, and its lusts; but the one who does the will of God remains forever.

The End of the Age

Matthew 24:1-3 Updated American Standard Version (UASV)

24 Jesus came out from the temple and was going away when[43] his disciples came up to point out the temple buildings to him. ² And he said

---

[42] MacArthur, John (2005-05-09). The MacArthur Bible Commentary (Kindle Locations 60742-60751). Thomas Nelson. Kindle Edition.

[43] Lit *and*

to them, "Do you not see all these things? Truly I say to you, not one stone here will be left upon another, which will not be torn down."

3 As he was sitting on the Mount of Olives, the disciples came to him privately, saying, "Tell us, when will these things be, and what will be the sign of your coming,[44] and of the end of the age?"

Here in verse three, we have Jesus and the disciples taking a seat on the Mount of Olives, looking down on the temple below. The temple compound was the ninth wonder of the ancient world. Jesus had just told the disciples that this marvel was going to be so devastated in a coming destruction, "there will not be left here one stone upon another that will not be thrown down." Looking down, the disciples asked Jesus what they thought to be but one question, not knowing the answer that Jesus would give, showed it to be three separate questions. Of course, the initial question **(1)** was their wondering when the destruction that Jesus spoke of was coming. There second portion of that question was **(2)** what will be the sign of your coming. The third portion of the question was **(3)** the end of the age.[45] Herein, we will focus on questions **(2)** and **(3)**. In short, **(1)** the destruction of Jerusalem took place in 70 C.E., just 37-years after the death, resurrection, and ascension of Christ.

They ask these questions about the destruction of Jerusalem and the temple, his own second coming (... [*parousia*], presence, common in the papyri for the visit of the emperor), and the end of the world. Did they think that they were all to take place simultaneously? There is no way to answer. At any rate Jesus treats all three in this great eschatological discourse, the most difficult problem in the Synoptic Gospels. ... It is sufficient for our purpose to think of Jesus as using the destruction of the temple and of Jerusalem which did happen in that generation in a.d. 70, as also a symbol of his own second coming and of the end of the world (... [*sunteleias tou aiōnos*]) or consummation of the age. In a painting the artist by skilful perspective may give on the same surface the inside of a room, the fields outside the window, and the sky far beyond. Certainly in

---

[44] Or *presence* (Gr *parousia*), which denotes both an "arrival" and a consequent "presence with."

[45] Whether one sees this as two questions or three questions is not that big of a difference. If it is two questions; then, the coming/presence of Christ and the end of the age are being treated as one event. However, if there are three; then, the coming/presence of Christ and the end of the age are being treated as two events. Either way, you have Christ's coming/presence and the end of the age. If the Greek word *parousia* carries the sense of both the arrival of Christ and his presence for a time before the end of the age, as explained by *Vine's Expository Dictionary*, this seems to better support it being a three part question. How long that interval is between the arrival, the presence and the conclusion, no one can truly know.

this discourse Jesus blends in apocalyptic language the background of his death on the cross, the coming destruction of Jerusalem, his own second coming and the end of the world. He now touches one, now the other. It is not easy for us to separate clearly the various items.[46]

In "what will be the sign of your **coming**," the Greek word behind "coming" (*parousia*) needs a little more in-depth explaining.

Parousia ... lit., "a presence," *para*, "with," and *ousia*, "being" (from *eimi*, "to be"), denotes both an "arrival" and a consequent "presence with." For instance, in a papyrus letter a lady speaks of the necessity of her *parousia* in a place in order to attend to matters relating to her property there. Paul speaks of his *parousia* in Philippi, Phil. 2:12 (in contrast to his *apousia*, "his absence"; see absence). Other words denote "the arrival" (see *eisodos* and *eleusis*, above). *Parousia* is used to describe the presence of Christ with His disciples on the Mount of Transfiguration, 2 Pet. 1:16. When used of the return of Christ, at the rapture of the church, it signifies, not merely His momentary "coming" for His saints, but His presence with them from that moment until His revelation and manifestation to the world. In some passages the word gives prominence to the beginning of that period, the course of the period being implied, 1 Cor. 15:23; 1 Thess. 4:15; 5:23; 2 Thess. 2:1; Jas. 5:7-8; 2 Pet. 3:4. In some, the course is prominent, Matt. 24:3, 37; 1 Thess. 3:13; 1 John 2:28; in others the conclusion of the period, Matt. 24:27; 2 Thess. 2:8.[47]

"What will be the sign of your coming" As we can see from the context of Matthew 24 and Vine's *Expository Dictionary*, parousia, describes not only the arrival of Christ, but his presence as well. This does not give us the sense of a coming and some swift departure. Rather, the presence aspect is a period of time that we cannot know the exact length of, so it does no good even to speculate by adding adjectives, like a "lengthy" or "short" presence.

"the end of the age" What is meant by the Greek word *aion*, which is translated "age." It refers to a certain period of time, an epoch, or age.

---

[46] A.T. Robertson, *Word Pictures in the New Testament* (Nashville, TN: Broadman Press, 1933), Mt 24:3.

[47] The reader should be aware that the Greek word parousia does mean presence, the word is derived from para (with) and ousia (being). However, it does not denote the idea of invisible as the Jehovah Witnesses attest to. See W. E. Vine, Merrill F. Unger, and William White Jr., *Vine's Complete Expository Dictionary of Old and New Testament Words* (Nashville, TN: T. Nelson, 1996), 111.

aion (αἰών, 165), "an age, era" (to be connected with *aei*, "ever," rather than with *ao*, "to breathe"), signifies a period of indefinite duration, or time viewed in relation to what takes place in the period.[48]

What period of time is being referred to here? If we look at God's use of Moses to help in the Exodus of his people from Egypt, and Moses penning of the Mosaic Law, we would say that from the Exodus to the sacrifice ransom death of Christ was an "age" (period of time or epoch) where the Israelite nation was the only way to God. Then, Jesus entered humanity into another age by his ransom sacrifice, which runs up unto his second coming/presence and the end of this age of Christianity.

Jesus answers this two or three-part question throughout the rest of Matthew 24 and chapter 25. Matthew gives us Jesus' presentation of the events that lead to Jesus coming and presence, to set up his kingdom to rule **over** the earth for a thousand years. Most will be shocked by my saying "over" the earth, as almost all translations render Revelation 5:10 as "and you have made them a kingdom and priests to our God, and they shall reign **on** the earth."

epí [2093] is in the genitive and can range from: "on, upon; over; at, by; before, in the presence of; when, under, at the time of;"[49] Below you are going to find a list of the genitive epi within Revelation that has a similar construction.

If we are to establish that some translations are choosing a rendering because it suits their doctrine, we must compare how they render the same thing elsewhere. I do believe that the English is a problem in trying to say, "They shall reign **on** the earth." First, because this is not a location issue: i.e., "where." The genitive *epi* is dealing not with where, but with authority over, which is expressed by having it over ... not on ...

Please also take special note that the context of all of these epi genitives that follow the active indicative verb and then are followed by the genitive definite article and noun are dealing with authority.

The verb "to reign" is properly used of kings and queens, and here implies complete power over the world and its inhabitants. So another

---

[48] W. E. Vine, Merrill F. Unger, and William White Jr., *Vine's Complete Expository Dictionary of Old and New Testament Words* (Nashville, TN: T. Nelson, 1996), 19.

[49] William D. Mounce, Mounce's Complete Expository Dictionary of Old & New Testament Words (Grand Rapids, MI: Zondervan, 2006), 1150.

way of expressing this is "and they shall rule over the world and its inhabitants" or "they shall have power over ...."[50]

Revelation 5:9-10 has a high level of theological content. It either says that Jesus and his co-rulers are going to over the earth, or on the earth. It is theological bias to have several cases of similar context and the same grammatical construction, rendering the verses the same every time, yet to then render one verse contrary to the others, simply because it aligns with one's theology. Please see Revelation 2:26; 6:8; 9:11; 11:6; 13:7; 14:18; 16:9; 17:18, and then look at Revelation **5:10**. Nowhere in Scripture does it say that Jesus is going to rule over the earth.

Signs of the End of the Age

Matthew 24:4 Updated American Standard Version (UASV)

⁴ And Jesus answered them, "See that no one leads you astray.

Jesus' disciples, like any other Jew of the day, would have seen the destruction of Jerusalem in 70 C.E., the first-century Jewish historian, Josephus, tells us 1,100,000 Jews were killed in the destruction of Jerusalem, with another 97,000 taken captive. (War VI. 9.3)[51] Therefore, here in advance (33 C.E.), Jesus wanted his disciples to be on the watch, to not be misled, as though the destruction of Jerusalem (66-70 C.E.) also meant "the end of the age."

Matthew 24:5 Updated American Standard Version (UASV)

⁵ For many will come in my name, saying, 'I am the Christ,' and they will lead many astray.

Yes, this would be one of the ways that many coming in Jesus' name would have led the disciples astray, claiming to be the Christ (Hebrew *Messiah*), namely the "anointed one." Therefore, it would not be Christians alone, who would be filling this role as false Christs/messiahs/anointed ones.

"From Josephus, it appears that in the first century before the destruction of the Temple [in 70 C.E.] a number of Messiahs arose promising relief from the Roman yoke, and finding ready followers ... Thus about 44, Josephus reports, a certain impostor, Theudas, who

---

[50] Bratcher, Robert G.; Hatton, Howard: A Handbook on the Revelation to John. New York: United Bible Societies, 1993 (UBS Handbook Series; Helps for Translators), S. 105

[51] Flavius Josephus and William Whiston, *The Works of Josephus: Complete and Unabridged* (Peabody: Hendrickson, 1987).

claimed to be a prophet, appeared and urged the people to follow him with their belongings to the Jordan, which he would divide for them. According to Acts v. 36 (which seems to refer to a different date), he secured about 400 followers. Cuspius Fadus sent a troop of horsemen after him and his band slew many of them, and took captive others, together with their leader, beheading the latter ... Another, an Egyptian, is said to have gathered together 30,000 adherents, whom he summoned to the Mount of Olives, opposite Jerusalem, promising that at his command the walls of Jerusalem would fall down and that he and his followers would enter and possess themselves of the city. But Felix, the procurator (c. 55-60), met the throng with his soldiery. The prophet escaped, but those with him were killed or taken, and the multitude dispersed. Another, whom Josephus styles an impostor, promised the people "deliverance and freedom from their miseries" if they would follow him to the wilderness. Both leader and followers were killed by the troops of Festus, the procurator (60-62; "Ant." xx. 8, § 10). Even when Jerusalem was already in the process of destruction by the Romans, a prophet, according to Josephus suborned by the defenders to keep the people from deserting announced that God commanded them to come to the Temple, there to receive miraculous signs of their deliverance. Those who came met death in the flames.

Unlike these Messiahs, who expected their people's deliverance to be achieved through divine intervention, Menahem, the son of Judas the Galilean and grandson of Hezekiah, the leader of the Zealots, who had troubled Herod, was a warrior. When the war broke out, he attacked Masada with his band, armed his followers with the weapons stored there, and proceeded to Jerusalem, where he captured the fortress Antonia, overpowering the troops of Agrippa II. Emboldened by his success, he behaved like a king and claimed the leadership of all the troops. Thereby he aroused the enmity of Eleazar, another Zealot leader, and met death as a result of a conspiracy against him (ib. ii. 17, § 9). He is probably identical with the Menahem b. Hezekiah mentioned in Sanh. 98b, and called, with reference to Lam. i. 17, "the comforter ["menaḥem"] that should relieve" (comp. Hamburger, "R. B. T." Supplement, iii. 80). With the destruction of the Temple, the appearance of Messiahs ceased for a time. Sixty years later a politico-Messianic movement of large proportions took place with Bar Kokba at its head. This leader of the revolt against Rome was hailed as Messiah-king by Akiba, who referred to him. *The Jewish Encyclopedia* lists 28 false Messiahs between the years 132 C.E. and 1744 C.E.[52]

---

[52] Vol. X, pp. 252-255.

Matthew 24:6 Updated American Standard Version (UASV)

⁶ You will be hearing of wars and rumors of wars. See that you are not alarmed, for those things must take place, but the end is not yet.

There have been religious leaders that have been misled by the two Great Wars of the 20th century, World War I and II, associating each of them with the "end of the age." The First Jewish–Roman War (66–73 C.E.),[53] at times called The Great Revolt, could have misled the disciples into thinking that the end was imminent. Therefore, Jesus tells them that they should not be alarmed and that the end is not yet. This counsel of Jesus has had to be applied from First Jewish–Roman War to the two Great Wars of the 20th century, every time a war came along, which seems to be an end all for humanity. Nevertheless, this one sign alone is not enough to signal the end, because imperfect humans are prone to war.

Matthew 24:7 Updated American Standard Version (UASV)

⁷ For nation will rise against nation, and kingdom against kingdom, and there will be famines and earthquakes in various places.

Here Jesus expounds on his previous comments about war because the conflicts of humankind have been so pervasive that there was a need for a reference book, *Dictionary of Wars* by George C. Kohn. Therefore, while we should take note of current events, wars, rumors of wars and even kingdom against kingdom is not enough alone to suppose that the end is here. Therefore, Jesus adds yet another two signs, famines, and earthquakes. These two have been a part of humankind's history. Of course, the impact is going to be far greater with seven billion living people on earth, as opposed to a hundred million in 100 C.E. Nevertheless, these are just the beginning. It seems that a war between the Islamic state and Christian nations is inevitable.

Matthew 24:8 Updated American Standard Version (UASV)

⁸ But all these are but the beginning of the birth pains.

Wars, rumors of wars, kingdoms again kingdom, famines and earthquakes are just the beginning of the things to come. However, they are not the goal post that the end is imminent. Such tragedies being merely a "beginning of the birth pains," the end was "not yet." Men

---

[53] The Second Jewish–Roman War (132–135 C.E.) Simon Bar Kokba, who claimed to be the long awaited Messiah, led a revolt against Roman Emperor Hadrian (76-139), for setting up a shrine to Jupiter (supreme Roman god), on the temple site in Jerusalem, as well as outlawing circumcision and instruction of the Law in public.

likely cannot appreciate this verse, because the woman only knows the pain of giving birth to a child. It is the most natural thing in her life and yet the most painful. Therefore, consider that what comes after this metaphorical concept is going to be far more painful for humankind. These pains will grow in severity until the birth of the end of the age, and the return of Jesus. Nevertheless, like any other birth that has finally reached the end, the joy of a newborn child makes one forget the prior pains. This is true after the tribulation, the joys from the Kingdom will outweigh the previous pains.

Matthew 24:9 Updated American Standard Version (UASV)

9 "Then they will deliver you up to tribulation, and will kill you, and you will be hated by all nations because of my name.

Verse 9 of the new section, 9-12, begins with "then" (Greek *tote*), which brings the reader into another section of signs, offering us more of the lines in the fingerprint, the full picture that we are in the time of to the end. "Then" can have the meaning coming *after, or at the same time*, or it could mean simply, *therefore*. It would seem that "then" is best understood as meaning 'at the same time,' because these signs, as well as those that we covered in 4-7, and those coming in verse 10 are of a composite sign. Meaning, you are looking for a time when they are all happening and on a worldwide scale.

Who are "they" that deliver Christians up to tribulation? It would be those Christians of verse 5, who were led astray, abandoning the Christian faith. The last 30 years, this has truly seen the abandonment of Christianity, as well as much tribulation for those that have remained faithful. What I am primarily referring to is liberal Christianity (80 percent of Christianity), who has abandoned the biblical truth, for the lie, so they can maintain a good relationship with the world, and progressivism. Christianity has never been more hated than it is today. Sadly, conservative Christians have been deeply opposed and persecuted by liberal Christianity, atheists, not to mention Islam and other religions.

Verse 9 says they will deliver you over (ESV), or hand you over (HCSB), to tribulation. If one is handed over, he must first be seized and then delivered to those, who are seeking to do him harm, even death. Why are the Christians hated so? Former Christians and liberal Christians hate the stand that conservative Christians take by truly living by God's Word, in a world that is anything but. Radical Islam is simply trying to impose themselves on everyone who stands in their way of dominating the world. Thus, being handed over is a result of one's true faith in Jesus Christ.

Matthew 24:10 Updated American Standard Version (UASV)

¹⁰ And then many will fall away,⁵⁴ will betray⁵⁵ one another, and will hate one another.

While early Christianity suffered horrible deaths through being martyred for simply being a Christian, the hatred today is just as vile by those that slaughter Christians around the world. Nevertheless, persecution through social media, news media, and by way of lawsuits, and protests in the streets, has become the new form of persecution in the Western world. Many have fallen away from Jesus, becoming apostates toward their former brothers and sisters, loathing their very existence.

Matthew 24:11 Updated American Standard Version (UASV)

¹¹ And many false prophets will arise and will lead many astray

What is a prophet? The primary meaning is one who proclaims the word of God, a spokesperson for God. Therefore, a false prophet would be a spokesperson giving the impression that he is a spokesman for God, but really he is far from it. These ones are very subtle and deceptive in their ability to present themselves as a person representing God. Some modern day examples would be, Jim Bakker, Kenneth Copeland, Benny Hinn, T.D. Jakes, Joyce Meyer, Juanita Bynum, Creflo Dollar, Eddie Long, Pat Robertson, and Joel Olsteen. Of course, these are just some of the televangelists, who are false prophets, with tens of millions of followers. Other false prophet religious leaders have tens of millions of followers as well. Then, there are charismatic Christian denominations that numbered over 500 million followers. These ones claim gifts of God (faith healing, speaking in tongues, etc.), which clearly are anything but. The true Christians are falling away in great numbers, being led astray by these false prophets, and those who have not, need to remain awake!

Matthew 24:12 Updated American Standard Version (UASV)

¹² And because lawlessness will be increased, the love of many will grow cold.

The world we live in is overflowing with murders, rapes, armed robberies, and assaults, not to mention war. It has grown so pervasive

---

⁵⁴ Lit *be caused to stumble*

24:10 many will be offended, lit. "caused to stumble," suggesting professing believers who fall away and even turn against "one another" in shocking acts of spiritual treachery. Those who fall away in such a manner give evidence that they never were true believers (see note on v. 13).—MacArthur, John. The MacArthur Bible Commentary (Kindle Locations 40393-40395). Thomas Nelson. Kindle Edition.

⁵⁵ Or *hand over*

that many have grown callused to seeing the newspapers, websites and television news filled with one heinous crime, one after another. In looking at just one city in the United States, in 2012, 532 people were murdered in the city of Chicago, with a population of 2.7 million. However, in San Pedro Sula of the country Honduras, 1,143 people were murdered with only a population of 719,447. Statistics from the United Nations report 250,000 cases of rape or attempted rape annually. However, it must be kept in mind that because of the savagery of the times, in "many parts of the world, rape is very rarely reported, due to the extreme social stigma cast on women who have been raped, or the fear of being disowned by their families, or subjected to violence, including honor killings."[56]

Verse 12 says that the love of "the love of many will **grow cold**," and indeed it has. There are atrocious crimes against individuals, groups, nations, which would cripple the mind of anyone living decades ago. However, because of seeing it every day, all day long, the world has grown hardened to the lawlessness that exists around them. Christians carry the hope of salvation in their heart, which Jesus addresses next.

Matthew 24:13 Updated American Standard Version (UASV)

¹³ But the one who endures to the end will be saved.

What are we to endure? We are to endure while we maintain our walk with God through false Christs who will lead many astray, the wars, and the natural disasters. We are to endure while we maintain our walk with God through the loss of many of our spiritual brothers and sisters who fall away, the betrayal of former Christians, and the hatred of humankind who is alienated from God. We are to endure while we maintain our walk with God through false prophets that have arisen and lead many astray, the increase of the lawlessness in this world, and the love of humanity growing colder. Yes, each of us, who survives to the end of the Christian era, to the return of Christ, will be saved from Jesus' destruction of the wicked. However, we are not to simply sit around, we have a work to accomplish that is the last sign of the end of the age.

Matthew 24:14 Updated American Standard Version (UASV)

¹⁴ And this gospel of the kingdom will be proclaimed in all the inhabited earth[57] as a testimony to all the nations, and then the end will come.

---

[56] http://en.wikipedia.org/wiki/Rape_statistics

[57] Or *in the whole world*

This is the last of the signs that Jesus gave that should concern us, as it is directly related to the end of the age, and the return of Christ, namely '**the gospel of the kingdom being proclaimed throughout the whole world**.' Jesus makes it very clear what he meant by "the whole world," by then saying "all nations" (Gk., *ethnos*). What Jesus meant here was more directed toward all races, not so much the "nations" that we know the world to be divided into today. Therefore, Jesus speaking of the whole world was a reference to "**a body of persons united by kinship, culture, and common traditions, *nation, people*.**"[58] Today, while for the most part, nations are made up of different races, the world is also becoming a melting pot.

In the phrase "**testimony** to all nations," we find the Greek word *martyrion*, which was a legal term of "**that which serves as testimony or proof, *testimony, proof*.**"[59] The testimony here that is to be shared by Christ's disciples has to with Jesus and the kingdom. Evidence, proof, testimony has the ability to overcome the false reasoning of those in the world, to win them over, as well as convict those who refuse to see the evidence for what it is. Elsewhere Jesus said very clearly,

Matthew 11:15 (UASV)	**Matthew 13:9** (UASV)	**Matthew 13:43** (UASV)
¹⁵ He who has ears to hear, let him hear.	⁹ The one who has ears, let him hear."	⁴³ Then the righteous will shine like the sun in the kingdom of their Father. He who has ears, let him hear.

No One Knows That Day and Hour

Matthew 24:36 Updated American Standard Version (UASV)

³⁶ "But of that day and hour no one knows, not even the angels of heaven, nor the Son, but the Father only.

While none of us can know the precise time of Jesus' return, we do know that we are to be busy in the work that he has given us. Regardless of the time left, how will you use it? Here is how we should use our time before Christ's return. We should **live as though it is tomorrow**, but **plan as though it is 50-years away**. What do we mean by this? We live as though Christ is returning tomorrow, by walking with God, having a

---

[58] William Arndt, Frederick W. Danker, and Walter Bauer, *A Greek-English Lexicon of the New Testament and Other Early Christian Literature* (Chicago: University of Chicago Press, 2000), 276.

[59] IBID, 619.

righteous standing before him. We plan as though it is 50-years away by living a life that makes strategies for a long-term evangelism that fulfills our end of the great commission. (Matt 24:14; 28:19-20; Ac 1:8)

Our sinful nature would not do well if we knew the exact day and hour. We do badly enough when we simply think Christ's return is close. You have had religions that have set dates for Christ's return, or are constantly saying, 'the end is near!' The ones who set actual dates for Christ's return: quit their jobs, sell their homes, take all their money out of the bank, and take their kids out of school, either (1) to have a good time before the end, or (2) to spend the last couple years yelling from the rooftops that "the end is coming!"

Those who are constantly saying, 'the end is near,' are similar, in that they do not take job promotions because it would cut into their evangelism, they do not allow their children to have university educations or plan careers because to them the end is near. Nevertheless, these groups are at least concerned about their evangelism, but fail to realize; we do not know when the end is coming.

We need to find a way in the time that remains, be it 5 years, 50 years, or 500 years, to encourage and foster "sincere brotherly love," and to display "obedience to the truth." What do we need to be obedient to? **(1)** We need to clean up the household of Christianity. **(2)** We need to then, carry out the great commission that Jesus assigned, to preach, to teach, and to make disciples! (Matt 24:14; 28:19-20; Ac 1:8) It is our assignment, in the time remaining, to assist God in helping those with a receptive heart, to accept the good news of the kingdom. Yes, we are offering those of the world, the hope of getting on the path of salvation, an opportunity at everlasting life. Just because we do not know the day or the hour, does not mean that we should be less urgent about this assignment. Remember Jesus' illustration,

Matthew 24:43 Updated American Standard Version (UASV)

43 But know this, that if the master of the house had known in what part of the night the thief was coming, he would have stayed awake and would not have let his house be broken into.

Moreover, remember Jesus' question,

Luke 18:8 Updated American Standard Version (UASV)

8 I tell you that he will bring about justice for them quickly. However, when the Son of Man comes, will he find the faith[60] on the earth?"

---

[60] Or *find this faith*

If we were to consider the chaos within Christianity today, the 41,000 different denominations of Christianity, all believing differently, could we honestly say that Jesus would truly find the faith?

Fairness Restored

Isaiah 2:1-4 Updated American Standard Version (UASV)

¹ The word that Isaiah the son of Amoz saw concerning Judah and Jerusalem.

² It will come to pass in the latter days
   that the mountain of the house of Jehovah
will be established on the top of the mountains,
   and will be lifted up above the hills;
and all the nations will stream to it,
³   and many peoples will come, and say:
"Come, let us go up to the mountain of Jehovah,
   to the house of the God of Jacob,
that he may teach us concerning his ways
   and that we may walk in his paths."
For the law[61] will go forth from Zion,
   and the word of Jehovah from Jerusalem.
⁴ He will judge between the nations,
   and will correct matters for many peoples;
and they shall beat their swords into plowshares,
   and their spears into pruning hooks;
nation shall not lift up sword against nation,
   neither shall they learn war anymore.

On these verses, Trent C. Butler writes, "**2:1**. This section begins with another introduction much like Isaiah 1:1, but this one only introduces the following sermons, not the entire book. What follows is a vision, what Isaiah ... saw. Interestingly, the first part of this vision also appears in Micah 4:1–5. The form of this sermon sounds like a call to worship introduced by a prophetic announcement of salvation. Apparently Isaiah and his younger contemporary Micah both used the same call to worship from the Jerusalem temple to speak to God's people. This would mean that God used the temple hymnody as a source for his inspired word."

"**2:2**. While the destruction of Jerusalem dominated chapter 1, the city's function as the center of salvation for all nations introduces this section. The last days are still within world history with separate nations

---

[61] Or *instruction* or *teaching*

acting. Israel used the same language as her Near Eastern neighbors in talking about the national temple as the highest mountain on earth where the deity fights battles for his people (cp. Pss. 46; 48). The prophet Isaiah applied this language to the temple in Jerusalem even though Jerusalem was obviously not the highest of the mountains Israel could see. Jerusalem would be high and lifted up because God was at work there, causing his purpose for the world to be realized in historical events. The emphasis is not on the height of Jerusalem. The emphasis is on the unheard-of foreign nations coming to Jerusalem to worship. God's hope always encompasses the world, not just one small nation (see Gen. 12:1–4)."

"**2:3–4**. The prophet, as he often did, took up the popular theology of the people's hymnody and subtly shifted it from present to future tense. Only in the last days would Zion occupy such an exalted position. God would no longer battle the nations. Jerusalem could no longer glory in the hope that nations would march to her with large gifts and tribute for her victorious king. The prophetic hope is that God's word will become the world's weapon. Military academies and weapons will vanish. People will learn to live according to God's ways. They will obey his teachings. Nations will come to Jerusalem, not because a victorious king forces them to, but because they are attracted to Jerusalem by the God who lives there and the wisdom he gives there. No longer will they have to fight to settle their differences. In Jerusalem God will be the great Mediator who settles all human disputes without battle. Military weapons will become obsolete. The world's only war will be on poverty and hunger."[62]

Isaiah 11:3-5 Updated American Standard Version (UASV)

³ And he will delight in the fear of Jehovah,
And he will not judge by what his eyes see,
 Nor make a decision by what his ears hear;
⁴ But with righteousness he shall judge the poor,
 And decide with fairness for the meek of the earth;[63]
And he shall strike the earth with the rod of his mouth,
 And with the breath of his lips he shall kill the wicked.
⁵ Righteousness shall be the belt of his waist,
 And faithfulness the belt of his loins.

---

[62] Anders, Max; Butler, Trent (2002-04-01). Holman Old Testament Commentary - Isaiah (p. 29-30). B&H Publishing.

[63] "The Messiah will reverse Israel's earlier dealings with the underprivileged (3:14, 15; 10:2)." – MacArthur, John (2005-05-09). The MacArthur Bible Commentary (Kindle Locations 27444-27445). Thomas Nelson. Kindle Edition.

On these verses, Trent C. Butler writes, "The wise king would enter the royal courtroom to judge his nation correctly. As judge, the king would be empowered with the breath of his lips, the same word translated "Spirit" in verse 2. By this he would protect the poor from the wicked, establishing the economic justice so central to prophetic preaching. The new age established by the new king would bring righteousness, a dominant theme for Isaiah. Coupled with faithfulness, this clothed the king for his royal reign."[64]

Isaiah 42:1 Updated American Standard Version (UASV)

42 Behold my servant, whom I uphold,
  my chosen one, in whom my soul delights;
I have put my Spirit upon him;
  he will bring forth justice to the nations.

On this verse, Trent C. Butler writes, "This is the first of four "Servant Songs" in Isaiah 40-55 (49:1–6; 50:4–9; 52:13–53:12). Here God formally presented the servant to an audience, although both the name of the servant and the nature of the audience remain mysteriously unclear. We do not have to find answers to all our questions about the servant. We need to understand that he is God's chosen one, God takes great delight in him, and God upholds or supports him."

"The servant's mission surprised Israel and it surprises us. His mission was not to deliver Israel from captivity and exile. The mission was for the nations. The servant gained power for his mission from the divine Spirit just as earlier rulers and prophets had. The servant's task was to bring justice to the nations. (For justice, see "Deeper Discoveries," ch. 1.) Justice involves a much broader meaning than the English term. In verse 4 it stands parallel to Torah, law or teaching. It is the verdict handed down by a judge (2 Kgs. 25:6); the whole court process (Isa. 3:14); the gracious and merciful judgment of God (Isa. 30:18); or the natural right and order claimed by a person or group of persons (Exod. 23:6)."

"In our text, the term for the servant's mission apparently encompasses a broad meaning. It refers to the natural world order and the rights expected by the nations of the earth within that order. God restores that order with its natural rights through his gracious and merciful judgment on the basis of his law or teaching."[65]

---

[64] Anders, Max; Butler, Trent (2002-04-01). Holman Old Testament Commentary - Isaiah (p. 83). B&H Publishing.

[65] Anders, Max; Butler, Trent (2002-04-01). Holman Old Testament Commentary - Isaiah (p. 232). B&H Publishing.

Isaiah 35:3-7 Updated American Standard Version (UASV)

³ Strengthen the weak hands,
   and make firm the feeble knees.
⁴ Say to those who have an anxious heart,
   "Be strong; fear not!
Behold, your God
   will come with vengeance,
with the recompense of God.
   He will come and save you."

⁵ Then the eyes of the blind shall be opened,
   and the ears of the deaf unstopped;
⁶ then shall the lame man leap like a deer,
   and the tongue of the mute sing for joy.
For waters break forth in the wilderness,
   and streams in the desert;
⁷ the burning sand shall become a pool,
   and the thirsty ground springs of water;
in the haunt of jackals, where they lie down,
   the grass shall become reeds and rushes.

On these verses, Trent C. Butler writes, "The revelation of God's glory provided the background for a new prophetic commission (vv. 3-4; cp. ch. 6). If God could change the dry wasteland so radically, how much more he could do so for humanity! The prophet was called to encourage the weak and feeble. Their reason for fear would vanish. God would come in vengeance. The divine appearance would destroy the enemy (34:8) but bring salvation to the people of God. Such salvation is not limited to a spiritual realm. The sick and disabled would find all their reasons for having an inferiority complex destroyed."[66]

Isaiah 65:20-23 Updated American Standard Version (UASV)

²⁰ No more shall there be in it
   an infant who lives but a few days,
   or an old man who does not fill out his days,
for the young boy shall die a hundred years old,
   and the sinner a hundred years old shall be accursed.
²¹ They shall build houses and inhabit them;
   they shall plant vineyards and eat their fruit.
²² They shall not build and another inhabit;
   they shall not plant and another eat;

---

[66] Anders, Max; Butler, Trent (2002-04-01). Holman Old Testament Commentary - Isaiah (p. 191). B&H Publishing.

for like the days of a tree will the days of my people be,
  and the work of their hands my chosen ones will enjoy to the full.
²³ They shall not labor in vain
  or bear children for calamity,
for they are the seed⁶⁷ made up of those blessed by Jehovah,,
  and their descendants with them.

On these verses, Trent C. Butler writes, "The injustices of life would disappear. Long life would be the rule for God's people, death at a hundred being like an infant's death that could only be explained as the death of a sinner. All of God's people would live to a ripe old age and enjoy the fruits of their life. The age of Messiah would clearly have dawned (cp. 11:6–9). No longer would people lose their property and crops to foreign invaders. Each of God's faithful people would enjoy the works of their hands. Labor would be rewarded in the field and in the birth place. Every newborn would escape the "horror of sudden disaster" (author's translation; NIV, misfortune). Curses would disappear. Every generation would be blessed by God."⁶⁸

Psalm 37:7-11 Updated American Standard Version (UASV)

⁷ Be still before Jehovah and wait patiently for him;
  do not fret because of the one who prospers in his way,
  because of the man who carries out evil devices!

⁸ Refrain from anger, and forsake wrath.
  Fret not yourself; it leads only to evildoing.
⁹ For the evildoers shall be cut off,
  but those who wait for Jehovah shall inherit the land.
¹⁰ Just a little while longer and the wicked one will be no more;
  And you will look carefully for his place and he will not be there.
¹¹ But the meek shall inherit the land
  and delight themselves in abundant peace.

On these verses, Stephen J. Lawson wrote, "David repeated his original advice: Do not fret when men succeed. He returned to the earlier thought of verse 2—sinners who seem to flourish for a season will eventually be destroyed (Eccl. 3:16–17). To point this out, he used a series of contrasts between the godly and the ungodly. **Refrain from anger**, he declared, because these **evil men** in the final day would be cut off and die before entering eternity damned. **But those who hope in the**

---

⁶⁷ I.e., *offspring*

⁶⁸ Anders, Max; Butler, Trent (2002-04-01). Holman Old Testament Commentary - Isaiah (p. 374). B&H Publishing.

LORD—the meek—**will inherit the land** (cp. Matt. 5:5). This indicated the fullness of God's blessing."[69]

Revelation 21:3-4 Updated American Standard Version (UASV)

3 And I heard a loud voice from the throne, saying, "Behold, the tabernacle of God is among men, and he will dwell[70] among them, and they shall be his people,[71] and God himself will be among them,[72] **4** and he will wipe away every tear from their eyes, and death shall be no more, neither shall there be mourning, nor crying, nor pain anymore, for the former things have passed away."

On these verses, Kendell Easley wrote, "For the third and final time John hears **a loud voice from the throne** (16:17; 19:5). The word for **dwelling** is traditionally translated "tabernacle" or "tent." When the Israelites had lived in the wilderness after the exodus, God's presence was evident through the tent (Exod. 40:34). Part of the reward for Israel's obedience to God was, "I will put my dwelling place [tabernacle] among you, and I will not abhor you. I will walk among you and be your God, and you will be my people" (Lev. 26:11–12). Israel's disobedience, of course, led finally to the destruction of the temple."

"The permanent remedy began when God became enfleshed in Jesus: "The Word became flesh and made his dwelling among us" (John 1:14). A form of the same verb translated "made his dwelling" in John 1:14 is now used by the heavenly voice: **he will live with them**. Here, then, is the final eternal fulfillment of Leviticus 26."

"They will be his people, and God himself will be with them and be their God is a divine promise often made, particularly in context of the new covenant (Jer. 31:33; 32:38; Ezek. 37:27; 2 Cor. 6:16). In eternity, it will find full completion in its most glorious sense. One striking note here is that the word translated "people," while often singular in Revelation (for example, 18:4), here is plural, literally "peoples." This points to the great ethnic diversity of those in heaven."

"The great multitude who came out of the Great Tribulation received the pledge of many blessings including the final removal of any cause for **tears** (7:15–17). Now this promise extends to every citizen-saint

---

[69] Anders, Max; Lawson, Steven (2004-01-01). Holman Old Testament Commentary - Psalms: 11 (p. 199). B&H Publishing.

[70] Lit *he will tabernacle*

[71] Some mss *peoples*

[72] One early ms *and be their God*

of the New Jerusalem. The picture of God himself gently taking a handkerchief and wiping away all tears is overwhelming. It pictures the removal of four more enemies:

- **death**—destroyed and sent to the fiery lake (20:14; 1 Cor. 15:26)

- **mourning**—caused by death and sin, but also ironically the eternal experience of those who loved the prostitute (18:8)

- **crying**—one result of the prostitute's cruelty to the saints (18:24)

- **pain**—the first penalty inflicted on mankind at the Fall is finally lifted at last (Gen. 3:16)"

"All these belonged to **the old order of things** where sin and death were present. The last thought could also be translated, "The former things are gone." No greater statement of the end of one kind of existence and the beginning of a new one can be found in Scripture." (Easley 1998, p. 395)

Resurrection of Life and Judgment

John 5:28-29 Updated American Standard Version (UASV)

28 Do not marvel at this, because an hour is coming when all who are in the memorial tombs will hear his voice **29** and come out, those who have done good things to a resurrection of life, and those who have practiced wicked things to the resurrection of judgment.

When Jesus returns, he will bring many angels, and wipe out the wicked. However, the righteous will not be destroyed, and the righteous prior to Jesus first coming back in the first century, will receive a resurrection. The unrighteous, which had never had the opportunity to know God, will also be resurrected for a chance to hear the Good News, and then, they will be judged on what they do during the millennial reign of Christ. (Acts 24:15) Therefore, the punishment for sin is death, the punishment for those, who "keep on sinning deliberately after receiving the knowledge of the truth, there no longer remains a sacrifice for sins," i.e., eternal death. However, "there will be a resurrection of both the just and the unjust [i.e., those who never heard the Good News]." – Acts 24:15

In death, Scripture show us as being unable to praise God. The Psalmist tells us, "For in death there is no remembrance of you; in Sheol [gravedom] who will give you praise?" (Psa. 6:5) Isaiah the prophet writes, "For Sheol [gravedom] cannot thank you [God], death cannot praise you; those who go down to the pit cannot hope for your faithfulness. 'It is the living who give thanks to you, as I do today; a father tells his sons about your faithfulness.'" – Isaiah 38:18-19.

Passing Over from Death to Life

John 5:24 Updated American Standard Version (UASV)

24 Truly, truly, I say to you, whoever hears my word and believes him who sent me has eternal life. He does not come into judgment, but has passed from death to life.

Regeneration is God restoring and renewing somebody morally or spiritually, where the Christian receives a new quality of life. This one goes from the road of death over to the path of life. (John 5:24) Here he becomes a new person, with a new personality, having removed the old person. (Eph. 4:20-24) **This does not mean** that the imperfection is gone, and the sinful desires are removed, but that he now has the mind of Christ, the Spirit and the Word of God to gain control over his thinking and his fleshly desires. Therefore, if one has truly experienced a conversion, it will be evident by the changes in one's new personality from the old personality, his life, and his actions. If this is the case, he will be fulfilling the words of Jesus, "let your light shine before others, so that they may see your good works and give glory to your Father who is in heaven."—Matthew 5:16.

Can we see one as truly a man of faith, a committed Christian, who attends the meetings, but never carries out any personal study, never shares the gospel with another, never helps his spiritual brothers or sisters (physically, materially, mentally, or spiritually), nor helps his neighbor, or any of the other things one would find within a man of faith? James had something to say about this back in chapter 1:26-27, "If anyone thinks he is religious and does not bridle his tongue but deceives his heart, this person's religion is worthless. A religion that is pure and undefiled before God, the Father, is this: to visit orphans and widows in their affliction, and to keep oneself unstained from the world." One who does not possess real faith, will not help the poor, he will not separate himself from worldly pursuits, he will favor those that he can benefit from (i.e., the powerful and wealthy), and ignore those that he cannot make gains from (i.e., orphans and widows), he will not know the love of God, nor his mercy.—James 2:8-9, 13.

Titus 3:5 Updated American Standard Version (UASV)

5 he saved us, not by deeds of righteousness that we have done, but because of his mercy, through the washing of regeneration and renewal by the Holy Spirit,

The Greek word *polingenesia* means to a renewal or rebirth of a new life in Christ, by the Holy Spirit. Jesus told Nicodemus, "unless someone is born of ... Spirit, he is not able to enter into the kingdom of God." (John 3:5). At the moment a person is converted, he is regenerated or renewed, passing over from death to life eternal. Jesus explains this at John 5:24, "the one who hears my word and who believes the one who sent me has eternal life, and does not come into judgment, but has passed from death into life." The principal feature of rebirth of a new life in Christ, by the Holy Spirit, regeneration, is the passing over from death to life eternal.

At that point, the Spirit dwells within this newly regenerated one. From the time of Adam and Eve, God has desired to dwell with man. God fellowshipped with Adam in the Garden of Eden. After Adam's rebellion, he chose faithful men, to walk with him in their life course, to communicate with them. Enoch, Noah, and Abraham walked with God. In the Hebrew language, the tabernacle is called *mishkan* meaning "dwelling place." In both the tabernacle and the temple, God was represented as dwelling with the people in the Most Holy. He also dwelt with the people through the Son, "And the Word became flesh and dwelt among us, and we have seen his glory, glory as of the only Son from the Father, full of grace and truth." (John 1:14) After Jesus' ascension, God dwelt among the Christians, by way of the Holy Spirit, in the body of each individual Christian, which begins at conversion.

APPENDIX P Does God Step in and Solve Our Every Problem Because We are Faithful?

Edward D. Andrews

Praising God as the Grand Savior

Psalm 42 depicts for us the circumstances of a Levite, one of the offspring's of Korah, who found himself in exile. His inspired words can be very beneficial to us in preserving thankfulness for friendship with fellow Christians and continuing steadfastly while going through hostile conditions.

Thirsting for God as a Deer Thirsts for Water

The psalmist stated,

Psalm 42:1-2 Updated American Standard Version (UASV)

42 As a deer longs for flowing streams of water,
  so my soul longs for you, O God.
2 My soul thirsts for God,
  for the living God.
When shall I come and appear before God?[73]

A female deer cannot survive long without water. If water is low, the deer will risk its life going out of cover to get at the lifesaving water, even though she knows that the prey could attack at any moment. Like the deer that longs for water because it is a matter of life or death, the psalmist longed for God. The word "pants" in the Hebrew means "to have a keen, consuming desire for." His driving passion was not for people, possessions, or prosperity but for God."[74]

---

[73] Some mss read *see the face of God*

[74] Anders, Max; Lawson, Steven (2004-01-01). *Holman Old Testament Commentary - Psalms: 11* (p. 224). B&H Publishing.

The Bible lands are a dry country, where the vegetation wastes away rapidly throughout the dry season, and water is a very valuable commodity, as it is limited in the extreme. That is why the Psalmist says that he was a 'soul thirsting for God.' He had been going without his essential spiritual needs being satisfied, that is the freedom of going to the sanctuary; therefore, he asks when he might again "appear before God."

He had been confined because of persecution, which prevented him from having contact with his fellow believers, which resulted in intense sadness, unhappiness, and hopelessness, as verse three indicates.

Psalm 42:3 Updated American Standard Version (UASV)

³ My tears have been my food
    day and night,
while they say to me all the day long,
    "Where is your God?"

Because of this hostile situation, the Psalmist was depressed to the point of being unable to eat. Therefore, his 'tears were his food.' Yes, "day and night" tears would roll down his cheeks into his mouth. His isolation and distress were not enough, as his enemies aggravated his wounds by provoking, ridiculing, in a hurtful or mocking way, as they would say all day long, "Where is your God?" He needed to find a way to reassure himself during this time of difficulty, to not be overrun by sorrow and heartache.

Why am I in Despair?

Psalm 42:4-6 Updated American Standard Version (UASV)

⁴ These things I remember,
    as I pour out my soul:
how I would go with the throng
    and lead them in procession to the house of God
with a voice of joy and thanksgiving,
    a multitude keeping festival.

    ⁵ Why are you cast down, O my soul,
    and why are you in turmoil within me?
Hope in God; for I shall again praise him,
    for the salvation of before him. ⁶ O my God, within me my soul is cast down within me;
    therefore I remember you
from the land of Jordan and the heights of Hermon,
    from Mount Mizar.

Here we find the Psalmist not living in the moment of suffering, but rather remembering a time before he was in exile. He 'pours out his soul,' reaching the depths of his inner self with such passion, as he reminisces within about the former days. The Levite recalls in his mind what life was like when he was in his land, as he lived and worshiped with his brother and sister Israelites, as they walked "to the house of God," to celebrate the festival. Initially, these memories did not bring joy, but the pain of knowing they were a thing of the past, deeply missed.

Then, he asked himself, "Why are you cast down, O my soul and why are you in turmoil within me"? At that moment, he realized that his hope of salvation was not in himself, but in God. Therefore, the sweet memories truly brought him relief! He knew that if he patiently waited, God would act in his behalf. He then knew that his unfavorable conditions were not going to define his faith that, in time God would aid him in his time of need. When that moment would happen, he would "praise him" for 'his salvation' and being 'his God.' He might have been far removed from the sanctuary, but the Psalmist kept his God at the forefront of his mind.

If we ever find ourselves in difficult times, unrelenting times, we need to follow the pattern set by the Psalmist. We need to remember that God is well aware of our circumstances, and he will not forsake us. We must realize that the issues that were raised by Satan in the Garden of Eden, the sovereignty of God, the rightfulness of his rulership, and the issues raised by Satan to God in the book of Job, the loyalty of God's creatures, are greater than we are.

Proverbs 3:25-26 Updated American Standard Version (UASV)

[25] Do not be afraid of sudden panic[75]
   or the storm of the wicked, when it comes,
[26] for Jehovah will be your confidence
   and will keep your foot from being caught.

Before delving into the rest of Psalm 42, let us take a moment to establish what these verses do not mean. Should we understand that these verses or any others in Scripture teach that because we are wisely walking with God that he will miraculously step in to protect each servant personally from difficult times, diseases, mental disorders, injury or death? No. These sorts of miracles are the extreme exception to the rule. Of the 4,000 plus years of Bible history, from Adam to Jesus, with tens of millions of people living and dying, we have but a few dozen miracles that we know of in Scripture. Even in Bible times, miracles were not

---

[75] Or *fear, dread, terror*

typical, far from it. Hundreds of years may pass with no historical record of a miracle happening at all.

If we are wisely walking with God, we can be confident that bodily disease, mental disorders, injury or early death is far less likely than if we were not. Moreover, we can draw on the resurrection hope. Does God miraculously move events to save us out of difficult times or miraculously heal us? Yes, he certainly can, but it is an extreme exception to the rule. He miraculously heals those who are going to play a significant role in his settling of the issues that were raised in the Garden of Eden.

What God's Word teaches us is this, that if we walk by using discernment and exercising sound judgment from Scripture, unless unexpected events befall us, we can be sure that we will not stumble into the difficulties that the world of humankind alienated from God faces every day. Conversely, the wicked do not have this protection as they reject the Word of God as foolish. In other words, Christians live by the moral values of Scripture, which gives them an advantage over those who do not. Therefore, God answers our prayers by our faithfully acting in behalf of those prayers, by applying Scripture in a balanced manner. If we have not taken in a deep understanding of God's Word, how can we have the Spirit-inspired wisdom, the very knowledge of God to guide and direct us in our ways? Just because we are not being rescued when we feel that we should, this does not mean that we have lost faith, or that God is displeased. Even though the Psalmist had no doubt that Jehovah God was coming to his aid, he still experienced grief.

Psalm 42:7 Updated American Standard Version (UASV)

7 Deep calls to deep
   at the roar of your waterfalls;
all your breakers and your waves
   have gone over me.

Yes, the Psalmist's surroundings of his exile were very beautiful; however, they brought him back to the reality of his difficulty! Verse 7 may very well be describing the snow on Mount Hermon when it melts. Marvelous waterfalls are fashioned, which pour into the Jordan, causing it to increase in size. It is as though one wave is speaking to another wave. This extraordinary spectacle of power brought to the Psalmist's mind that he had been consumed by distress as if being overcome by a flood. Nevertheless, his faith in God does not waiver

Psalm 42:8 Updated American Standard Version (UASV)

⁸ By day Jehovah commands his steadfast love,
  and at night his song is with me,
  a prayer to the God of my life.

There is no doubt in the Psalmist's mind that Jehovah God will engulf him with his steadfast love, freeing him of anxiety. This will empower him to praise God in song and to offer a prayer of thanks 'to the God of his life.'

The Korahite Levite thinks,

Psalm 42:9-10 Updated American Standard Version (UASV)

⁹ I say to God, my rock:
  "Why have you forgotten me?
Why do I go mourning
  because of the oppression of the enemy?"
¹⁰ As with a shattering of my bones,
  my adversaries taunt me,
while they say to me all the day long,
  "Where is your God?"

Then, it seems that the Psalmist slips, even though he views God as 'his rock,' a place of protection from one's enemies. Yes, he now asks, "Why have you forgotten me?" Yes, the Psalmist was allowed to remain in his circumstances of sadness, feeling depressed, as his enemies took pleasure in what appeared to be a victory. The psalmist speaks of himself as being criticized in an unbearable way. So malicious was the mockery and disdain that it could be likened 'as with a deadly wound in his bones.' However, the Levite again comes to himself with self-talk, challenging his irrational thinking with rational thinking.

Wait for God

Psalm 42:11 Updated American Standard Version (UASV)

¹¹ Why are you cast down, O my soul?
  And why are you disturbed within me?
Hope in God; for I shall again praise him,
  my salvation and my God.

It is not the troubles of the Psalmist, which actually caused him to feel bad. It is what he told himself that contributed to how he felt. Self-talk is what we tell ourselves in our thoughts. In fact, self-talk is the words we tell ourselves about people, self, experiences, life in general, God, the future, the past, the present; it is specifically all the words we say to ourselves all the time. Destructive self-talk, even subconsciously, can be very harmful to our mood: causing mood slumps, our self-worth plummeting, our body feeling sluggish, our will to accomplish even the smallest of things is not to be realized and our actions defeat us.

Intense negative thinking of the Psalmist led to his feeling forsaken, resulting in painful emotions, and depressive state. However, his thoughts based on a good mood were entirely different from those based on his being upset. Negative thoughts that flooded his mind were the actual contributors of his self-defeating emotions. These very thoughts were what kept the Psalmist sluggish and contributed to his feeling abandoned. Therefore, his thinking was also the key to his relief.

Every time the Psalmist felt down because of his irrational self-talk, he attempted to locate the corresponding negative thought he had to this feeling. It was those thoughts that created his feelings of low self-worth. By offsetting them and replacing them with rational thoughts, he actually changed his mood. The negative thoughts that move through his mind did so with no effort, and were the easiest course to follow, because imperfect human tendencies gave him that way of thinking, a pattern of thinking. However, the Psalmist challenged those irrational thoughts of being forsaken with rational ones, saying that he would hope in God and that he would continue to praise him as in the end God is his salvation, even if that salvation comes in the form of a resurrection.

The centerpiece to it all is our Christlike mine. Our moods, behaviors and body responses result from the way we view things (fleshly or spiritual). It is a proven fact that we cannot experience any event in any way, shape, or form unless we have processed it with our mind first. No event can depress us; it is our perception of that event that will contribute to intense sadness, even depression. If we are only sad over an event, our thoughts will be rational, but if we are depressed or anxious over an event, our thinking will be bent and irrational, distorted and utterly wrong.

If we are to remain rational in our thinking, we need to grasp the fact that God does not always step in when we believe he should, nor is he obligated to do so. As was stated earlier, he has greater issues that need resolving, which have eternal effects for the whole of humankind. There is far more times that when God does not step in, meaning that our relief may come in the hope of the resurrection. However, for his servants that apply his Word in a balanced manner, fully, God is acting in their best interest by way of his inspired, inerrant Word.

APPENDIX Q How Are We to Understand the Indwelling of the Holy Spirit?

Edward D. Andrews

1 Corinthians 3:16 Updated American Standard Version (UASV)

¹⁶ Do you not know that you are a temple of God and that the Spirit of God dwells in you?

Before delving into the phrase, "indwelling of the Holy Spirit, let us consider the **mistaken view** of New Testament scholars Simon J. Kistemaker and William Hendriksen, who wrote,

> The Spirit of God lives within you." The church is holy because God's Spirit dwells in the hearts and lives of the believers. In 6:19 Paul indicates that the Holy Spirit lives in the physical bodies of the believers. But now he tells the Corinthians that the presence of the Spirit is within them and they are the temple of God.
>
> The Corinthians should know that they have received the gift of God's Spirit. Paul had already called attention to the fact that they had not received the spirit of the world but the Spirit of God (2:12). He teaches that Christians are controlled not by sinful human nature but by the Spirit of God, who is dwelling within them (Rom. 8:9).
>
> The behavior—strife, jealousy, immorality, and permissiveness—of the Christians in Corinth was reprehensible. By their conduct the Corinthians were desecrating God's temple and, as Paul writes in another epistle, were grieving the Holy Spirit (Eph. 4:30; compare 1 Thess. 5:19).[76]

First, it must be told that I am almost amazed at how so many Bible scholars say nonsensical things, contradictory things when it comes to the Holy Spirit. Bible Commentators use many verses to say that the Holy Spirit literally,

(1) **dwells in** the individual Christian believers,

(2) having **control over** them,

---

[76] Simon J. Kistemaker and William Hendriksen, *Exposition of the First Epistle to the Corinthians*, vol. 18, New Testament Commentary (Grand Rapids: Baker Book House, 1953–2001), 117

(3) **enabling them** to live a righteous and faithful life,[77]

(4) with the believer **still being able to sin**, even to the point of grieving the Holy Spirit (Eph. 4:30).

Let us walk through this again, and please take it slow, ponder whether it makes sense, is reasonable, logical, even Scriptural. The Holy Spirit literally dwells in individual believers, controlling them so they can live a righteous and faithful life, yet they can still freely sin, even to the point of grieving the Holy Spirit. Does this mean that the Holy Spirit is not powerful enough to prevent their sinful nature from affecting them? The commentators say the Holy Spirit now controls the Christian, not their sinful nature. If that were true, it must mean the Holy Spirit is ineffectual and less powerful than their sinful nature of the Christian, because the Christian can still reject the Holy Spirit and sin to the point of grieving the Holy Spirit. If the Holy Spirit is controlling the individual Christian, how is it possible that he still possesses free will?

Let us return to the phrase of "indwelling of the Holy Spirit." Just how often do we find "indwelling" in the Bible? I have looked at over fifty English translations and found it once in the King James Version ad two in an earlier version of the New American Standard Bible. One reference is to sin dwelling within us, and the other reference is to the Holy Spirit dwelling within us.

The Updated American Standard Version removed such usage. We may be asking ourselves since "indwelling" is almost nonexistent in the Scriptures, why the commentaries, Bible encyclopedias, Hebrew and Greek word dictionaries, Bible dictionaries, pastors and Christians using it to such an extent, especially in reference to the Holy Spirit? I say in reference to the Holy Spirit because some scholars refer to the indwelling of Christ and the Word of God.

Before addressing those questions, we must take a look at the Greek word behind 1 Corinthians 3:16 "the Spirit of God **dwells [οἰκέω]** in you." The transliteration of our Greek word is *oikeo*. It means "'to dwell' (from *oikos*, 'a house'), 'to inhabit as one's abode,' is derived from the Sanskrit, *vic*, 'a dwelling place' (the Eng. termination —'wick' is connected). It is used (a) of God as 'dwelling' in light, 1 Tim. 6:16; (b) of the 'indwelling' of the Spirit of God in the believer, Rom. 8:9, 11, or in a church, 1 Cor. 3:16; (c) of the 'indwelling' of sin, Rom. 7:20; (d) of the

---

[77] Millard J. Erickson, *Introducing Christian Doctrine* (Grand Rapids: Baker Book House, 1992), 265–270

absence of any good thing in the flesh of the believer, Rom. 7:18; (e) of the 'dwelling' together of those who are married, 1 Cor. 7:12-13."[78]

Thus, for our text, it means the Holy Spirit is dwelling in true Christians. The TDNT tells us, "Jn.'s μένειν [menein] corresponds to Paul's οἰκεῖν [oikein], cf. Jn. 1:33: καταβαῖνον καὶ μένον ἐπ' αὐτόν [descending and remaining upon him]. The new possession of the Spirit is more than ecstatic."[79] What does TDNT mean? It means that John is using *meno* ("to remain," "to stay" or "to abide") in the same way that Paul is using *oikeo* ('to dwell').

When we are considering the Father or the Son alone, and even the Father and the Son together, we are able to have a straightforward conversation. However, when we get to the Holy Spirit, we tend to get off into mysterious and mystical thinking. When we think of humans, and the words *dwell* and *abide*, both have the sense of where we 'live or reside in a place.'

However, there is another sense of 'where we might stand on something,' 'our position on something.' Thus, in English dwell and abide can be used interchangeably, similarly, just as Paul and John use *meno* "abide" or "remain" and *oikeo* "dwell" similarly. Let us look at the apostle John's use of meno,

1 John 4:16 Updated American Standard Version (UASV)

16 We have come to know and have believed the love which God has for us. God is love, and the one who remains **[meno]** in love remains in God, and God remains **[meno]** in him.

Here we notice that God is the embodiment of "love" and if we **abide in** or **remain in** that love, God then **abides in** or **remain in** us. We do not attach any mysterious or mystical sense to this verse, such as God literally being in us and us being in God. If we suggest that this verse, i.e., God being in us, means his taking control of our lives, does our being in God, also mean we control his life? We would think to suggest such a thing is unreasonable, illogical, nonsensical, and such. Commentator Max Anders in the *Holman New Testament Commentary* says, "This is the test of true Christianity in the letters of John. We must recognize the basic character of God, rooted in love. We must experience that love in our own relationship with God. Others must

---

[78] W. E. Vine, Merrill F. Unger, and William White Jr., *Vine's Complete Expository Dictionary of Old and New Testament Words* (Nashville, TN: T. Nelson, 1996), 180.

[79] Gerhard Kittel, Geoffrey W. Bromiley, and Gerhard Friedrich, eds., *Theological Dictionary of the New Testament* (Grand Rapids, MI: Eerdmans, 1964–)

experience this God kind of love in their relationships with us." (Walls and Anders 1999, 211) Our love for God and man is the motivating factor in what we do and not do as Christians. John is saying that we need to remain in that love if we are to remain in God and God is to remain in us. We may be thinking, well, is it not true that God guides and direct us? Yes, however, this is because we have given our lives over to him.

1 John 2:14 Updated American Standard Version (UASV)

¹⁴ I have written to you, fathers, because you know Him who has been from the beginning. I have written to you, young men, because you are strong, and the word of God remains [*meno*] in you, and you have overcome the evil one.

Here we see that the Word of God abides or remains in us. Does this mean that the Word of God is literally within our body, controlling us? No, this means that our love for God and our love for his Word is a motivating factor in our walk with God. We are one with the Father as Jesus was and is one with the Father, and he is one with us. Listen to the words of Paul in the book of Hebrews,

Hebrews 4:12 Updated American Standard Version (UASV)

¹² For the word of God is living and active and sharper than any two-edged sword, and piercing as far as the division of soul and spirit, of both joints and marrow, and able to judge the thoughts and intentions of the heart.

Is the Word of God literally living, and an animate thing? No, it is an inanimate object. Is our Bible literally sharper than a two-edged sword? No, if we decide to stab someone with it, it would look quite silly. Is the Word of God literally able to pierce our joints and marrow? No, again, this would seem ridiculous. If we literally hold the Bible up to our head, is it able to discern our thinking, what we intend to do? What did Paul mean? The Word of God does these things by our being able to evaluate ourselves by looking into the light of the Scriptures, which helps us to identify the intentions of our heart, i.e., inner person. When we meditatively read God's Word daily and ponder what the author meant, we are taking into our mind, God's thoughts and intentions. When we accept the Bible as the inspired, inerrant Word of God, take its counsel and apply its principles in our lives, it will have an impact on our conscience. The conscience is the moral code that God gave Adam and Eve, our mental power or ability that enables us to reason between what is good and what is bad. (Rom. 9:1) Then, the inner voice within us is not entirely ours, but is also God's Word, empowering us to avoid choosing the wrong path.

1 John 2:24 Updated American Standard Version (UASV)

²⁴ As for you, let that remain [*meno*] in you which you heard from the beginning. If what you heard from the beginning remains [*meno*] in you, you also will remain [*meno*] in the Son and in the Father.

Those who had followed Jesus **from the beginning** of his three and half ministry cleaved to what they had heard about the Father and the Son. Therefore, if the same truths are within our heart, inner person, our mental power or ability, we too can **abide** or **remain [*meno*]** in the Son and the Father. (John 17:3) It is as James said, if we draw close to God, through his Word the Bible, he will draw close to us. (Jam. 4:8) In other words, God becomes a part of us and we a part of him through the Word of God that is "living and active, sharper than any two-edged sword, piercing to the division of soul and of spirit, of joints and of marrow, and discerning the thoughts and intentions of the heart."

In John chapter 14, we see this two-way relationship more closely. Jesus said, "Believe me that I am in the Father and the Father is in me, or else believe on account of the works themselves." **(14:11)** He also said, "In that day you will know that I am in my Father, and you in me, and I in you." **(14:20)** We see that the Father and Son have a close relationship, a relationship that we are invited to join.

All through the above discussion of the Father and the Son, we likely had no problem following the line of thought. However, once we interject the Holy Spirit, it is as though our common sense is thrown out. Christians know that the Father and the Son reside in heaven. They also understand that when we speak of the Word of God, the Father and the Son dwelling in us, it is in reference to our being one with them, our unified relationship, by way of the Word of God. However, when we contemplate the Holy Spirit, it is as though our mental powers shut down, and we enter the realms of the mysterious and mysticism. However, we just understood John **14:11** and **14:20**, i.e., how Jesus is in the Father, the Father in Jesus, and their being in us. So, let us now consider the verses that lie between verse **11** and **20**.

Jesus Promises the Holy Spirit

John 14:16-17 English Standard Version (ESV)

¹⁶ And I will ask the Father, and he will give you another Helper, to be with you forever, ¹⁷ even the Spirit of truth, whom the world cannot receive, because it neither sees him nor knows him. You know him, for he dwells [*meno*] with you and will be in you.

John 14:16-17 Updated American Standard Version (UASV)

16 And I will ask the Father, and he will give you another Helper, that he may be with you forever; **17** the Spirit of truth, whom the world cannot receive, because it does not see him or know him, but you know him because he remains [*meno*] with you and will be in you.

Do we not find it a bit disconcerting that, all along when looking at John's writings as to the Son and the Father abiding [*meno*] in one another, in us, and us in them. In those places, the translation rendered *meno* as abiding, but now that the Holy Spirit is mentioned, they render *meno* as "dwell."

Do these verses call for us to; drive off the path of reason, into the realms of mysteriousness and mysticism talk? No, these verses are very similar to our 1 John 2:24 that we dealt with above, but will quote again, "Let what you heard from the beginning **abide [meno]** in you. If what you heard from the beginning **abides [meno]** in you, then you too will **abide [meno]** in the Son and in the Father." In 1 John 2:24, we are told that if the Word of God that we heard from the beginning of being a Christian, **abides [meno]** in us, we will **abide [meno]** in the Son and the Father. In John 14:15-17, if we keep Jesus' commands, the Holy Spirit will **dwell**, actually **abide [meno]** in us. In all of this, the common denominator has been the spirit inspired, fully inerrant Word of God. It is what we are to take into our mind and heart, which will affect change in our person, and enable us to abide or remain in the Father and the Son, and they in us, as well as the Holy Spirit, abiding or remaining in us.

The Holy Spirit, through the Spirit-inspired, inerrant Word of God is the motivating factor for our taking off the old person and putting on the new person. (Eph. 4:20-24; Col. 3:8-9) It is also the tool used by God so that we can "be transformed by the renewal of your mind, so that you may approve what is the good and well-pleasing and perfect will of God." (Rom. 12:2; See 8:9) *The Theological Dictionary of the New Testament* compares this line of thinking with Paul's reference, at Romans 7:20, to the "sin that dwells within me."

The dwelling of sin in man denotes its dominion over him, its lasting connection with his flesh, and yet also a certain distinction from it. The sin which dwells in me (ἡ οἰκοῦσα ἐν ἐμοὶ ἁμαρτία) is no passing guest, but by its continuous presence becomes the master of the house (cf. Str.-B., III, 239).[80] Paul can speak in just the same way, however, of the lordship of the Spirit. The community knows (οὐκ οἴδατε, a reference to catechetical

---

[80] Str.-B. H. L. Strack and P. Billerbeck, *Kommentar zum NT aus Talmud und Midrasch*, 1922 ff.

instruction, 1 C. 3:16) that the Spirit of God dwells in the new man (ἐν ὑμῖν οἰκεῖ, 1 C. 3:16; R. 8:9, 11). This "dwelling" is more than ecstatic rapture or impulsion by a superior power.[81]

How does the Holy Spirit control a Christian? Certainly, some mysterious or mystical feeling does not control him.

Paul told the Christians in Rome,

Romans 12:2 Updated American Standard Version (UASV)

2 And do not be conformed to this world, but be transformed by the **renewing of your mind**, so that you may prove what the will of God is, that which is good and acceptable and perfect.

Just how do we **renew our mind**? This is done by taking in an accurate knowledge of Biblical truth, which enables us to meet God's current standards of righteousness. (Titus 1:1) This Bible knowledge, if applied, will allow us to move our mind in a different direction, by filling the void, after having removed our former sinful practices, with the principles of God's Word, principles that guide our actions, especially ones that guide moral behavior.

Psalm 119:105 Updated American Standard Version (UASV)

105 Your word is a lamp to my feet
and a light to my path.

The Biblical truths that lay in between Genesis 1:1 and Revelation 22:21 will transform our way of thinking, which will in return affect our mood and actions and our inner person. It will be as the apostle Paul said to the Ephesians. We need to "to put off your old self, which belongs to your former manner of life and is corrupt through deceitful desires, and to be renewed in the spirit of your minds, and to put on the new self, created after the likeness of God in true righteousness and holiness ..." (Eph. 4:22-24) This force that contributes to our acting or behaving in a certain way, for our best interest is internal.

Paul told the Christians in Colossae,

Colossians 3:9-11 Updated American Standard Version (UASV)

9 Do not lie to one another, seeing that you have put off the old man[82] with its practices **10** and have put on the new man[83] who is being

---

[81] Gerhard Kittel, Geoffrey W. Bromiley, and Gerhard Friedrich, eds., *Theological Dictionary of the New Testament* (Grand Rapids, MI: Eerdmans, 1964–), 135

renewed through accurate knowledge[84] according to the image of the one who created him, **11** where there is not Greek and Jew, circumcised and uncircumcised, barbarian, Scythian, slave, free; but Christ is all, and in all.

Science has indeed taken us a long way in our understanding of how the mind works, but it is only a grain of sand on the beach of sand in comparison to what we do not know. We have enough of these basics to understand some fundamental processes. When we open our eyes to the light of a new morning, it is altered into and electrical charge by the time it arrives at the gray matter of our brain's cerebral cortex. As the sound of the morning birds reaches our gray matter, it comes as electrical impulses. The rest of our senses (smell, taste, and touch) arrive as electrical currents in the brain's cortex as well. The white matter of our brain lies within the cortex of gray matter, used as a tool to send electrical messages to other cells in other parts of the gray matter. Thus, when anyone of our five senses detects danger, at the speed of light, a message is sent to the motor section, to prepare us for the needed action of either fight or flight.

Here lies the key to altering our way of thinking. Every single thought, whether it is conscious or subconscious makes an electrical path through the white matter of our brain, with a record of the thought and event. This holds true with our actions as well. If it is a repeated way of thinking or acting, it has no need to form a new path; it only digs a deeper, ingrained, established path.

This would explain how a factory worker who has been on the job for some time, gives little thought as he performs his repetitive functions each day; it becomes unthinking, automatic, mechanical. These repeated actions become habitual. There is yet another facet to be considered; the habits, repeated thoughts, and actions become simple and effortless to repeat. Any new thoughts and actions are harder to perform, as there need to be new pathways opened up.

The human baby starts with a blank slate, with a minimal amount of stable paths built in to survive those first few crucial years. As the boy grows into childhood, there is a flood of pathways established, more than all of the internet connections worldwide.

Our five senses are continuously adding to the maze. Ps. 139:14: "I will give thanks to you, for I am fearfully and wonderfully made. . . ."

---

[82] Or *old person*

[83] Or *new person*

[84] See Romans 3:20 ftn.

(NASB) So, it could never be overstated as to the importance of the foundational thinking and behavior that should be established in our children from infancy forward.

Paul told the Christians in Ephesus,

Ephesians 4:20-24 Updated American Standard Version (UASV)

20 But you did not learn Christ in this way, **21** if indeed you have heard him and have been taught in him, just as truth is in Jesus, **22** that you take off, according to your former way of life, the old man, who is being destroyed according to deceitful desires, **23** and to be **renewed in the spirit of your minds**, **24** and put on the new man,[85] the one created according to the likeness of God in righteousness and loyalty of the truth.

How are we to understand being **renewed in the spirit of our minds**? Christian living is carried out through the study and application of God's Word, in which, our spirit (mental disposition), is in harmony with God's Spirit. Our day-to-day decisions are made with a biblical mind, a biblically guided conscience, and a heart that is motivated by love of God and neighbor. Because we have,

- Received the Word of God,
- treasured up the Word of God,
- have been attentive to the Word of God,
- inclining our heart to understanding the Word of God,
- calling out for insight into the Word of God,
- raising our voice for understanding of the Word of God,
- sought the Word of God like silver,
- have searched for the Word of God like gold,
- we have come to understand the fear of God, and have
- found the very knowledge of God, which now
- leads and directs us daily in our Christian walk.

---

[85] An interpretive translation would have, "put on the new person," because it does mean male or female.

Proverbs 23:7 New King James Version (NKJV)

⁷ For as he thinks in his heart, so is he. "Eat and drink!" he says to you, But his heart is not with you. [Our thinking affects our emotions, which in turn affects our behavior.]

Irrational thinking produces irrational feelings, which will produce wrong moods, leading to wrong behavior. It may be difficult for each of us to wrap our mind around it, but we are very good at telling ourselves outright lies and half-truths, repeatedly throughout each day. In fact, some of us are so good at it that it has become our reality and leads to mental distress and bad behaviors.

When we couple our leaning toward wrongdoing with the fact that Satan the devil, who is "the god of this world," (2 Co 4:4) has worked to entice these leanings, the desires of the fallen flesh; we are even further removed from our relationship with our loving heavenly Father. During these 'last days, grievous times' has fallen on us as Satan is working all the more to prevent God's once perfect creation to achieve a righteous standing with God and entertaining the hope of eternal life. – 2 Timothy 3:1-5.

When we enter the pathway of walking with our God, we will certainly come across resistance from three different areas (Our sinful nature, Satan and demons, and the world that caters to our flesh). **Our greatest obstacle** is **ourselves** because we have inherited imperfection from our first parents Adam and Eve. The Scriptures make it quite clear that we are **mentally bent toward bad**, not good. (Gen 6:5; 8:21, AT) In other words, our natural desire is toward wrong. Prior to sinning, Adam and Eve were perfect, and they had the natural desire of doing good, and to go against that was to go against the grain of their inner person. Scripture also tells us of our inner person, our heart.

Jeremiah 17:9 Updated American Standard Version (UASV)

⁹ The **heart is more deceitful** than all else,
and desperately sick;
who can understand it?

Jeremiah's words should serve as a wake-up call, if we are to be pleasing in the eyes of our heavenly Father, we must focus on our inner person. Maybe we have been a Christian for many years; maybe we have a deep knowledge of Scripture, perhaps we feel that we are spiritually strong, and nothing will stumble us. Nevertheless, our heart can be enticed by secret desires, where he fails to dismiss them; he eventually commits a serious sin.

Our conscious thinking (aware) and subconscious thinking (present in our mind without our being aware of it) originates in the mind. For good, or for bad, our mind follows certain rules of action, which if entertained one will move even further in that direction until they are eventually consumed for good or for bad. In our imperfect state, our bent thinking will lean toward wrong, especially with Satan using his world, with so many forms of entertainment that simply feeds the flesh.

James 1:14-15 Updated American Standard Version (UASV)

14 But each one is tempted when he is carried away and enticed by his own desire.[86] 15 Then the desire when it has conceived gives birth to sin, and sin when it is fully grown brings forth death.

1 John 2:16 Updated American Standard Version (UASV)

16 For all that is in the world, the lust of the flesh and the lust of the eyes and the boastful pride of life, is not from the Father, but is from the world.

Matthew 5:28 Updated American Standard Version (UASV)

28 but I say to you that everyone who looks at a woman with lust[87] for her has already committed adultery with her in his heart.

1 Peter 1:14 Updated American Standard Version (UASV)

14 As children of obedience,[88] do not be conformed according to the desires you formerly had in your ignorance,

If we do not want to be affected by the world of humankind around us, which is alienated from God, we must again consider the words of the Apostle Paul's. He writes (Rom 12:2) "Do not be conformed to this world, but be transformed by the renewal of your mind that by testing you may discern what is the will of God, what is good and acceptable and perfect." Just how do we do that? This is done by taking in an accurate knowledge of Biblical truth, which enables us to meet God's current standards of righteousness. (Titus 1:1) This Bible knowledge, if applied, will enable us to move our mind in a different direction, by filling the void with the principles of God's Word, principles that guide our actions, especially ones that guide moral behavior.

---

[86] Or "own *lust*"

[87] ἐπιθυμία [*Epithumia*] to strongly desire to have what belongs to someone else and/or to engage in an activity which is morally wrong—'to covet, to lust, evil desires, lust, desire.'— GELNTBSD

[88] I.e., *obedient children*

Psalm 119:105 Updated American Standard Version (UASV)

¹⁰⁵ Your word is a lamp to my feet
and a light to my path.

We have said this before but it bears repeating. The Biblical truths that lay in between Genesis 1:1 and Revelation 22:21 will transform our way of thinking, which will in return affect our mood and actions and our inner person. It will be as the apostle Paul set it out to the Ephesians. We need to "to put off your old self, which belongs to your former manner of life and is corrupt through deceitful desires, and to be renewed in the spirit of your minds, and to put on the new self, created after the likeness of God in true righteousness and holiness ..." (Eph. 4:22-24) This force that contributes to our acting or behaving in a certain way, for our best interest is internal.

Bringing This Transformation About

The mind is the mental ability that we use in a conscious way to garner information and to consider ideas and come to conclusions. Therefore, if we perceive our realities based on the information, which surrounds us, generally speaking, most are inundated in a world that reeks of Satan's influence. This means that our perception, our attitude, thoughts, speech, and conduct are in opposition to God and his Word. Most are in true ignorance to the changing power of God's Word. The apostle Paul helps us to appreciate the depths of those who reflect this world's disposition. He writes,

Ephesians 4:17-19 Updated American Standard Version (UASV)

¹⁷ This, therefore, I say and bear witness to in the Lord, that you no longer walk as the Gentiles [unbelievers] also walk, in the futility of their mind [emptiness, idleness, slugishness, vanity, foolishness, purposelessness], ¹⁸ being darkened in their understanding [mind being the center of human perception], alienated from the life of God, because of the ignorance that is in them, because of the hardness of their heart [hardening as if by calluses, unfeeling]; ¹⁹ who being past feeling gave themselves up to shameless conduct,[89] for the practice of every uncleanness with greediness.

---

[89] Or "loose conduct," "sensuality," "licentiousness" "promiscuity" Greek, *aselgeia*. This phrase refers to acts of conduct that are serious sins. It reveals a shameless condescending arrogance; i.e., disregard or even disdain for authority, laws, and standards.

Hebrews 4:12 Updated American Standard Version (UASV)

¹² For the word of God is living and active and sharper than any two-edged sword, and piercing as far as the division of soul and spirit, of both joints and marrow, and able to judge the thoughts and intentions of the heart.

By taking in this knowledge of God's Word, we will be altering our way of thinking, which will affect our emotions and behavior, as well as our lives now and for eternity. This Word will influence our minds, making corrections in the way we think. If we are to have the Holy Spirit controlling our lives, we must 'renew our mind' (Rom. 12:2) "which is being renewed in knowledge" (Col. 3:10) of God and his will and purposes. (Matt 7:21-23; See Pro 2:1-6) All of this boils down to each individual Christian digging into the Scriptures in a meditative way, so he can 'discover the knowledge of God, receiving wisdom; from God's mouth, as well as knowledge and understanding.' (Pro. 2:5-6) As he acquires the mind that is inundated with the Word of God, he must also,

James 1:22-25 Updated American Standard Version (UASV)

²² But be doers of the word, and not hearers only, deceiving yourselves. ²³ For if anyone is a hearer of the word and not a doer, he is like a man who looks intently at his natural face[90] in a mirror.

²⁴ for he looks at himself and goes away, and immediately forgets what sort of man he was. ²⁵ But he that looks into the perfect law, the law of liberty, and abides by it, being no hearer who forgets but a doer of a work, he will be blessed in his doing.

---

[90] Lit *the face of his birth*

CHAPTER I

Paragraph 3. Subject of class essay: Paul and the other Apostles: Points of Connection and Contrast.

5. Subject of class essay: Relation of Christianity to Learning and Intellectual Gifts: its Use of them and its Independence of them.

9. Quote passages of Scripture in which Paul's destination to be the missionary of the Gentiles is expressed.

CHAPTER II

On the external features of the period embraced in this chapter compare the corresponding pages of Hausrath; on the internal features see Principal Rainy's lecture on Paul in "The Evangelical Succession Lectures," Vol. I.

14. On the chronology of Paul's life see the notes at the end of Conybeare and Howson, and Farrar, II. 623.

The principal dates may be given at this stage from Conybeare and Howson for reference throughout:

36. Conversion.

38. Flight to Tarsus.

44. Brought to Antioch by Barnabas.

48. First Missionary Journey.

50.   Council at Jerusalem.

51–54.   Second Missionary Journey. 1 and 2 Thessalonians written at Corinth.

34–58.   Third Missionary Journey.

57. 1 Corinthians written at Ephesus; 2 Corinthians, in Macedonia; Galatians, at Corinth.

58. Romans written at Corinth. Arrest at Jerusalem.

59. In prison at Cæsarea.

60.   Voyage to Rome.

62. Philemon, Colossians, Ephesians, Philippians, written at Rome.

63. Release from prison.

67. 1 Timothy and Titus written.

68. In prison again at Rome. 2 Timothy.

Death.

15. The goats'-hair cloth was called Cilicium, from the name of the province.

16. Dean Howson's "Metaphors of St. Paul." Also Hausrath, p. 15.

23. Subject for class essay: Paul's First Sight of Jerusalem.

27. A startling picture of the state of society in Jerusalem might be constructed from the materials supplied in Matt. 23.

28. Detailed comparison of the experience of Paul with that of Luther: their early religious ideas; the state of religion around them; their failure to find peace and their sufferings of conscience; their discovery of the righteousness of God.

On the religious associations of Paul's early life see the first one hundred pages of Reuss' "Christian Theology in the Apostolic Age."

31. On the history of Christianity between the death of Christ and the conversion of St. Paul see Dykes' "From Jerusalem to Antioch."

34. The question whether Paul was married. His views on the subject of the place of woman.

35. Perhaps Acts 26:11 may not imply that any of the Christians yielded to his endeavors to make them blaspheme.

15. What was the Latin name for a town enjoying the political privileges possessed by Tarsus?

16. What are Paul's principal metaphors?

17. Where does he make this boast?

19. What was the Latin name for the Roman citizenship, and what privileges did it include? On what occasions is Paul recorded to have used it? On what occasions might he have been expected to use it when he omitted to do so? What reasons may be given for the omission?

20. Name friends of Paul who were engaged in the same trade as he.

21. Give Paul's quotations from the Greek poets. Do you know the authors he quoted from? Explain "Septuagint" and "Diaspora."

22. Where does Paul refer to the sophists and rhetoricians?

26. Make a collection of Paul's quotations from the Old Testament, showing whence each of them was taken.

28. What does Paul mean by the Law?

32. Trace out the points of contact between the language and views of Stephen's speech and those of Paulvg.

Explain—

"*Si Stephanus non orasset,*

Ecclesia Paulum non haberet."

34. Where is it said that Paul voted in the Sanhedrin?

35. Collect Paul's references to the persecution and bring out how severe it was.

CHAPTER III

On Paul's mental processes before and at the time of his conversion see Principal Rainy's lecture, already quoted.

The conversion of Paul is one of the strong apologetic positions of Christianity. See this worked out in Lyttelton's "Conversion of St. Paul." But it might be worked out afresh on more modern lines.

40. Principal Rainy, in the lecture above referred to, says that he sees no evidence of such a conflict as this in Paul's mind; but what then is the meaning of "It is hard for thee to kick against the pricks"?

41. The general tenor of the earliest Christian apologetic as it is to be found in the speeches of the Acts of the Apostles.

44. Nothing could be more alien to the spirit of the New Testament than to turn this round the other way, and, assuming that what Paul saw was only a vision, argue that the other appearances of Christ, because they are put on the same level, may have been only visions too. This is a mere stroke of dialectical cleverness, which shows no regard to the obvious intention of the writers.

There are three accounts of the conversion of Paul in the Acts. What is the significance of this reduplication in so small a book? Enumerate the differences between these accounts and explain them.

38. Prove that the first Christians called Christianity The Way, and explain the signification of this name.

CHAPTER IV

On the subject of this chapter see the relevant portions of any of the Handbooks of New Testament Theology—Weiss, Reuss, Schmid, Van Oosterzee; also Neander's "Planting of Christianity," and Pfleiderer's "Paulinismus." Hausrath's sketch is so out of proportion as to be really a caricature. Weiss' exposition is perhaps the most solid and trustworthy. He divides Paulinism into four sections:

  I. The Earliest Gospel of Paul during the Heathen Mission (gathered from Thessalonians). One chapter—the Gospel as the Way of Deliverance from Judgment.

  II. The Doctrinal System of the Four great Doctrinal and Controversial Epistles (Corinthians, Romans, Galatians). Chapter 1. Universal Sinfulness of Man; chap. 2. Heathenism and Judaism; chap. 3. Prophecy and Fulfilment; chap. 4. Christology; chap. 5. Redemption and Justification; chap. 6. The New Life; chap. 7. The Doctrine of Predestination; chap. 8. The Doctrine of the Church; chap. 9. The Last Things.

  III. The Development of Doctrine in the Epistles Written in Prison (Colossians, Ephesians, Philippians, Philemon). Chap. 1. The Pauline Foundations; chap. 2. Further Development of Doctrine.

  IV. The Teaching of the Pastoral Epistles. One chapter—Christianity as Doctrine.

52. Luther in the Wartburg.

54–65. As these paragraphs are nothing but a paraphrase of Rom. 1–8, pupils ought to be asked to compare with them the corresponding paragraphs of the Epistle.

65. On Paul's Psychology see the Handbooks of Delitzsch and Beck: also Heard, "The Tripartite Nature of Man," and Laidlaw, "The Bible Doctrine of Man."

51. Where does Paul mention his journey to Arabia?

56. What is the connection between moral and intellectual degeneracy?

62. Where does Paul speak of the gospel as a "mystery," and what does he mean by this word?

65. Does Paul divide human nature into two or into three sections? Do you know the theological names for these alternatives? Does Paul regard the unregenerate man as possessing the part of human nature which he calls "spirit"?

67. Enumerate the incidents of Christ's earthly life referred to by Paul.

CHAPTER V

On this subject see the first two chapters of Conybeare and Howson; "New Testament Times" of Hausrath and Schürer.

72. Subject of class essay: The Origin and Significance of the name "Christian."

72. By what other names were the Christians called in New Testament times, among themselves or among their enemies?

78. What did the Greeks, the Romans, and the Jews severally contribute to Christianity?

CHAPTER VI

The aim of this Handbook, as of "The Life of Jesus Christ" in the same series, being to show at a single glance the general course of the life and the principal objects it touched, a good many details have been omitted. This is especially the case in this chapter and in chapter X. The omissions cause those great features to stand out more prominently which details are apt to obscure. In this chapter an endeavor has been made to show in this way what were the different regions into which the apostle travelled, and what the peculiarities and the extent of the work he did in each. But in an extended Bible-class course the lessons will naturally go more into detail, and perhaps the incidents which took place in each town may generally form a lesson. Here, therefore, and at the beginning of chap. X, a few hints may be given of the view-points for the lessons, in so far as they are not already given in the text.

Acts 13:1–12.	First Footsteps of Christian Missions.
Acts 13:14–52.	Antioch. Paul's Missionary Method.
Acts 14:1–6.	Iconium. Among the Jews.
Acts 14:6–20.	Lystra. Among the Heathen.
Acts 14:21–28.	Paul as a Pastor.
Acts 15.	Paul as an Ecclesiastic.
Acts 16:1–6.	The New Companion.
Acts 16:6–10.	Opening up Virgin Soil.
Acts 16:12–40.	Philippi. Transfiguration and Disfiguration of Humanity.
Acts 17:1–9.	Thessalonica. An Honorable Reproach.
Acts 17:10–14.	Beroea. See the text.
Acts 17:15–34.	Athens. The Gospel and Intellectual Curiosity.
Acts 18:1–3.	Corinth. Paul's earthly Home.

Acts 18:4–17. The Missionary's Discouragements and Encouragements.

Acts 18:23–28. A polished Shaft in God's Quiver.

Acts 19. Ephesus. See the text. Also, Conflict of Christianity with Vested Interests and Mob Violence.

79. Howson's "Companions of St. Paul."

81. A minute inspection of Acts 13:9 will confirm the view here given of the change of name, though it is difficult to get quit of the idea that the conversion of the governor, who bore the same name, had something to do with it.

84. On the worship of the synagogue see Farrar's "Life of Christ," I. 220.

89. On the Council of Jerusalem, which took place between the first and second journey, see chap. IX.

93. What is here said of the plan of the Acts explains still more strikingly the meagreness of the record of the third journey.

97. Berœa was to the south of the Via Egnatia.

99. Subject of class essay: The Influence of Christianity on the Lot of Woman.

103. Subject of class essay: Paul at Athens.

104. Subject of class essay: Paul and Socrates.

113. A strong argument against the mythical theory of the miracles of our Lord may be constructed from the paucity of the miracles attributed to Paul. If that age naturally wove miraculous legends round great names, why did it not encircle Paul with a continuous web of miracle? and why does the New Testament admit that the Baptist worked no miracle?

79. Give a list of Paul's companions and friends mentioned in the New Testament.

84. What were the charges generally brought against him before the authorities?

91. Where in his writings does he mention Barnabas and Mark?

93. Give the places in Acts where the items of this catalogue are recorded.

94. Mention other classical associations of this region.

98. What two kings of Macedonia are famous in history?

102. Expand these allusions to Greek history.

103. Give a number of the names associated with the golden age of Athens and mention what they were famous for.

108. Find out all the visions mentioned in Paul's life, and prove that they were given him at the crises of his history.

110. Distinguish our Asia and Asia Minor from the Asia of the New Testament.

CHAPTER VII

In the chronological table, p. 170, the dates of the Epistles have already been given and the points of the history indicated where they come in. It is a pity the Epistles are not arranged in chronological order in our Bibles. Their characteristics may be mentioned:

1 and 2 Thessalonians. Simple beginnings. Attitude to Christ's second coming.

1 Corinthians. Picture of an apostolic church.

2 Corinthians. Paul's portrait of himself.

Galatians. Vehement polemic against Judaizers.

Romans. Paul's gospel.

Philemon. Example of Christian courtesy.

Colossians and Ephesians. Paul's later gospel.

Philippians. Picture of Roman imprisonment.

1 Timothy and Titus. Form of the church.

2 Timothy. The last scenes.

118. On Paul's style see Farrar's Excursus at the close of Vol. I. The comparison of it to that of Thucydides is more dignified than that of the text, but less true.

119. Inspiration did not interfere with natural characteristics of style. It made the writer not less but more himself, while of course it imparted to the products of his pen a divine worth and authority.

120–127. Howson's "Character of St. Paul;" Hausrath, 45–57; Baur's remarks (II. 294 ff.) on his intellectual character are very good. But the principal sources are 2 Corinthians and Acts 20.

122. Farrar's treatment of Paul's bodily infirmities is a serious blot on his book. They are obtruded with a frequency and exaggeration which

produce an impression quite different from that made by the references to them in Scripture. For a treatment of the same subject, realistic, but full of sympathy and delicacy, see Monod.

122 ff. Illustrate these paragraphs fully from Scripture.

123. Compare Paul with Livingstone and other missionaries.

CHAPTER VIII

On this subject compare Neander's "Planting of Christianity," Book II. chap. 7, and Schaff's "Church History;" also Bannerman's "Church of Christ." This chapter is only a piecing together of the information scattered through 1 Corinthians. It would be well to get pupils to seek out the passages of the Epistle which correspond to the different paragraphs. A picture of a Pauline church of a later date might be compiled in the same way from the Pastoral Epistles.

136. The doctrine of the Holy Spirit was revealed "at sundry times and in divers manners," and the complete doctrine is to be obtained by uniting the representations of the various writers of Scripture. In the New Testament there are four phases—1. In the Synoptical Gospels the Holy Spirit is set forth in His influence on the human nature of Christ; 2. In the Acts and Paul, as the power for founding the church and converting the world; 3. In Paul as the principle of the new life of Christians; 4. In John as the Comforter.

138. Compare the irregularities of other periods of vast change, e. g. the Reformation.

144. On the extent to which an authoritative ecclesiastical system is given in the New Testament, compare "Jus Divinum Presbyterii" and Hooker's "Ecclesiastical Polity."

130. Give the names of the principal games of ancient times, derived from the places where they were held.

131. Where are churches mentioned as meeting in the houses of individuals?

132. Explain the words "barbarian," "Scythian," in Col. 3:11.

136. What modern divine endeavored to revive these phenomena, and what is the name of the church he founded? What is the meaning of the word "charism"? Were the tongues of Pentecost the same as those of 1 Corinthians? Give instances in which New Testament prophets did predict future events.

CHAPTER IX

The criticism which seeks to disintegrate the New Testament writings and set the apostles against one another other is founded on a revival of the claim of the Judaizers that their propaganda had the sanction of Peter and the other original apostles. In a Handbook like this it is impossible to discuss at any length the Tubingen Theory. But some of its points are silently met in the text; and the whole theory is met by an attempt to give a view of the course of the controversy which covers all the facts. The distinction drawn in paragraphs 159 ff. between the central question in dispute and a subordinate aspect of the controversy will be found to clear up many intricacies. Compare Sorley's "Jewish Christians and Judaism."

This chapter is full of references to passages in Acts and Galatians, which pupils ought to be asked to produce.[91]

---

[91] James Stalker, *The Life of St. Paul.* (New York: American tract society, 1888), 5–181.

www.ingramcontent.com/pod-product-compliance
Lightning Source LLC
LaVergne TN
LVHW041332080426
835512LV00006B/412